Father Robert J. Kus

Hormiga Junction

Journal of a Missionary Priest - 2021

Red Lantern Press
WILMINGTON NORTH CAROLINA
www.redlanternpress.com

Publications of Red Lantern Press

Journals by Fr. Robert J. Kus

- Dreams for the Vineyard: Journal of a Parish Priest - 2002
- For Where Your Treasure Is: Journal of a Parish Priest – 2003
- There Will Your Heart Be Also: Journal of a Parish Priest – 2004
- Field of Plenty: Journal of a Parish Priest – 2005
- Called to the Coast: Journal of a Parish Priest – 2006
- Llamado a la Costa - Diario de un párroco – 2006
- Then Along Came Marcelino: Journal of a Parish Priest – 2007
- Y Después Llegó Marcelino - Diario de un párroco – 2007
- Living the Dream: Journal of a Parish Priest – 2008
- Viviendo el Sueño: Diario de un Párroco - 2008
- A Hand to Honduras: Journal of a Parish Priest – 2009
- Una Mano a Honduras: Diario de un Párroco - 2009
- Beacon of Hope: Journal of a Parish Priest – 2010
- Luz de Esperanza: Diario de un Párroco - 2010
- Serving God by Serving Others: Journal of a Parish Priest – 2011
- Servir a Dios Sirviendo a Los Demás: Diario de un Párroco – 2011
- The Year of Clifton: Journal of a Parish Priest – 2012
- Basilica: Journal of a Parish Priest – 2013
- Crucifix: Journal of a Parish Priest – 2014
- Holy Doors: Journal of a Parish Priest – 2015
- Amazing!: Journal of a Parish Priest – 2016
- Clear and Misty: Journal of a Parish Priest – 2017
- Honduras Calling: Journal of a Missionary Priest – 2018
- Home in Honduras: Journal of a Missionary Priest – 2019
- MissionPriest.com: Journal of a Missionary Priest – 2020
- Hormiga Junction: Journal of a Missionary Priest – 2021

Reitocan Books by Fr. Robert J. Kus

- Reitocan Grace – Gracia Reitoqueña: A Honduran Parish in Photos and Scripture
- Reitocan Faith – Fe Reitoqueña: A Honduran Parish in Photos and Scripture
- Reitocan Joy – Alegria Reitoqueña : A Honduran Parish in Photos and Scripture

Publications of **Red Lantern Press Cont.**

Homily Collections by Fr. Robert J. Kus

- Flowers in the Wind 1 – Story-Based Homilies for Cycle B
- Flowers in the Wind 2 – Story-Based Homilies for Cycle C
- Flowers in the Wind 3 – Story-Based Homilies for Cycle A
- Flowers in the Wind 4 – More Story-Based Homilies for Cycle A
- Flowers in the Wind 5 – More Story-Based Homilies for Cycle B
- Flowers in the Wind 6 – More Story-Based Homilies for Cycle C
- Flowers in the Wind 7 – Still More Story-Based Homilies for Cycle A
- Flowers in the Wind 8 – Still More Story-Based Homilies for Cycle B
- Flowers in the Wind 9 – Still More Story-Based Homilies for Cycle C
- Flowers in the Wind 10 – Even More Story-Based Homilies for Cycle A
- Flowers in the Wind 11 – Even More Story-Based Homilies for Cycle B
- Flowers in the Wind 12 – Even More Story-Based Homilies for Cycle C

Nursing and Saints by Fr. Robert J. Kus

- Saintly Men of Nursing: 100 Amazing Stories
- Hombres Santos de la Enfermería: Cien Historias Asombrosas

Dedication

In Loving Memory of

Msgr. Girard "Jerry" Michael Sherba

June 6, 1952 – October 26, 2021

Diocese of Raleigh

North Carolina

U.S.A.

Acknowledgments

Many thanks go to the parishioners and priests of the parish of San Francisco de Asís, Reitoca, F.M., Honduras. They have welcomed me and helped me feel treasured and helpful.

I especially thank Cardinal Óscar Andrés Rodríguez Maradiaga, S.D.B., who graciously invited me to become a missionary in the Archdiocese of Tegucigalpa.

Thanks go to Pat Marriott of the Basilica Shrine of St. Mary in Wilmington, North Carolina, who edited and designed this journal.

Special thanks also go to the fine folks of Kindle Direct Publishing, who helped bring this book to life.

Introduction

The purpose of this book is to provide a glimpse into the daily life of a Catholic priest who transitioned from being a pastor of a North Carolina parish to a missionary priest in the mountains of Honduras – at the age of 75.

A secondary purpose of this book is to add to the rich histories of the Parish of San Francisco de Asís in Reitoca, F.M., Honduras and the Catholic Archdiocese of Tegucigalpa.

This journal is a personal reflection of just one priest, so in no way should it be seen as the official position of other priests or the parishes in which the author has served.

Furthermore, I remind the reader that this journal is a one-year "snapshot" of my life. Hopefully, the person who wrote this in 2021 is not the same person who lives today.

Father Robert J. Kus
Reitoca, F.M., Honduras
May 2022

JANUARY 2021

January 1, 2021 – Friday – Mary, Mother of God
Reitoca, F.M., Honduras – 7:20 p.m.
Mostly clear – 79 F

Today is the first day of a new year, and I have a feeling that it's going to be the best year ever! Usually I'm not crazy about New Year's Day, because it is a symbol of the end of Christmas vacation and the taking down of the Christmas tree and decorations. This year, however, I'm leaving my two trees up for at least a week more. I was going to toast the New Year with sparkling grape juice that Aaron brought for me, but I couldn't get the top open. Juan can probably it for me tomorrow when he comes to work.

This morning when I stepped on the scale, it read 119 pounds. That's a good weight for me. For several months I've been fluctuating between 117 and 122.

Blackie hasn't been himself the last couple of days. Last night he slept in my bedroom closet which he has made into his private little get-away, and he hardly has eaten a thing all day. This morning, he was on the deck making sounds like a coyote. He has done that before, and the sounds are very eerie. I have no idea what they mean. After a full day of rest, he decided to go out on the town late this afternoon with his friends Andy and Henry.

Speaker of the U.S. House of Representatives, Nancy Pelosi, has appointed retired Rear Admiral Margaret Grun Kibben as the House Chaplain upon the retirement of Fr. Pat Conroy. Admiral Kibben is a Presbyterian minister with a wealth of experience in the Navy and the Marines.

Today the Republican-majority US Senate overrode Donald Trump's veto of the annual Defense bill that gives the military a three percent pay raise among other things. This is the first override of a veto President Trump has had in his presidency.

Thirty-three countries have now identified cases of the new "omicron" coronavirus variant that is supposed to be highly contagious.

Like last year, this year I am only making one New Year's resolution in print, and that is to produce a volume of Catholic "mission heroes" taken from the first year of my blog, *MissionPriest.com*. That will be a fun and relatively easy project. I plan to do an additional volume each year from the same blog.

January 2, 2021 – Saturday – Ss. Basil the Great & Gregory Nazianzen
Reitoca, F.M., Honduras – 7 p.m.
Light rain – 80 F

Little Blackie is worn to a frazzle and has slept most of the day, has eaten almost nothing, and has no desire to go for walks. But he appears to be enjoying a "day off" from his ramblings to who-knows-where.

January 3, 2021 – Epiphany Sunday
Reitoca, F.M., Honduras – 8:50 p.m.
Mostly clear – 75 F

Blackie slept many hours yesterday and last night, so first thing this morning he ate breakfast and left the campus for the day. I haven't seen him all day, nor Andy or Henry.

I had to ask Juan to come to the campus today as I had no water. He came with his good friend Mainor. Because it was Mainor's first time on the Holy Cross campus, I showed him around a bit. Mainor's father died a few months ago, so now he lives only with his mother and a younger brother in the district of Reitoca called El Higuerito, where Juan lives. Juan quickly solved the water problem.

Today I mostly worked on my selected bibliography for my first Catholic missionary heroes' book.

January 4, 2021 – Monday – St. Elizabeth Ann Seton
Reitoca, F.M., Honduras – 6:25 p.m.
Mostly clear – 82 F

Perhaps the most intriguing news of the weekend is the report of a phone call that Donald Trump made to the Secretary of State of Georgia, telling him to "find" enough votes to make his total more than what Joe Biden got in the presidential election. The secretary of state told Donald Trump that he could not do that, for the votes had been counted three different times, and every time, Joe Biden came up with tens of thousands more votes than Trump.

Also intriguing to me was an article that discussed how the pandemic has affected the workplace. More and more people have been able to work from home, and the overwhelming majority love it; they do not want to go back to the office except for maybe a day or two per week. This, in turn, is leaving many office buildings empty, and that is leading some to consider turning the buildings into living quarters. Another good thing about being able to work from home is that many workers can live anywhere; they do not have to locate in cities with sky-high housing prices. It will be interesting to see how this all plays out in the future.

Little Blackie returned home this morning, limping because he hurt his right front leg. He ate and then slept all day. After having a snack around 5 p.m., he limped out for the night once again. I fear that one day he'll be killed by a bigger dog, by human bullies, or a truck. Blackie truly lives a dangerous life.

January 5, 2021 – Tuesday – St. John Neumann
Reitoca, F.M., Honduras – 7:40 p.m.
Partly cloudy – 78 F

Today Catholic Christians celebrate the feast of St. John Neumann, a Redemptorist who came to the United States from Bohemia (now a region of the Czech Republic). Bohemian-Irish-Americans like myself celebrate this nineteenth-century man who helped build the American Church, especially in Philadelphia where he served as the fourth bishop.

Today in the United States, all eyes were on the state of Georgia where people were voting for two people to become U.S. senators.

Juan and I worked today on clearing the pavement in the back of my house. Though Juan did the majority of the work, I helped by loading rocks and soil into the wheelbarrow. I'm not used to such work, so I'm sure I'll sleep very well tonight.

Chele dropped by my house today with his cousin Alexi. He was checking in to see what his next project on the Holy Cross campus will be. There are not many projects for him, but the ones that need to be done are rather tricky, such as installing ceiling fans and centering the overhead lamp over my kitchen table.

After five days off, Emilio was back to work this evening. He has been getting treatment for his right eye, which has bits of glass in it. He thinks he got the bits of glass while riding on a motorcycle a week ago, on his way to a party in Lodo Negro celebrating Danilo's nephew's graduation from engineering school. Emilio was not wearing goggles on the trip, and the journey from Reitoca to Lodo Negro is about one-and-a-half hours. Next week he'll be seeing a specialist in Tegucigalpa.

January 6, 2021 – Wednesday – St. André Bessette
Reitoca, F.M., Honduras – 9:15 p.m.
Mostly cloudy – 75 F

The election results from Georgia are in. The two new U.S. senators are both Democrats – Rev. Raphael Warnock and Jon Ossoff. Rev. Warnock will be the first African American from Georgia to be in the senate. He is the pastor of the historic Ebenezer Baptist Church, where Rev. Dr. Martin Luther King, Jr. was pastor before he was assassinated. Jon Ossoff, who is Jewish, will be the youngest U.S. senator at the age of 33.

The election of the two Georgians means that the Democrats will be the majority party in the Senate, for they have 48 members plus two independents who caucus with them. In the case of a tie, the vice president, Democrat Kamala Harris, will cast the deciding vote.

I read an interesting article today about how marijuana stocks are rising on hopes that a Democratic senate will decriminalize marijuana nationally. It is worth noting that "decriminalization" is not the same as "legalization," but it will go a long way to end the sexist and racist application of anti-marijuana laws that have destroyed the lives of so many, especially African American men.

Today, thousands of supporters of Donald Trump stormed the Capitol Building. Five people have been killed. People around the world are appalled, as are many Americans. Even many Republicans have condemned the Trumpian thugs who stormed the Capitol, ransacked private offices, and stole items. They say the protestors are bringing disgrace to their party and the country.

Twitter, Facebook, and You Tube have all banned Donald Trump. Political leaders and observers say that Donald Trump has always exhibited "autocratic tendencies" – ya think? – and now this is the result. I'm sure many sociologists would say the behavior of the thugs is a characteristic of the "true believer" type.

Donald Trump remained silent during most of the uproar but intervened when coaxed by family members. He told his followers, "We love you; you are very special," and "go home now."

Many people in the Trump administration, including Secretary of Transportation Elaine Chao, wife of the current Senate Majority Leader Mitch McConnell, have resigned over today's violence attributed to Donald Trump's behavior.

Though this president has brought disgrace to the nation and to the office of president, he has certainly been a wildly colorful character whose antics have kept the whole world entertained and wondering what he would do next. I guess Americans, and the rest of the world, will have to find other sources of drama for entertainment after January 20th.

Rudy Giuliani, former mayor of New York City who was once hailed as an American hero for his leadership during the 9-11 disaster, has been making an increasing number of statements out of touch with reality, spinning unfounded conspiracy theories that don't even make sense. His contribution to today's wild events was this statement: "Let's have trial by combat."

The priests of the Diocese of Raleigh received word today that Passionist Fr. Hector Galvan, who is assisting at St. Ann parish in Clayton, N.C., was admitted to UNC Health in Smithfield and is in ICU on a ventilator for COVID-19. Meanwhile, Fr. Trent Watts, pastor of St. Therese in Wrightsville Beach, is still in New Hanover Regional Medical Center and needs a ventilator to assist his breathing.

Blackie is back home, thinner and with a hurt left front leg. He doesn't seem to be in any pain, however, and he has an excellent appetite.

January 7, 2021 – Thursday – St. Raymond of Peñafort
Reitoca, F.M., Honduras – 7:30 p.m.
Partly cloudy – 77 F

Blackie has been resting all day, and Juan gave him a bath. He is eating well, though he is still limping around, holding his left front leg in the air.

Juan began painting the metal frame that will hold the laminate roofing outside my kitchen windows. He's about one-fourth finished. It's an intricate paint job that requires two coats of paint, so it's slow work.

Speaker of the U.S. House of Representatives, Nancy Pelosi, and others are calling for Donald Trump to be impeached a second time if the vice president and cabinet refuse to remove him from office via the 25th Amendment.

Today, Donald Trump admitted that Joe Biden won the election and that there would be a peaceful transition of power. However, Mr. Trump told his supporters, "… I also want you to know that our incredible journey is only just beginning." I hope those in power take those words seriously and watch this man's every move from now on.

January 8, 2021 – Friday
Reitoca, F.M., Honduras – 7:15 p.m.
Mostly clear – 81 F

More people from the Trump administration have resigned because of the Wednesday rioting at the Capitol. This includes Betsy DeVos, who has been a very polarizing Secretary of Education.

Today Twitter, Donald Trump's favorite platform of communicating with his followers, has banned him permanently.

Donald Trump has confirmed that he will not attend Joe Biden's inauguration. It is customary that the outgoing president and his spouse invite the incoming president and his spouse to the White House, show them around, and make them feel welcome. It is also customary for the outgoing president to attend the inauguration as the most visible evidence of the orderly transition of power that our society cherishes. Mr. Trump will do neither of those things.

Juan went home early today because he wasn't feeling well, and Blackie has remained at home resting. Henry is back on the deck, but there has been no sign of Andy for days now.

January 9, 2021 – Saturday
Reitoca, F.M., Honduras – 7:20 p.m.
Mostly clear – 75 F

Today I celebrated Masses in La Libertad and San Miguelito. There were more people in the churches than are usually there for weekend Masses, and both Danilo and I were delighted by that.

It's been an incredibly beautiful day here in Reitoca with sunshine, blue skies, fluffy white clouds, and very brisk breezes. The breezes are especially noticeable on my deck, and Henry is back, so Blackie and his friends loved hanging out there all day.

Juan continued painting today, and Chele and two other young men fixed some of the doors that have not worked since I moved into the house in October. It's nice to be able to close doors with no problem!

On the news today, President Trump's son, Donald Jr., was bragging that he recently went on a hunting expedition to Alaska with one of his sons, and they did "some toxic masculine stuff." I looked up "toxic masculinity" on the Internet, and I was surprised to learn it is an actual concept. Even after reading about it, I'm not sure what it is.

Another news item caught my attention that is occurring in Murdock, Minnesota. I am familiar with that town because a friend of mine was pastor of the St. Isidore Catholic Community, which has an oratory and four parish churches including Sacred Heart Church in Murdock. Apparently, a group called Asatru has bought the abandoned Lutheran church in the town, and the people of Murdock are very upset. The Asatru group in Murdock is highly racist, although internationally that religion has not been racist. Apparently, racists have infiltrated the religion and incorporated many of its symbols. The international leaders of Asatru are beside themselves, wondering what to do about the racist infiltration. Despite the popular clamor, the mayor said the town must grant Asatru permission to buy the building because of "religious freedom" laws. The world gets crazier by the minute, and more intriguing.

January 10, 2021 – Baptism of Jesus Sunday
Reitoca, F.M., Honduras – 6 p.m.
Mostly clear – 83 F

This was a nice, quiet day at my house. Juan had the day off, and Blackie decided to stay home as he still has trouble putting weight on his left front leg.

I spent some of the day working on my mission hero book and finished reading Richard Chamberlain's book, *Shattered Love: A Memoir.* I thoroughly enjoyed Richard's book. I loved his acting, especially as

Dr. Kildare on television and in the movie, *The Thorn Birds*. Now I've begun reading Basil De Pinto's *Wonder: A Memoir*.

Today I requested some money from the Red Lantern Foundation for four projects: a new sacristy for Our Lady of Candelaria Church in Curarén; an under-floor concrete base for the altar in the church of San Miguelito in the pueblo of the same name; a plaza for the Church of San José in Lodo Negro, a community of Curarén; and shirts for the band of Santa Rita, a community of Alubarén. Happily, we have the money in our checking account, so I'll have it by Wednesday from the United States.

January 11, 2021 – Monday
Reitoca, F.M., Honduras – 6:55 p.m.
Partly cloudy – 81 F

The weather for the next nine days is supposed to be the same as today: high of 91 F and low of 69 F with no rain in sight.

Danilo dropped by today because he needed to take my car to Tegucigalpa to buy some parts for his pickup truck. It's very difficult for people who live in this part of Honduras to get many items such as automotive parts, for Tegucigalpa, a couple of hours away, is the nearest place with a lot of shopping.

Danilo and four relatives have started a chicken business, and it is doing well. They have 700 chickens for sale, and the demand for them is great. I'm delighted for Danilo and the others, for they have worked very hard to get this project off the ground. Their hard work seems to be paying off well for them.

January 12, 2021 – Tuesday
Reitoca, F.M., Honduras – 8:55 p.m.
Clear – 79 F

For much of my adult life, especially when I lived in the states of Montana, Washington, and Oklahoma, I did not watch television. But in my priesthood in North Carolina, I often watched too much. Since coming to Honduras, however, I have not watched any except in hotel rooms when I travel. Because I don't watch TV, I've been able to do much more writing, reading, and reflecting.

I have found, though, that although I enjoy being knowledgeable about current events, a steady diet of news can become toxic. The toxicity is especially keen in times of political elections.

I thought of that the other day when I read about a woman who loved to read books – cookbooks, to be specific. As some people sit and read novels, this woman reads cookbooks cover to cover. I remember doing something similar during times of heavy political advertisements. Instead of reading cookbooks, however, I found myself enjoying non-controversial TV shows such as The Weather Channel or cooking shows. I even found myself, from time to time, watching baseball on television, for it was so "normal." Baseball has rules that don't change. If you have three strikes, you are out. You could throw a mini temper-tantrum, but you were still out.

Now, to enter the world of "normal" when the news is toxic, I find solace in reading about how people "do life" – memoirs are my favorite type of reading nowadays.

January 13, 2021 – Wednesday – St. Hilary
Reitoca, F.M., Honduras – 8:45 p.m.
Clear – 75 F

The U.S. House of Representatives voted today 232-197 to impeach Donald Trump. Ten Republicans joined all the Democrats in impeaching him. He is the first president in history to be impeached twice. Now the Senate is charged with having a trial. The trial cannot begin until at least January 19, the day before Joe Biden is inaugurated.

Law enforcement officials are investigating whether the storming of the Capitol building on January 6 was aided by people inside the government, including people in the Congress. This is all very scary stuff.

The group of Ancient Order of Hibernians in Wilmington, North Carolina, of which I was the chaplain for many years, may begin conducting meetings via Zoom. If it did, I would be able to attend on occasion if my schedule permitted it. For me, the pandemic has made being socially connected much easier, thanks to Zoom.

This evening, my Rotary Passport 7730 Club had its annual meeting, and all four of us here in Honduras attended via Zoom. We have two new members from Denmark who now live on the North Carolina coast, and my dear friend, Richard Creech, who has been to visit Reitoca at least four times in the past.

January 14, 2021 – Thursday
Reitoca, F.M., Honduras – 7:50 p.m.
Partly cloudy – 79 F

This morning I made my first pie ever, a cherry pie. It turned out great. Aaron and Valencia stopped by late this afternoon after clinic hours to have a piece of pie and visit. Next week, Aaron will come over to discuss the possibility of applying for Rotary scholarships for worthy candidates.

Danilo came to the Holy Cross campus today, so he helped Juan and me move the remaining items from my room at the rectory and clean the room. I'm now officially out of the rectory.

January 15, 2021 – Friday
Reitoca, F.M., Honduras – 8:05 p.m.
Partly cloudy – 79 F

Danilo stayed on the Holy Cross campus last night, the first night that he spent in the Blessed James Miller *casita*, more commonly called "the blue house." Danilo spent the morning working on various projects on the campus with Juan. He has found that the afternoons here in Reitoca are just too hot to do much work outside. In the community where he is from, Lodo Negro in Curarén, the climate is much cooler. In fact, coffee is one of Lodo Negro's main crops because of its climate.

Fr. Carlos took my truck today to Quebracho to celebrate Mass. Quebracho is a community of Reitoca where I've celebrated Mass only one or two times in the past. The roads to that community are very bad.

January 16, 2021 – Saturday
Reitoca, F.M., Honduras – 7:05 p.m.
Mostly cloudy – 79 F

This past week I've been transfixed by articles on Donald Trump and his followers, the so-called Christian right, racism, violence, and talk of civil war. Donald Trump has supposedly said, as have many of his followers, "This is just the beginning." It will be interesting to see how the right-wingers, especially the extremist fringe, carry out their agendas into the future without their leader in the presidency.

The scariest thing that is being uncovered is that many of the people who supported the riots on the United States capitol were in the military, government, and political party leadership. As the light shines on many of these individuals and groups, they are trying their best to distance themselves from domestic terrorist activity.

Today Juan and I trimmed some of the overgrown trees in front of the rectory. The branches hung so low that they were banging into the top of the pickup trucks using the driveway. Now, the drive looks so much better.

The next project I'd like to do for the Holy Cross campus is to build a drive from the church rectory to the campus. I'm putting Danilo in charge of that project.

This afternoon, three cows made the mistake of coming onto the Holy Cross campus, and Blackie, Andy, and Henry had a great time chasing them off.

January 17, 2021 – Second Sunday in Ordinary Time
Reitoca, F.M., Honduras – 7 p.m.
Partly cloudy – 79 F

Today I celebrated Masses in three Alubarén communities: Concepción, El Hatillo, and Alubarén itself. In Alubarén, I also had six baptisms. The churches of Concepción and Alubarén were full, and everyone had their masks on.

Today the Diocese of Raleigh reported that Fr. Trent Watts, pastor of St. Therese parish in Wrightsville Beach, died from COVID-19 in New Hanover Regional Medical Center today. I will celebrate a Mass for him this week.

January 18, 2021 – Monday – Martin Luther King, Jr. Day
Reitoca, F.M., Honduras – 7:05 p.m.
Mostly cloudy – 82 F

Blackie and I were alone most of today because Juan had the day off. It was a beautiful day here with fresh breezes.

Today is Martin Luther King, Jr. Day in the United States. I clearly remember the day he was shot, for I was on a bus traveling from a ghetto in Cleveland where I had just taught a class to African American women who were preparing to take a practical nurse licensing exam. As the bus got to E. 55th and Euclid Avenue, a man jumped on the bus and shouted, "Martin Luther King has just been shot!" I was the only white person on the bus, and the area we were in was a black neighborhood. I was not at all afraid, for I have always felt that if I were ever attacked, there would be others who would come to my rescue. So far, it's worked.

In 1968, when Martin Luther King was shot, the civil rights movement in the United States was focused on racial minorities, specifically African Americans. Later, the movement would be expanded to include ethnic minorities, especially Hispanics. Later still, it would embrace sexual minorities. One day, God willing, all people will be treated with dignity and respect as children of God.

And speaking of which, today begins the Week of Prayer for Christian Unity. Although I have been part of many interfaith ministerial groups, ecumenical activities have never taken center stage in my life. I appreciate those who do lead in that area, however, and wish them well.

January 19, 2021 – Tuesday
Reitoca, F.M., Honduras – 6:50 p.m.
Clear – 81 F

Today Danilo and I traveled to Tegucigalpa for banking and shopping. It was a productive but tiring day. Danilo agreed to oversee the driveway project connecting the rectory drive to the Holy Cross drive.

Today is Donald Trump's last full day as President of the United States. On the floor of the U.S. Senate, the majority leader of the U.S. Senate, Mitch McConnell (R-KY), denounced Donald Trump and his supporters. U.S. Senate minority leader Chuck Schumer (D-NY) said that he would like the Senate to bar Donald Trump from holding any future federal office in the future.

I have been re-reading the late Fr. Andrew Greeley's *My Love: A Prayer Journal.* Yesterday, I came across a passage about how train whistles touched something in his spirit. He was always intrigued by train whistles as a child, and now that he is an older man, the sound still triggers emotions in him. Where are the people headed? Why are they traveling? What will greet them at their destination?

I recall as a child in Maple Heights, Ohio riding in the back seat of the car with my grandfather driving and my grandmother riding shotgun. When we stopped at a railroad crossing my grandma loved to count the freight cars, and I loved waiting for the caboose. I always thought how wonderful it would be to ride in a caboose across the country, passing little towns and waving to the people looking at the train as it passed by. As an adult, I even thought that one day, when I lived in my retirement home,

I'd be sure it was somewhere near railroad tracks so I could hear the train go by. So, now I live in Honduras where there are no trains. Funny how life works!

Senator Mitch McConnell (R-KY), current majority leader, told senators in a speech on the senate floor that the January 6th riots in the capitol were fueled by the president's lies about the election being stolen and by other power figures. Until the riots, Sen. McConnell backed the president, at least in public.

January 20, 2021 – Wednesday – St. Fabian; St. Sebastian
Reitoca, F.M., Honduras – 4:50 p.m.
Sunny – 88 F

Today is Inauguration Day in the United States. President Joe Biden is the 46th president in American history, and the second Catholic president. If Congress approves all the president's picks, President Biden will have the most Catholic cabinet in history, with over one-third of the members being Catholic. These would include the Secretaries of Defense; Interior; Health and Human Services; Agriculture; Commerce; Labor; Veterans Affairs; and Energy. In addition, the incoming Presidential Envoy for Climate, a cabinet-level position, is also Catholic.

President Trump and his wife left Washington this morning. As they stood on the top step of Air Force One, they waved good-bye and walked into the plane that was blaring the Village People's song, "YMCA." In four years, Mr. Trump has been impeached twice and oversaw his Republican party lose the presidency and both houses of Congress. Also, on his watch, millions of people lost their jobs in the pandemic, and over 400,000 Americans have died from the virus. And as his presidency came to an end, the nation watched many of his followers rioting at the Capitol with his encouragement. Now, the former president is faced with a slew of legal issues, not the least of which is how to deal with over $400,000,000 in debt that will come due in the next few years.

The latest news from the former president is that he is thinking of forming his own political party. That would be an incredibly interesting happening!

Today is the feast of St. Sebastian, patron saint of Reitoca. Firecrackers went off at 6 a.m. to celebrate the occasion, but because of the pandemic, there was no festival or procession. However, Fr. Carlos dropped by with four young people from Curarén who were in Reitoca for the commemorative Mass that Fr. Carlos conducted.

January 21, 2021 – Thursday – St. Agnes
Reitoca, F.M., Honduras – 7:30 p.m.
Partly cloudy – 82 F

One of the most fascinating ideas that has been floating around in American society is a loose-knit set of ideas called QAnon theory. Though it has many forms, its major tenet is that former President Trump is heading up a special movement to destroy the "bad guys," that is, the "Democrats." The theory holds that Democrats are evil cannibals and pedophiles. Q refers to the inventor of the theory, and the "anon" refers to the idea that nobody knows for sure who Q is or are. Some believe it could be Donald Trump himself.

When Donald Trump's presidency came and went with no apocalyptic event, QAnon followers were faced with making sense of the theoretical system they had believed. The entire failure of such a system reminds me of a sociological study published in 1956 by Leon Festinger, Henry Riecken, and Stanley Schachter called, "When Prophecy Fails: A Social and Psychological Study of a Modern Group That Predicted the Destruction of the World." The study explored how members of a small UFO-worshipping religion in Chicago dealt with the fact that the apocalypse did not occur as expected. Basically, the study, and later similar studies, found that the more individuals have invested in the belief system – such as selling their houses and giving up their jobs – the more likely they were to continue following the theory.

Now, many people of QAnon feel lost without their leader, Donald Trump. Many, in fact, are very angry at him for letting them down, and many are condemning him for abandoning them.

This morning, Fathers Carlos and Sebastián were at my house for a Zoom meeting with the cardinal and other priests who work in the Archdiocese of Tegucigalpa. It was part inspirational, and part informational.

President Biden has been busy signing executive orders, undoing many of the policies of the past president, just as Trump did with Obama's policies four years earlier. His biggest challenge right now is creating and implementing a national plan to combat COVID-19. In the last administration, there was no national plan, so every state had to figure out how to combat the pandemic.

January 22, 2021 – Friday
Reitoca, F.M., Honduras – 8 p.m.
Clear – 81 F

Today a young policeman from Azacualpa was killed in Tegucigalpa. He was only 24 years old. I don't know the details yet.

The *New York Times* reported today that Donald Trump tried to get the Department of Justice to overturn Georgia's presidential election votes. I'm sure that will be very big news for some time to come.

I got a nice message today from a dear friend, Rojann, who lives in Arizona. She and I used to teach at The University of Iowa together, and she recently retired from her professorship at Arizona State University. She is loving retirement.

January 23, 2021 – Saturday – St. Vincent; St. Marianne Cope
Reitoca, F.M., Honduras – 8:25 p.m.
Clear – 79 F

Today I celebrated Masses in La Libertad and San Miguelito. I was very happy to give money from the Red Lantern Foundation to San

Miguelito to build a concrete foundation under their altar area. Right now, the altar sits on a wooden platform that could one day collapse from old age.

In my homily, I told the people that Pope Francis had proclaimed the Third Sunday in Ordinary Time to be known as the "Sunday of the Word of God." The purpose of this day is to renew our love for the Bible.

In honor of the young police officer who was killed in a motorcycle accident recently, there was a large procession in Reitoca with many police attending. I didn't attend, but I did see the group from a distance and heard the continual police sirens. I believe the young man's name was Freddy Chévez.

Danilo stayed in the Blessed James Miller casita for the night.

January 24, 2021 – Third Sunday in Ordinary Time
Reitoca, F.M., Honduras – 7:40 p.m.
Mostly clear – 81 F

Yesterday when Juan left for the day around 4:30 p.m., the cistern was full of water, but this morning there wasn't any. Fortunately, Danilo was here, and he discovered that a broken pipe connected to the Blessed Stanley Rother (yellow) *casita*, whose floor was covered with water. So, he turned off the water to that little house and got rid of the water on the floor. I would not have known how to turn off the water to the house, so I'm very glad he was here.

Later, Danilo made a little stone bridge so he could drive his pickup truck from the drive to the side of the *mayordomo's* house.

Because I had Mass in Curarén this afternoon at 4 p.m., Juan came to the Holy Cross campus at 2:30 and stayed until Danilo and I returned at 5:30. Juan brought his friend Mainor (pronounced "Minor") with him to keep him company. Mainor and Juan love to hear the English words "refrigerator" and "congratulations," which they think are the most hilarious words they ever heard.

It was wonderful to celebrate Mass in Curarén once again, for I hadn't been there since around February of 2020. The altar servers are renovating the sacristy with money from the Red Lantern Foundation and are doing a very good job. Sr. Teresa and another Sister, Lillian I think is her name, came to see me after Mass to say hello, as did some of the other members of the community. Curarén has always been one of my favorite places to serve.

I preached about César Chávez and how well he lived his vocation serving migrant workers in the United States. I also told them that the new president, Joe Biden, has an image of César Chávez in the White House.

January 25, 2021 – Monday – Conversion of St. Paul
Reitoca, F.M., Honduras – 8:30 p.m.
Clear – 81 F

The Diocese of Raleigh reported today that Fr. Daniel Pal, OFM Conv, Administrator of Holy Cross parish in Durham, is being transferred out of the diocese by his Order. Deacon Philip E. Rzewnicki, who is assigned to diaconal ministry at Holy Cross parish, will fill in as administrator of the parish until a new pastor can be assigned.

January 26, 2021 – Tuesday – Ss. Timothy & Titus
Reitoca, F.M., Honduras – 8:30 p.m.
Clear – 81 F

Danilo went into Tegucigalpa today to bring two workers to the Holy Cross campus, Carlos and Nelson. Both men worked on the building of the campus. They were here to measure the distance for connecting the drive of the rectory with the drive of Holy Cross campus. They hope to give an estimate of the cost tomorrow. A man from Reitoca who also worked on the project, Jorge, joined us. As I understand it, Jorge is an expert on concrete.

After the men were finished with their measurements, Danilo took them back to Tegucigalpa and then returned to Holy Cross around 7 p.m. It was a very long day for him, driving at least seven hours. When he arrived back on the campus, he discovered that the leak from the pipes going into the yellow *casita* was active again, and the floors were again covered with water. For some unknown reason, Carlos turned the water supply back on after Danilo had turned it off. Danilo and I got most of the water out, and tomorrow morning Juan and I will get the place dry.

January 27, 2021 – Wednesday – St. Angela Merici
Reitoca, F.M., Honduras – 7:15 p.m.
Clear – 82 F

The first thing on this morning's "to-do" list for Juan and me was to dry out the yellow *casita*. It was easier than we thought it would be, and now the house is in good shape though the water is cut off to it.

Today I read an interesting article in the *National Catholic Reporter* about the radical traditionalists, sometimes called the "rad-trads," in the Diocese of Charlotte. One of the main persons it featured was a priest who transferred from the Diocese of Raleigh a couple of years ago. The article noted that parishes that have been taken over by radical traditionalists have lost members, many of them becoming Lutherans or Episcopalians. It also talked about how some of the rad-trads have been burning books by Catholic writers who don't fit into their worldview, writers such as Fr. Henri Nouwen and the Trappist priest and activist Thomas Merton. Hate never takes a holiday.

On a similar note, the Department of Homeland Security has issued a nationwide terrorism alert against "violent domestic extremists," such as those who stormed the Capitol on January 6. Today I read about a newly elected member of the U.S. House of Representatives from Georgia, Marjorie Taylor Greene, who has made incredibly hateful statements against people with whom she disagrees.

Tonight's full moon is known as the "wolf moon," and it is dazzling on this clear night in the mountains.

January 28, 2021 – Thursday – St. Thomas Aquinas
Reitoca, F.M., Honduras – 8 p.m.
Clear – 81 F

Danilo and I went to Tegucigalpa today for banking and shopping.

On the way home from Tegucigalpa, I stopped at a house in the vicinity of El Higuerito to bless the grave of Mainor Euceda's father, Santos Evelio Euceda Osorto. Mr. Euceda did not want to be buried in the cemetery in Reitoca, so the family chose a nice little hill on their property as a gravesite. Mainor and his mother Carmen were with Danilo and me for the grave blessing.

Before the blessing, I noticed a wall filled with photos of the family, and Mainor took me in to look at them. I was delighted that one of the photos was one I had taken eleven years ago of a young father, mother, and little son heading to the clinic in Reitoca. It turns out that the young father in the photo was Mainor's brother, who is now working in Houston, and the little boy is now 14 years old. I used that very photo in my web post for this past Holy Family Sunday.

Carmen, who has lived in the house for over thirty years, is an expert gardener. The yard is filled with huge bushes of all types of colorful flowers in bloom.

Late this afternoon, Aaron was at my house to help me with a few projects. I'd be lost without his help.

January 29, 2021 – Friday
Reitoca, F.M., Honduras – 8 p.m.
Mostly clear – 79 F

Juan dropped by for lunch today to get a paper he needed to prove he had a full-time job here at Holy Cross campus. I think I need to design a stamp for "Holy Cross Catholic Ministries," for Hondurans love having documents stamped. I'll mention to Aaron that we need a Holy Cross stamp, for he loves doing artistic things like that.

This morning I made a batch of chili. Juan had some for lunch while he was here, and Miguel from the clinic came by to get some to take to Dr. Aaron. I love to share my food, for I'm more into cooking than eating. Juan told me that his family had enjoyed eating pizza that I bought for them yesterday when we were in Tegucigalpa. I was amazed to learn that Juan's father had heard of pizza in the past but had never tasted it. He loved it.

Fr. Carlos also dropped by this morning to discuss my Masses this coming week. I'll be celebrating in Reitoca, Curarén, and Pueblo Nuevo.

The Diocese of Raleigh announced openings for pastors for the coming year. This the "first round" of announcements. There were four parishes listed as needing new pastors: Basilica Shrine of St. Mary in Wilmington (my former parish); Holy Cross in Durham; St. Mildred in Swansboro; and St. Therese in Wrightsville Beach.

I was at the Basilica Shrine of St. Mary as pastor and rector from 2006 to 2018, so I'm very familiar with it. The parish suffered greatly from Hurricane Florence and has not yet been able to fully repair the buildings that were damaged.

Holy Cross parish in Durham has a primarily African American congregation that has been staffed by Conventional Franciscan priests. That order has discerned that they can no longer staff the parish, for the decline in vocations to the religious order priesthood is even more severe than vocations to the diocesan priesthood.

St. Mildred in Swansboro was run by a La Salette Missionary priest, but that order doesn't have anyone to send to St. Mildred.

Finally, St. Therese parish in Wrightsville Beach in the Wilmington area, is open because of the death of Fr. Trent Watts. This parish is right on the beach in a very well-to-do area.

The electrical power went out today at 3 p.m. in my house, and it stayed off. This evening, as I sat at my kitchen table reading on my iPad, I glanced up to see if the moon had come over the mountains yet. At that very moment, the moon rose over the mountains on this very clear night.

January 30, 2021 – Saturday
Reitoca, F.M., Honduras - 8:20 p.m.
Mostly clear – 79 F

The electricity finally came back on today at 6:30 this morning. I truly don't understand the system.

There were high winds today, so even though it was in the low 90s, it didn't feel too hot. Blackie loved being out on the deck all day.

Today I noticed a strange thing with Blackie. While his friend Henry was here for the day, Blackie would occasionally bark at something but Henry would remain silent. Usually if someone comes on the campus, both dogs go into high gear, barking wildly. Maybe Blackie is seeing things that nobody else sees or hears; spooky.

January 31, 2021 – 4th Sunday in Ordinary Time
Reitoca, F.M., Honduras – 8 p.m.
Clear – 81 F

Juan went to Tegucigalpa on Friday to visit the store where he plans to buy a new motorcycle. The people there said the paper I sent with him, indicating he was a full-time employee on the Holy Cross campus, was perfect except for its lack of an official stamp. So, today Juan will take it to Fr. Carlos to have a parish stamp put on it.

I've asked Aaron to make a stamp design for me so I can have it handy in the future. It'll be for Holy Cross Catholic Ministries, *Ministerios Católicos de la Santa Cruz.*

This morning I walked from the Holy Cross campus to San Francisco de Asís in Reitoca. The walk takes only fifteen minutes. I haven't been to the Reitoca church in about ten months, so it was good to see everyone again. I told the story of Annalena Tonelli, an Italian martyred in Somalia, for my homily. It showed how an unmarried person was free to do many things that a married person would generally not. Annalena served as a lawyer, teacher, and nurse. The homily was in harmony with today's reading from

St. Paul's First Letter to the Corinthians extolling the glories of the single state (7: 32-35).

Engineers Brajans and Gustavo plan to visit the Holy Cross campus on Monday, February 8 to see how everything is going. They'll also explore the possibility of building my planned drive connecting the rectory with the Holy Cross campus, and they'll investigate the water problem with the yellow Blessed Stanley Rother guesthouse. While they are here, I'll ask them about the possibility of designing a new garden area that I would like next to my house.

For fun, I've been re-reading Fr. Andrew M. Greeley's *The Bishop in the West Wing*. Though it was published in 2002, many of the novel's political intrigues are very like those of January 2021.

Today I read an interesting article about Rep. Adam Kinzinger (R-IL) who is founding a political action committee (PAC) to counter the pro-Trump influence on the Republican party. Adam Kinzinger was one of ten Republicans in the U.S. House of Representatives who voted for Donald Trump's second impeachment. He notes that the current Republican party bears little resemblance to the traditional Republican party he signed up for.

January will end in a few hours, and here in Reitoca we are ending it with sunshine, blue skies, a nice breeze, and a high temperature of 95 F.

January 2021 was a most interesting month. In this month, pro-Trump radicals stormed the Capitol in Washington, Donald Trump was impeached again, and the United States inaugurated a new president, Joe Biden. President Biden, the nation's second Catholic president, went to work immediately. This month also saw the death of Fr. Trent Watts, pastor of St. Therese parish in Wrightsville Beach, North Carolina. Finally, after many months off during the pandemic, I'm once again "back in the saddle" celebrating Masses on a regular basis.

I am very ready to jump into February to see what riches it has in store for me. I hope it will be a bit mellower than January.

FEBRUARY 2021

February 1, 2021 – Monday
Reitoca, F.M., Honduras – 7:20 p.m.
Clear – 81 F

As the curtain opens on February, we see a military coup in Myanmar, ousting its president, Aung San Suu Kyi and declaring a year-long "state of emergency" because their candidate did not win the November elections.

Meanwhile in Russia, people are protesting against the persecution of Alexei Navalny, a leader of the opposition, by the Vladimir Putin government.

In the United States, Oregon's new law that decriminalizes hard drugs begins today, Donald Trump loses five lawyers who were going to defend him at his second impeachment trial, a major snowstorm is blanketing the Great Lakes and northeastern states, and protestors in Los Angeles blocked the vaccination site at Dodger Stadium saying that the pandemic is a "hoax."

At Vatican City, Pope Francis has declared the fourth Sunday of July to be henceforward known as the annual "World Day for the Grandparents and Elderly." This year, that day will fall on July 25.

Here in Reitoca, there is some bad news. Aaron told me that usually Clínica Santa María confirms two to four cases of COVID-19 per week. Today, however, it confirmed five cases. So, I'm instituting some new safety precautions on the Holy Cross campus. Because of my age, it would be very dangerous for me to get COVID-19. I hope I can stay safe until the vaccines are available to us here in Honduras.

February 2, 2021 – Tuesday – Presentation of the Lord; Groundhog Day
Reitoca, F.M., Honduras – 7:35 p.m.
Clear – 72 F

A cool breeze is blowing right now in Reitoca making it feel just perfect.

Today is Groundhog Day in the United States, and each year a groundhog named Punxsutawney Phil comes out of his home in Gobbler's Knob in Punxsutawney, Pennsylvania to predict if there will be six more weeks of winter, or if spring weather is right around the corner. Today, while snow was falling, he predicted six more weeks of winter.

Today I celebrated Mass in Curarén for the feast of Our Lady of Candelaria as this feast, the Presentation of the Lord, is their patronal feast day. There were seven altar servers. The electricity kept going on and off throughout the Mass, but we made it through just fine. One of the altar servers will be coming with Danilo and me to Pueblo Nuevo tomorrow to celebrate that community's patronal feast day, Our Lady of Suyapa.

Today I was reading how U.S. Senate Minority Mitch McConnell (R-KY) blasted the craziness that has taken over many in his party. He said, "Looney lies and conspiracy theories are cancer for the Republican Party and our country." Though he did not mention her by name, many people believe he was targeting a freshman representative, Marjorie Taylor Greene (R-GA) who is known for calling the terrorist attacks of September 11 a hoax, school shootings in the United States hoaxes, agreeing with a QAnon supporter who called for U.S. House Speaker Nancy Pelosi's murder, and theorizing that the California wildfires may have been caused by a secret Jewish space laser. Rep. Greene, who is also rabidly homophobic, replied to Sen. McConnell's criticism by saying, that it is "weak Republicans" who are the "real cancer" of the party.

On a positive note, the U.S. stock market was up, and Pete Buttigieg became the first openly gay man to become a member of a presidential cabinet when Congress voted to approve his nomination. Pete, 39-year- old former mayor of South Bend, Indiana, will become Secretary of Transportation.

February 3, 2021 – Wednesday – Our Lady of Suyapa
Reitoca, F.M., Honduras – 7:30 p.m.
Clear – 77 F

Today is a national holiday in Honduras, the feast of Our Lady of Suyapa, patron saint of Honduras. She is also the Commander-in-Chief of the Honduran Armed Forces. Ordinarily, hundreds of thousands of people flock to the Basilica of Suyapa for the special day, but because of the pandemic, that will not happen this year. This morning, I was awakened by firecrackers at 5 a.m. from Reitoca in honor of the holiday.

Today I celebrated Mass in Pueblo Nuevo, a community of Curarén. Their new church is named Our Lady of Suyapa, so it was a particularly special Mass. Danilo and I took an altar server from Curarén, Misael, with us. When we got to the church, we discovered that nobody had told the community about the Mass. The community had been to an all-night vigil in Comayagua, but within twenty minutes, the entire community was present for the Mass and had the altar area completely decorated with flowers from the people's gardens. This is an amazing community, filled with faith and joy. And it has a tremendous number of children.

After bringing Misael back to Curarén and me to Reitoca, Danilo took Juan to Tegucigalpa to the place where Danilo is doing the paperwork for Juan's new motorcycle, for Juan does not have a valid identification card. This is Juan's third visit to the store.

Pope Francis declared that from now on, July 29 will be the feast of Saints Mary, Martha, and Lazarus.

Aaron was here this afternoon to put some movies on my MacBook and help with various computer-related odds and ends.

February 4, 2021 – Thursday
Reitoca, F.M., Honduras – 9:10 p.m.
Clear – 73 F

Danilo and Juan got back from Tegucigalpa after 8 p.m. yesterday. Danilo had taken with him the new paper I had written about his employment, and the people in Pueblo Nuevo stamped it as we didn't have a stamp. The people who run the store said the stamp was fine, but that I hadn't described what job, exactly, Danilo had at Holy Cross campus. So, Danilo must go back once again with a new paper on Monday. This is not surprising, for that is how Honduras works. It took me five visits to get my Honduran identification card. So, I wrote a new paper and Danilo will get it stamped with the parish stamp and take the new paper to Tegucigalpa on Monday. I hope that he'll be able to pick up a new motorcycle for Juan on Tuesday.

Juan stayed the whole night on the deck keeping Emilio company, and took today off.

Today was a very quiet day here on the Holy Cross campus. I spent the day cooking, copying some films to put on my main computer, gardening, reading, and writing.

February 5, 2021 – Friday – St. Agatha
Reitoca, F.M., Honduras – 7:20 p.m.
Mostly clear – 79 F

This afternoon I had a 4 p.m. Mass in Alubarén. I talked about the concept of martyrdom and especially the martyr heroes here in Central America such as Blessed James Miller and Blessed Stanley Rother, martyrs of Guatemala; Servant of God Casimir Cypher of Honduras; St. Oscar Romero and Venerable Rutilio Grande; the four women martyrs of El Salvador (Ms. Jean Donovan, Maryknoll Sisters Maura Clarke and Ita Ford, and Ursuline Sr. Dorothy Kazel); and the six Jesuit martyrs of El Salvador, their housekeeper, and the housekeeper's daughter.

In my homily, I related that I went to Catholic school as a child and had always loved hearing stories of saints. However, I took the stories very seriously, and often at night before falling asleep, I would try to imagine being a martyr. I was very worried that I would not be brave enough to be a martyr. So, one day when I was seven or eight-years old, I asked a Sister about this. She said that when it is time to be a martyr, God sends special graces to the person to be brave. That made me much more comfortable. I'm counting on those special graces should that day ever come for me!

February 6, 2021 – Saturday – Ss. Paul Miki & Companions
Reitoca, F.M., Honduras – 7:25 p.m.
Clear – 79 F

Cardinal Rodríguez, our Archbishop of Tegucigalpa, has been diagnosed with COVID-19 and is in the hospital. Characteristically, he left a message that doesn't want any fuss made, but to keep him in our prayers. I'm sure he is getting the absolutely best medical treatment and nursing care possible. He is truly a most remarkable man who radiates love, joy, humor, and humility.

February 7, 2021 – Fifth Sunday in Ordinary Time
Reitoca, F.M., Honduras – 12:30 p.m.
Sunny – 97 F

This morning I celebrated two Masses. In both communities, the churches were mostly full, with no social distancing and with people of all ages, from little babies to older folks.

In the first community, the Delegados and all the people in the congregation wore masks. In the second community, absolutely no one wore masks except for me at Communion time and when I entered and left the church. I'll have to tell Fr. Carlos about this experience because the lack of masks is putting everyone at danger, and the coronavirus is running rampant in Honduras.

The two communities are not far from each other, yet they are approaching the pandemic in radically different ways. As a sociologist, I couldn't help but think what an interesting case study these two communities would make in terms of the effects of leadership, or lack thereof, on community behaviors. I'd love also to know the incidence of COVID in each of the two communities.

Blackie went out last evening and didn't come back until this morning. After eating breakfast, he basically slept all day. After having dinner, he went out into the night once again. I have no idea where he goes, but I suspect it's to see his girlfriend, Gingersnap.

February 8, 2021 – St. Jerome Emiliani; St. Josephine Bakhita
Reitoca, F.M., Honduras – 3:55 p.m.
Sunny – 97 F

This morning I received terrible news about the murder yesterday of a young man right outside the gate of the Holy Cross campus. It was Mainor Fúnez, about 21-years old, who was one of the workers who helped build the Holy Cross campus. He was shot by a masked gunman sometime in the morning. Danilo came to the campus around 7 a.m. yesterday to pick me up for Masses, but neither he nor I saw anything out of the ordinary. Danilo thinks the young man was buried in the Reitoca Cemetery today. I'll celebrate a Mass for Mainor. One of Mainor's brothers, Rosman, is a *Delegado de la Palabra* in Reitoca.

This was a very busy day here on the Holy Cross campus due to a visit from civil engineers Brajans and Gustavo, and from Chele and two others he brought. Brajans and Gustavo checked the water situation in the yellow (Blessed Stanley Rother) house and addressed other items needing attention. I also asked them to revise their estimate for the drive that I'd like to connect the rectory campus with the drive on the Holy Cross campus.

The Associated Press reported that many smaller countries are tired of waiting for bigger countries to help them get the COVID vaccine, so they are looking for ways to buy the vaccines themselves. Featured in the article were countries such as Honduras, Mexico, and Serbia.

In the United States yesterday, Super Bowl LV featured the Tampa Bay Buccaneers vs. the Kansas City Chiefs. Tampa Bay won 31-9. The game was played in Tampa, Florida, and thousands of people attended the event without wearing masks. This dismayed the mayor of Tampa and all who worry about the spread of the virus from irresponsible people.

February 9, 2021 – Tuesday
Reitoca, F.M., Honduras – 9:25 p.m.
Clear – 77 F

Brajans and Gustavo gave me a new bid for constructing the new road connecting the rectory drive to that of the Holy Cross campus drive, but I had to reject it as it was way beyond my budget. However, perhaps I'll be able to work with them on another project in the future.

Poor Danilo had no luck at the motorcycle store for the fourth time. Today, they said the stamp he had on his paper wasn't the parish's stamp; he had the stamp of Clínica Santa María, which is part of the parish, but they didn't accept that.

Drs. Aaron and Valencia came to my house this afternoon. Valencia's last day as the microbiologist of the Clínica Santa María laboratory will be on March 11. Valencia, the founding microbiologist of the laboratory, has done amazing work for the past four-and-a-half years. She will be living in Tegucigalpa and hopes to learn new aspects of her field. Fortunately, she will remain a member of our Rotary club (Passport 7730) and will work on establishing relationships with other Rotary clubs in Tegucigalpa. We need relationships with Honduran clubs to improve our chances of getting a Rotary global grant.

While Aaron and Valencia were visiting, all the electricity in my house went out, but Aaron was able to call Edwin, an electrical engineer, and fixed the problem. Edwin thinks we need to remove the washer and dryer from the solar system and put them exclusively on the "city" system. All of this is totally over my head, but Aaron grasps it very easily. He is a total gem for a person like me who is close to illiterate on technical matters.

Today I got some wonderful news from my friend Joe Lakatos in Wilmington. He has received a job offer at Holy Cross College in South Bend, Indiana. Joe, who has advanced degrees in Business Administration and Law, will be the Brother John Driscoll, C.S.C. Professor of Business Administration beginning in the 2021-2022 academic year. Very importantly, he is granted immediate tenure. While at Holy Cross, Joe plans to study for a Master's degree in theology. To my delight, he hopes to somehow connect his students and alumni with my own Holy Cross campus here in Reitoca. Joe visited me here in July of 2019 when the Holy Cross campus buildings were still under construction. I'm very excited about Joe's good fortune, and I look forward to playing some role in his journey.

Today began the second impeachment trial of Donald Trump. The defending lawyer did a terrible job; even Donald Trump and his Republican allies had nothing positive to say. The Democrats, however, presented a powerful video of the storming of the capitol by Trumpian "patriots."

I also read today about a Religious Sister in Europe who recovered from COVID. Sister is 116 years old, the second-oldest person in the world according to the folks who keep track of such information. She said she didn't even know she had COVID until others told her she had tested positive for it!

February 10, 2021 – Wednesday – St. Scholastica
Reitoca, F.M., Honduras – 8:25 p.m.
Clear – 79 F

This was another day in which the temperature reached 97 F.

Today the priests of the Diocese of Raleigh received a note from the chancery to remember two priests in our special prayers: Msgr. Jerry Sherba and Fr. Hector Rangel Galván.

Msgr. Jerry Sherba, who is now retired, is in UNC Hospital in Chapel Hill undergoing treatments for two cancers, myeloma and acute myeloid leukemia (AML). The note says that Jerry has "…his usual joy-filled spirit" despite a great deal of pain.

Fr. Hector is a Passionist priest stationed at St. Ann parish in Clayton. He is being treated for long-term effects of COVID.

This evening, Dr. Aaron joined me at my house for our monthly Rotary Passport Club meeting. This month we had a special presentation on the importance of storytelling and how the use of video and graphics can build relationships. The presenter was Cody Milewski of Cassian Films in Wilmington, North Carolina. It was a very interesting and informative presentation. I wonder if Cody would like to visit us here in Honduras. He would probably jump at the chance. But first we need to make enough progress in the pandemic that travel is possible again.

February 11, 2021 – Thursday – Our Lady of Lourdes
Reitoca, F.M., Honduras – 9:25 p.m.
Mostly clear – 75 F

Today the Catholic Church celebrates the World Day of the Sick as well as Our Lady of Lourdes. Every year, an estimated six million pilgrims visit the shrine of Lourdes, many of them hoping for a cure for whatever illness they have.

This afternoon, as I was writing in my study, I noticed a brown dog on the deck and assumed it was Andy. But when I opened the door to the deck, the dog jumped up and dashed into the house and into the kitchen. She knocked over a couple of cans on the shelf in the laundry room next to the kitchen, and then tried to get to the dogfood supplies. I immediately remembered Chispa, a puppy with the same personality, whom I used to call Trouble before learning her actual name. Sure enough, the brown dog was Chispa, now full-grown. She is making herself right at home and immediately began protecting the campus by barking at Emilio as he was walking to the house for his night shift.

I have not been watching the Senate trial of Donald Trump, but today I watched a fascinating presentation by Rep. Jamie Raskin of Maryland, the lead Impeachment Manager for the Democrats. He presented an amazing video of Donald Trump inciting his followers to violence. Political pundits are sure the Republicans in the Senate will acquit the ex-president to avoid the wrath of the hard-core Trumpian "true believer" voters. Many Republicans not in Congress are talking of forming an alternative, center-right political party.

This evening I celebrated Mass in the "mother church" of the parish, San Francisco de Asís in Reitoca. I preached on St. Bernadette Soubirous.

I walked to the church from the Holy Cross campus which takes only about fifteen minutes. When I was almost at the church, I received a call from Danilo saying he had come from his home to bring me to the Mass. So, he and his nephew Ober drove my truck to church and gave me a ride home. It was Ober's first time on the Holy Cross campus.

February 12, 2021 – Friday
Reitoca, F.M., Honduras – 7:40 p.m.
Clear – 79 F

Today is Lunar New Year, the beginning of the Year of the Ox. I predict it will be an excellent year, but I predict that every year.

Today I celebrated Mass in Alubarén. Because the Scriptures were about the healing ministry of Jesus, I told the story of the creation of the Ronald McDonald House Charities.

After the Mass, Danilo and I gave a ride to a young man who was going to Reitoca to attend an A.A. meeting. He said that the A.A. group in Reitoca meets every evening from 7-9 p.m. and that there are usually seven people. I have seen a sign advertising the meeting, but it doesn't show the time, day, or place.

This afternoon I attended a Zoom discussion regarding ordination of women as deacons in the Catholic Church. It was hosted by Gail De George, and the panelists were Phyllis Zagano and Colleen Gibson. The three women who led the meeting made their case very clearly. I especially enjoyed Phyllis' presentation. Regrettably, I was not able to attend the entire meeting as I had to leave for Mass.

Fr. Carlos dropped by the Holy Cross campus this evening and gave me my Mass schedule for next week. He said that in Honduras, the plan is to distribute Ash Wednesday ashes in the regular way (on the forehead) despite the pandemic. In the Diocese of Raleigh, however, the priests will "sprinkle ashes" on top of people's heads. The ashes used for Ash Wednesday often leave terrible stains on white albs. I can't imagine how the sprinkling rite will turn out.

February 13, 2021 – Saturday – Blessed James Miller
Reitoca, F.M., Honduras – 6:45 p.m.
Partly clear – 81 F

Today the U.S. Senate voted 57-43 to find Donald Trump guilty of inciting the violence in the Capitol on January 6, 2021, far short of the two-thirds majority required to convict the ex-president. Seven Republicans joined all the Democrats in voting to convict Donald Trump.

Today a group of about ten youths from Curarén and their chaperone came to visit my house. They were in Reitoca for a special Mass and a meeting with Fr. Carlos. That group has a lot of spirit.

Little Chispa did not show up today. From what Juan tells me, she only wants to be on the campus when I'm here. If I'm not here, she leaves.

Today is the feast of Blessed James Miller, a Christian Brother from Wisconsin who was martyred in Guatemala. His memory is special here on the Holy Cross campus because the mayordomo's *casita* is dedicated to him.

February 14, 2021 – 6th Sunday in Ordinary Time
Reitoca, F.M., Honduras – 7:15 p.m.
Clear – 81 F

Today is Valentine's Day and World Day of Marriage in the Catholic Church. My blog post today features a photo of one of the last couples whose wedding I officiated before coming to Honduras – Vicente Antonio and Ilse del Carmen López.

Little Chispa showed up this morning at my house, had breakfast, and then disappeared.

This morning I had Masses in La Libertad and San Miguelito. I told the story of St. Dulce of Brazil and how she helped the poor and sick. My favorite story of Dulce is how she turned a chicken coop into a 1,500-bed hospital. When her group of poor people grew to about seventy, Sr. Dulce asked her superior if she could use the chicken yard of the convent as a temporary place for the people to stay. The superior gave Dulce permission, provided that she care for the chickens. Dulce did; she fed the chickens to the patients. The chicken coop became San Antonio Hospital.

On the way home from San Miguelito, I learned that the killer of Mainor Funes has plans to kill all four of the remaining brothers, but I have no idea why. So, the brothers are in hiding and making plans to leave the area. It must be a very scary time for the brothers.

February 15, 2021 – Monday
Reitoca, F.M., Honduras – 8:20 p.m.
Mostly clear – 79 F

Today is Presidents' Day in the United States, but here in Honduras it is a regular Monday.

Danilo made his fifth trip to Tegucigalpa today to buy a motorcycle for Juan. Once again, he was unable to buy it because of various bureaucratic issues. I suggested he try another store: this one doesn't deserve our business.

I'm reading books by two of my favorite writers and am fascinated by the similarities that I'm finding. The books are *The House by the Sea: A Journal* by May Sarton; and *My Love: A Prayer Journal* by Fr. Andrew Greeley. Both were very prolific writers, and both treasured their solitude and quiet time to write. But both were always scheduling events, such as giving lectures, because neither one was able to say "No." Then, finding themselves tired and frazzled, both would get angry at themselves. But both recognized that only they were to blame for always saying "Yes" to others.

That happens to people who are natural "givers" in life, myself included. In academics, that often happened to professor friends and to me. We'd think nothing of saying, "Oh, sure, I can do that" to an engagement way into the future. But then when the date for the gig would come closer, we'd be scrambling to get our papers written for our presentations. And every time, we would be acutely aware that we had nobody to blame but ourselves, for nobody forced us to say "yes" to the request.

February 16, 2021 – Tuesday – Mardi Gras
Reitoca, F.M., Honduras – 7:20 p.m.
Partly cloudy – 81 F

Today is Mardi Gras, but because of the pandemic, there are not the usual wild parties in New Orleans and other places. In New Orleans, instead of parades with floats, some people are decorating their houses as though they were floats.

Big storms have been causing problems all over the United States. In Texas, for example, snow is causing major power outages, and a tornado in Brunswick County, North Carolina killed three people. Millions of Americans are without electricity.

February 17, 2021 – Ash Wednesday
Reitoca, F.M., Honduras – 7 p.m.
Mostly cloudy – 79 F

Today we begin the season of Lent with the celebration of Ash Wednesday. I celebrated two Masses today in La Libertad and San Miguelito.

In La Libertad, right before the Mass was to begin, I noticed that the ashes were missing. One of the *Delegadas* of the community quickly got some ashes from a nearby cook-fire so I could put ashes on foreheads after the homily. I later learned that a young man who is known to be a drug addict had stolen the ashes that were sitting on the Communion rail right before Mass, put them in his pocket, and left the church before Mass. I have no idea what he was planning to do with a little bag of ashes. He probably had no idea either.

In San Miguelito, the people are getting ready to begin building a new foundation under the altar. The current platform is old and wooden, and the people are afraid that one day it will collapse, sending the altar, ambo, priest, and lectors to the floor below.

The road from Reitoca to the communities of La Libertad and San Miguelito are worse than ever. It's hard to imagine what they will be like during the rainy season.

February 18, 2021 – Thursday
Reitoca, F.M., Honduras – 8 p.m.
Mostly cloudy – 82 F

Today I celebrated Mass in Curarén and told the story of Sr. Dorothy Stang, an Ursuline missionary sister from Ohio. Dorothy was a martyr of the Amazon. Because Danilo was busy in Lodo Negro, his nephew Mainor gave me a ride to and from Curarén.

Cardinal Rodríguez is out of the hospital now and will continue recovering from COVID at home. That is great news.

Juan was a *padrino* (godfather) this morning for a baptism in Rebalse, a community of Reitoca. He got a whole new set of clothes for the occasion. The Rebalse community set off firecrackers this morning and this evening as part of the baptismal celebration. Fr. Carlos celebrated the Mass and Baptisms for seven children.

The robotic Mars explorer Perseverance, nicknamed "Percy" by staff, landed on Mars. The craft has a helicopter aboard, called Ingenuity. The landing on the "red planet" went flawlessly. Scientists around the world, and everyone interested in outer space, will be eagerly waiting for new discoveries. Mars is about 126 million miles from Earth.

February 19, 2021 – Friday
Reitoca, F.M., Honduras – 8:30 p.m.
Clear – 81 F

Today Juan and I started cleaning up litter on the road to the gate of the Holy Cross property. I call the road Calle Calvario (Calvary Street) because it such a terribly difficult "road." We filled four trash bags and ended that project for the day. We plan to continue working on it little by little, maybe filling up at least four trash bags per day.

The rest of the day I took as a "Greenleaf Day," a day where I rested from most work by watching many episodes of the television series *Greenleaf.* The show features a black mega-church and the Greenleaf family that runs it. The family has one problem after another, and every member of the family has plenty of drama in their life. The show is rather addictive to me, but I needed a break from reading and writing.

This afternoon a young family of father, mother, and two-year-old daughter came to the Holy Cross campus to visit me. They wondered if I could give them money to build a house in Rebalse, a community of Reitoca. I explained that we had no program that could help individual families with construction projects. If we did have such a project, the demand would be unbelievably huge.

If I could, I'd build the whole world beautiful houses and give each person a million dollars. Unfortunately, however, I can't do this. I do truly wish I could do much more than I'm currently doing to help the people of Honduras. I need to learn more about what Habitat for Humanity is doing in Honduras and how we might be able to involve that organization here in the mountains.

I learned that ten countries of the world have administered 75% of the world supply of COVID vaccine, while 130 nations, including Honduras, have received none.

February 20, 2021 – Saturday
Reitoca, F.M., Honduras – 9:15 p.m.
Mostly cloudy – 75 F

This morning I attended an excellent course in grant-writing for Rotary via Zoom. We learned about preparing small district grants as well as global grants, and we learned who are the key persons who can help us in such preparations.

Aaron came up with design for a stamp for what I'm calling Holy Cross Catholic Ministries to endorse documents for our ministry (and for cases like poor Juan's motorcycle). So, as soon as the stampers arrive, I'll be able to stamp documents to my heart's content.

In the Andrew Greeley book that I'm re-reading, Fr. Greeley talks about growing older and what that means mentally and physically. In the journal, he is 70-71 years old. He notes the changes the body goes through, but also and how growing old allows one to see more clearly the hand of God in one's life. I find that is so true. In my life, it is only in looking back on my life that I can see how God was leading me.

Though my body has slowed down and there are more aches and pains, I continue to find that each decade of life is more exciting and fruitful than the one before it. And I'm so grateful that I'm able to experience that, for many people talk about aging as a negative thing rather than a positive experience.

In May Sarton's *A House by the Sea: A Journal*, she writes, "One of the good elements of old age is that we no longer have to prove anything, to ourselves or to anyone else. We are what we are." Well, I'm not sure I've gotten to that stage yet, and as a matter of fact, I'm not even sure I fully grasp what May was trying to say. But it sounds good.

February 21, 2021 – Second Sunday of Lent
Reitoca, F.M., Honduras – 9:15 p.m.
Clear – 79 F

This morning I had Mass in Reitoca, so Juan came to watch over Holy Cross campus while I was at church. His friend, Mainor Euceda, came over with him. I walked to church, so Blackie and his little friend Chispa had to be kept in the house until I returned, for otherwise they would have followed me and hung out near the altar during the whole Mass. Blackie once followed me to church and stayed near me through the whole Mass. Fortunately, he was good as gold, but having him "assist" me at Mass was a distraction for the congregation (though they greatly enjoyed his presence).

The Diocese of Raleigh sent word to all the priests of the diocese that Fr. J. Hector Rangel Galván died last night from the effects of COVID-19 following a lengthy hospitalization in Smithfield. Fr. Hector was a Passionist priest from Mexico who had been serving at St. Ann parish in Clayton.

Fr. Carlos dropped by this evening to give me this coming week's Mass assignment. I'll be celebrating Mass in La Laguna on Saturday and in Alubarén and Curarén next Sunday. I haven't been to La Laguna in over a year.

February 22, 2021 – Monday – Chair of St. Peter
Reitoca, F.M., Honduras – 7:35 p.m.
Mostly clear – 82 F

I have been awake since 4:30 a.m., worrying about our parish health care projects. My main concern is that I have little information about the finances and how *SaludHondu*, our fund-raising organization in the US, faring. But worry won't accomplish anything except insomnia.

Danilo and I went to Tegucigalpa this morning, and I met Marco at Banco Atlántida to pay salaries for our clinic staff. Danilo and I also went in search of a gasoline-powered generator for our water system in case of an electric blackout, but we could not find any that met our needs. We'll keep looking.

On the way home from Tegucigalpa, Danilo and I stopped in at Gabriela's Ferretería on CA-5 to see what they have. We need some laminate for the overhang outside my kitchen. We saw some red material, but I'll have to take photos of the red roofs on my house to be sure to buy a matching design.

The United States reached a milestone today: over a half-million people in the country have died of COVID-19. The government noted that the number is greater than all the Americans – almost all of them men –

who were killed in World War I, World War II, and the Vietnam War combined. The COVID-19 death tolls, however, are not sexist; they reflect both men and women in about equal numbers.

February 23, 2021 – Tuesday – St. Polycarp
Reitoca, F.M., Honduras – 9:45 p.m.
Clear – 79 F

Today I woke at 3 a.m., once again worrying about *SaludHondu* and our clinic staff and whether we will have sufficient money for the future.

This afternoon, Drs. Aaron, Marco, Valencia and I met at my house for a meeting of the International Projects Committee of our Rotary Passport 7730 Club. I told them that the international group of the Wilmington, N.C. Club would like to help us with a global grant, but Rotary global grants require strict date commitments, and we can't make any firm commitments because we have no idea when we will be vaccinated.

I shared my worries with the group, and that was very therapeutic for me. I have much less stress now. "A problem shared is a problem halved; a problem kept secret is a problem doubled" is the little saying that comes to mind.

February 24, 2021 – Wednesday
Reitoca, F.M., Honduras – 10 p.m.
Mostly clear – 79 F

Today I took most of the day off to relax by watching the remaining episodes of *Greenleaf.* That was a remarkable series about "big religion" and the fall and redemption of human beings in everyday life, especially religious leaders.

Juan is off for two days, so Blackie and I are alone to enjoy the solitude of Holy Cross campus.

I have been running out of some of my medicines because I'm not able to travel to the United States to pick up supplies. Fortunately, Dr. Marco can get what I need from our two pharmacies that he oversees – Farmacia San Francisco de Asís in Reitoca and Farmacia Candelaria in Curarén.

February 25, 2021 – Thursday
Reitoca, F.M., Honduras – 8:55 p.m.
Clear – 81 F

Though the outdoor temperature is in the middle 90s during the day, I have only to open the doors to the living room and deck area for a tremendous breeze to blow through the house, making it very comfortable. Because I don't have door stoppers, I'm using jugs of water to prevent the doors from slamming from the wind.

I got my two homilies done for this weekend and am now preparing blog posts for the week after next.

February 26, 2021 – Friday
Reitoca, F.M., Honduras – 6:15 p.m.
Clear – 88 F

As I write this note, a beautiful full moon has risen over the northeastern mountains. According to the Farmer's Almanac, it is called the Full Snow Moon. What a beautiful name for it, though of course we never have snow in Honduras.

Today Juan and I enjoyed watching a helicopter fly by the Holy Cross campus to land somewhere in Reitoca for a political rally. Primary elections for national and local candidates will be on March 14.

Today I picked and pickled about thirty *habanero* peppers. They are very hot and can burn skin if they are touched. I sent one jar to Dr. Aaron, and on Sunday I'll give Fr. Carlos the other jar. Both love hot peppers.

February 27, 2021 – Saturday
Reitoca, F.M., Honduras – 9 p.m.
Clear – 81 F

Today I celebrated a Mass in La Laguna, a Curarén community that is a one-hour drive from Reitoca. There were many people because we had six baptisms. I performed five of the baptisms after the homily, and then I did another after the Mass for a little boy who arrived late. It all worked out well. I posed with the baptismal families after the Mass. That is a very friendly community.

Two *Delegados* from neighboring communities came to the Mass to help with the music ministry – Rubén of San Román and Israel of Pueblo Nuevo. After the Mass, Danilo and I gave a ride to Rubén to his home. Rubén, and the San Román community, want me to come to celebrate Mass for them on March 25. I told Rubén he would have to ask Fr. Carlos, for he manages my schedule. Rubén and Danilo immediately said that Fr. Carlos knows all about it already and has approved. So, I suspect the community wants to give formal thanks to the Red Lantern Foundation for giving it money to redo their church. I also promised we'd give them 4000 *lempiras* on Tuesday to buy paint. Four-thousand lempiras is about US $167.

Danilo tried my *habanero* peppers, but they were too hot for him.

February 28, 2021 – 2nd Sunday of Lent
Reitoca, F.M., Honduras – 7:15 p.m.
Mostly clear – 88 F

Fr. Carlos walked over to my house this morning from the rectory to give me my Mass assignment for the week. I'll be celebrating Masses in Alubarén, El Limón, La Libertad, and San Miguelito. I gave him a jar of my pickled *habanero* peppers. I'm eager to see if they were hot enough for him.

The Mass in Alubarén was uneventful, but in Curarén, I performed ten baptisms. I stayed after the Mass for photos with the baptism families. The altar server, Noel, took photos for the individual families. He is so incredibly helpful, as well as very knowledgeable about liturgy. I predict he will make a fine priest one day.

February was an interesting month. Cardinal Rodríguez was hospitalized with COVID-19, but he is recovering nicely. Passionist priest Fr. J. Hector Rangel Galván of St. Ann parish in Clayton, North Carolina, died from the disease. He's the second priest working in the Diocese of Raleigh to die from COVID.

Little Chispa, whom I had named "Trouble" when she was a puppy because of her amazing ability to cause chaos wherever she goes, has returned to my life. She is as energetic as ever and filled with unbridled love. I must be very careful walking when she's around, however, for she has a habit of walking in between my legs and tripping me.

Also, this month, Juan and I have begun to clean up the trash that litters Calle Calvario, the road to the side of the Holy Cross campus. We plan to make this an ongoing project.

Dr. Valencia, the founding microbiologist of the laboratory in Clínica Santa María, will be leaving her job to take advantage of new learning opportunities that are only offered in Tegucigalpa. Her last day will be March 11. She will remain a member of the Rotary Passport 7730 Club and plans to help establish relationships between clubs in Tegucigalpa and our group here in Reitoca.

Perseverance safely landed on Mars on February 18. Now, its helicopter Ingenuity will explore the planet and send back data to Earth.

Finally, the Wilmington Rotary Club has contacted me to let me know it would love to help with obtaining a global grant for us here in Honduras. Until we get the COVID vaccine, however, we can't make concrete plans. However, I'm very grateful and excited that the Wilmington Rotary Club has expressed its support and interest.

Now, I'm ready for a productive and exciting March.

MARCH 2021

March 1, 2021 – Monday
Reitoca, F.M., Honduras – 7 p.m.
Mostly clear – 88 F

Irish Heritage Month arrived here in Reitoca with a temperature of 96 F this afternoon. The national Ancient Order of Hibernians is planning a month-long series of presentations on Irish history and celebrations. Unfortunately, many of the presentations will be on the weekends when I'm out and about in the mountain pueblos and villages celebrating Masses, but perhaps I'll be able to check in for some of the celebrations.

Juan is staying over tonight in the St. Oscar Romero House because Danilo, Emilio and I will be leaving at 6 a.m. tomorrow, and we didn't want the campus to be unattended. I want to be on time for my 9 a.m. appointment at the American Embassy to renew my passport.

Today I chose my themes and stories for this coming week's homilies, so now I have only to put them into prose. The hardest part is done.

This afternoon, Aaron brought over two rubber stamps for "Holy Cross Catholic Ministries" that he designed. In addition to the words in both English and Spanish, there is a large Latin cross with two guest houses. I am very pleased with them.

March 2, 2021 – Tuesday
Reitoca, F.M., Honduras – 7:35 p.m.
Partly cloudy – 82 F

Danilo, Emilio and I left the Holy Cross campus at 6 a.m. for Tegucigalpa so I'd be at the embassy on time for my 9 a.m. appointment. Because we left so early, I thought for sure we'd get there much too early. In fact, we made it just in time. The embassy staff told me that the appointment could take an hour, and people are not allowed to bring in a watch or phone. So, I could not call Danilo when I was finished. After leaving me at the embassy, he took Emilio to a motorcycle store to get a license plate for his son's motorcycle, and then they went to the bank and a restaurant.

It turned out that my appointment took fifteen minutes. So, I waited for Danilo for two hours. Fortunately, it was a beautiful day in Tegucigalpa. Unlike Reitoca, where it got up to 97 F today, in Tegucigalpa it was in the low 80s with refreshing breezes. Passports are delivered only on Fridays, and they may be picked up between 8 and 10 a.m. I can get mine on March 26. So, it was a successful day for me, for without a U.S. passport, I can't travel. Now I'm good to go till 2031.

One excellent accomplishment was purchasing a new gasoline-powered generator at La Mundial (True Value) for the cistern. We need that when the public electricity goes off. We also got one watermelon each as this is watermelon season, and all the roadside stands are filled with them.

March 3, 2021 – Wednesday - St. Katharine Drexel
Reitoca, F.M., Honduras – 2:30 p.m.
Sunny – 97 F

It is a scorcher outside, but there is a nice breeze. I'm enjoying the day, for I have no Masses, no Zoom meetings, and no appointments. I'm using the day to write homilies and do odds and end around the house.

Today I ordered a year of the digital version of the *Washington Post*. That, with my *New York Times* subscription, should keep me well informed.

March 4, 2021 – Thursday – St. Casimir
Reitoca, F.M., Honduras – 8 p.m.
Mostly clear – 81 F

This afternoon I had Mass in Alubarén. As always, there was a good number of people for the Mass.

In the United States, today, Congress did not meet because a right-wing group threatened to engage in violence. The group believed that former president Donald Trump would return and become president again.

March 5, 2021 – Friday
Reitoca, F.M., Honduras – 8:40 p.m.
Mostly clear – 79 F

Today is Emilio's birthday, so he is taking a few days off with family. It was 97 F today here in Reitoca.

Juan and I planted *habanero* and watermelon seeds and garlic cloves, and we potted a new cactus plant that I bought in Tegucigalpa on Tuesday. The cactus looks beautiful sitting on one of the kitchen counters.

This coming Thursday will be Dr. Valencia's last day at Clínica Santa María, so the staff will have a little party in her honor that afternoon here on my deck.

March 6, 2021 – Saturday
Reitoca, F.M., Honduras – 3:55 p.m.
Sunny – 97 F

This morning Danilo and I went to the Reitocan community of El Limón, where I celebrated Mass and baptized nine children. We also celebrated the Presentation of a small baby named Dylan. This community reserves consecrated hosts to take to the homebound sick and for Communion services. Having Communion services is rather new in this parish. It would be nice to have more of our churches be able to have such services, for only five of our more than 80 churches have a Mass each week. Most of the churches have a Liturgy of the Word run *by Delegados de la Palabra* on Thursdays and Sundays.

I had been scheduled to celebrate Masses in La Libertad and San Miguelito tomorrow, but Fr. Carlos changed the schedule due to high COVID-19 cases in La Libertad. So, instead I'll have Masses in Concepción and El Hatillo. That's fine with me, for it means we'll be back an hour earlier than if we had gone to the original places.

March 7, 2021 – Third Sunday of Lent
Reitoca, F.M., Honduras – 9:30 p.m.
Clear – 79 F

The Masses in Concepción and El Hatillo went very well today. An elderly man from Concepción told Danilo and me that there will probably not be any people at Mass next Sunday because it is primary election day in Honduras. But since people have all day to vote, I suspect we'll have people for Mass.

Fr. Carlos warned Danilo and me not to pick up any passengers next Sunday on election day. He said that there could be troublemakers out and about, and if there is any trouble with such people in our truck, the whole truck would be suspect. So, Danilo and I won't pick anyone up, even though we very often give rides to folks on our journeys.

Today it was 97 F, but there were strong winds, so it didn't feel too hot. The wind did knock out our electricity for a short period of time.

March 8, 2021 – Monday – St. John of God
Reitoca, F.M., Honduras – 8:50 p.m.
Clear – 79 F

Today is International Women's Day, so there are many articles on the internet about inspirational women and their contributions to the world. In my blog post for today, I included a photo of the cake the men of Clínica Santa María bought for the women of the clinic in honor of this day in 2019.

It is also the feast day of St. John of God, a spectacular nurse who founded the Brothers Hospitallers. He is one of the men featured in my book, *Saintly Men of Nursing: 101 Amazing Stories.*

We had strong winds here in Reitoca today, so the high temperature was only in the low 90s.

Today there were three cows grazing on the Holy Cross campus. One of them was in the triangle where I have a little *almendro* tree, and I was afraid she would either eat the tree or clumsily knock it over. She left it alone, however. Juan told me that cows don't eat *almendro* trees. Later in the day, a couple of horses came and did some grazing.

Little Chispa was here this afternoon, but Blackie went out on the town.

March 9, 2021 – Tuesday – St. Frances of Rome
Reitoca, F.M., Honduras – 9:20 p.m.
Partly cloudy – 79 F

Today I walked with Juan to Anita's store in the center of Reitoca, and Blackie and Chispa tagged along. I should take more walks into the town to get exercise. I took some photos of the town for a PowerPoint presentation I'll make one day.

Today all the priests of the Diocese of Raleigh received an invitation to the ordination of three men to the transitional diaconate on April 10. "Transitional" refers to the fact that the men are "passing through" the diaconate on their way to priesthood ordination. The three men, and the places where they will celebrate their first Masses as deacons, are Andrés Guillermo Arévalo Quinchangegua (Our Lady of Lourdes in Ralcigh); John Michael Prudente de Guzman (St. Joseph in Raleigh); and Erik Reyes Reyes (Sacred Heart in Whiteville). I hope they have as wonderful a priesthood as I have had.

March 10, 2021 – Wednesday
Reitoca, F.M., Honduras – 8 p.m.
Partly cloudy – 81 F

The U.S. Congress passed a 1.9-trillion-dollar pandemic relief bill today, and the president is expected to sign it tomorrow.

I'm thinking of traveling to the United States in April after Easter if possible. While there, I can get my healthcare checkups and yearly supply of medicines.

This afternoon and evening I hosted a farewell party for Dr. Valencia, who founded our St. Mary Laboratory at Clínica Santa María.

She'll be learning new microbiological procedures in Tegucigalpa. All the clinic staff was here for the party except for Nurse Yesenia. The new microbiologist, Dr. Shelsie Vásquez Banegas, was welcomed at the party, and our pastor, Fr. Carlos, led us in a prayer. My deck is an absolutely perfect place for a party in the late afternoons and evenings when the heat of the day dissipates.

March 11, 2021 – Thursday
Reitoca, F.M., Honduras – 6:35 p.m.
Partly cloudy – 86 F

This morning I celebrated Mass in Lodo Negro, the community of Curarén where Danilo lives. We had eleven baptisms in addition to the Mass, and I stayed after the Mass for photos with each of the baptism families.

This afternoon, Dr. Aaron stopped by to help me with a few computer things. He noted that Dr. Marco will be preparing a PowerPoint presentation for our May Rotary Passport Club meeting. It will feature what we are doing for the health needs of this rural mountain area, and we'll include a discussion of the lodging and sightseeing that visitors from the United States can expect.

I suggested to Aaron that after the elections, we should plan a party on my deck for the mayors of Alubarén, Curarén, and Reitoca. Perhaps we could also invite those of La Libertad and San Miguelito. Those are the five municipalities of our parish. We'd like to see what they think of our plans for applying for Rotary global grants. What we really want is a new space for a polyclinic or a little hospital.

President Biden gave a speech last evening, and he hopes that the United States can be back to at least a semblance of "normality" by the Fourth of July, Independence Day.

March 12, 2021 – Friday
Reitoca, F.M., Honduras – 7:45 p.m.
Clear – 82 F

Danilo drove his new (used) red Nissan pickup truck to the Holy Cross campus. This is Danilo's first vehicle ever, so it is very special to him. We drove in my truck, however, to the community of Samalares Abajo.

That community has a big new church called Espíritu Santo (Holy Spirit). This was the first time that Danilo and I had been inside the new church, though it is only about a twenty-minute drive from Reitoca. This a an incredibly peppy community with an excellent band, choir, and leadership. In addition to the Mass, I celebrated four baptisms. Fr. Carlos had told me that the Mass was at 10 a.m., so we got there about 9:45. Unfortunately, he told the community the Mass was at 9 a.m. I apologized for the lateness, and the community seemed very willing to forgive.

Today the Diocese of Raleigh announced that Fr. Bill Upah, pastor of Annunciation parish in Havelock, is appointed pastor of St. Therese parish in Wrightsville Beach, and that Fr. Pius S. Wekesa, administrator of St. John the Baptist parish in Roanoke Rapids, is appointed pastor of Holy Cross parish in Durham. Bill Upah and I were ordained together in 1998 at St. Michael the Archangel church in Cary, and as far as I know, we're the only two priests of the diocese whose ethnic backgrounds are half Bohemian and half Irish. I hope both Frs. Bill and Pius are very happy in their new assignments that will begin June 29.

March 13, 2021 – Saturday
Reitoca, F.M., Honduras – 8:40 p.m.
Clear – 81 F

Blackie was out all night, returning around 7 a.m. He didn't want any breakfast, and he slept the day away. Then around 8 p.m., he went out into the night once again.

March 14, 2021 – 4th Sunday of Lent
Reitoca, F.M., Honduras – 8:30 p.m.
Clear – 81 F

There was a pickup truck accident last night in Reitoca, in which a parishioner named Enma Osorto was killed. I offered the 7 p.m. Mass in Reitoca for her this evening, and her funeral Mass will be tomorrow morning.

Today is Primary Election Day in Honduras. Here in Reitoca, the big contest is between the current mayor, Marlon Osorto, and a lawyer named Johel Zelaya. This morning I met Zelaya in the central plaza area. He has a reputation for helping the poor. I also took some photos of the crowds registering to vote and waiting to vote.

Today I celebrated Mass in Reitoca at 9 a.m. and 7 p.m. I walked to both Masses. Though I went by myself this morning, this evening Juan walked with me. Danilo, who was unable to get to Reitoca, asked Juan to do that, for he felt that there was too great a chance for violence with so many people out and about from the election. Although the central plaza area in front of our church was packed with people, it was quite safe because of the presence of many soldiers and police.

On the walk back home, Juan and I stopped to admire the crystal-clear sky and all the stars.

Blackie has been regularly going out all night, coming back in the morning, and then sleeping all day.

March 15, 2021 – Monday
Reitoca, F.M., Honduras – 8:30 p.m.
Clear – 81 F

Today was the funeral Mass for Enma Osorto in the church of San Francisco de Asís, the "mother church" of our parish. I'm not sure which priest celebrated the Mass.

Juan stayed in the St. Oscar Romero house last night, for he didn't want to be traveling in Reitoca on election day. Now he is off for two days.

This morning I talked with Ramon, a man from Wilmington, N.C., who is living as a religious hermit. He is currently exploring the possibility of becoming a canonical hermit, one who makes public vows, in the Archdiocese of Atlanta. Canonical hermits can be either clergy or laity (which includes religious sisters and brothers). Ramon has my full support.

Today the Diocese of Raleigh sent all the priests of the diocese, and other priests who work in the diocese, its second posting of parishes that will need a new pastor. The openings are three: Annunciation in Havelock (554 families); St. John the Baptist in Roanoke Rapids (202 families); and St. Peter in Greenville (1,488 families).

I ordered a year's supply of medicines today from Express Scripts, so when they're delivered to Richard Creech's house in Wilmington, N.C., I'll try to get a flight to pick them up. Life is so much more complicated without post office or FedEx deliveries.

March 16, 2021 – Tuesday
Reitoca, F.M., Honduras – 8:45 p.m.
Clear – 81 F

This was a 99 F day, and it definitely felt like it. Fortunately, however, the evening temperatures, combined with breezes, make it ideal to be outside in the late afternoons and evenings. I spent the day relaxing.

March 17, 2021 – Wednesday – St. Patrick
Reitoca, F.M., Honduras – 9:30 p.m.
Mostly clear – 77 F

Today I learned that Marlon Osorto, current mayor of Reitoca, won the primary election to be the Liberal Party's candidate for mayor of Reitoca later in the year. Each of the five municipalities in our parish has its own *alcalde* (mayor).

Today I also learned that "almost all" of the healthcare staff of our parish received an anti-COVID vaccination today. It was a great surprise, for I didn't know that the vaccine had arrived in Honduras. People over 75 years of age are high on the list to receive the vaccine when available in Honduras, so Aaron will make sure it is available for me.

The Archdiocese of Tegucigalpa sent the priests working in the archdiocese instructions on celebrating Holy Week during this time of pandemic. Among changes include no processions, no feet-washing at the Mass of the Lord's Supper on Holy Thursday, and others.

This morning Juan and I spruced up the St. Oscar Romero guesthouse so I could take some photos for Marco, who is putting together a PowerPoint presentation for our Rotary club to show what kind of lodgings they can expect if they come to visit.

Fr. Carlos stopped by this evening to give me the Mass schedule for the coming weekend. I'll be celebrating Mass in the Reitocan community of San José this Friday on their patronal feast day. The Feast of St. Joseph is also Father's Day in Honduras, as it is in many predominantly Catholic countries. On Sunday, I'll be celebrating Masses in the Alubarén communities of Concepción and El Hatillo.

March 18, 2021 – Thursday – St. Cyril of Jerusalem
Reitoca, F.M., Honduras – 8:30 p.m.
Mostly cloudy – 77 F

I had no Masses today, so I used the day to relax. This afternoon we had a wonderful rain for about two hours. It was our first good rain in a couple of months, so it is very much appreciated.

March 19, 2021 – Friday – St. Joseph
Reitoca, F.M., Honduras – 4:55 p.m.
Mostly cloudy – 72 F

Today is one of the two feast days in honor of St. Joseph, the Feast of St. Joseph the Husband of Mary. (The other one is May 1, the Feast of St. Joseph the Worker.) On this Father's Day, I celebrated Mass in the

Reitocan community of San José. The band from the Reitocan community of El Higuerito showed up and provided lively music before the Mass and during the Mass. That was a wonderful surprise.

The San José community has revitalized their plaza and put in playground equipment, lanterns, and a bandstand. It's beautiful but it needs more shade trees. This is a community with many children and lots of spirit. A *Delegado* named Natividad is the primary leader of the church community in San José.

Fr. Carlos is celebrating Mass today in the church of San José in the Curarén community of Lodo Negro. I'm not sure where Fr. Sebastian is today.

March 20, 2021 – Saturday
Reitoca, F.M., Honduras – 7 p.m.
Partly cloudy – 79 F

Today is the first day of spring in the northern hemisphere. Here, in Reitoca, it is still "summer." Here in Honduras, we have approximately twelve hours of light and twelve hours of darkness every day. The only thing that is different between what we call "summer" (November to April) and "winter" (May to October), is that there is rain at times in "winter." In the "summer" months, Reitoca becomes very dry from a lack of rain.

March 21, 2021 – Fifth Sunday of Lent
Reitoca, F.M., Honduras – 10 p.m.
Partly cloudy – 77 F

This morning I had Masses in Concepción and El Hatillo. In both communities, the *Delegados* read the cardinal's letter explaining the COVID-required changes for Holy Week liturgies. In both communities, everyone wore masks. I think Fr. Carlos must have gotten the word out to do this, for the last time I was in one of the communities, nobody wore masks except Danilo and me.

March 22, 2021 – Monday
Reitoca, F.M., Honduras – 7:35 p.m.
Clear – 73 F

Danilo and I went to Tegucigalpa today and accomplished quite a bit. We were able to buy supplies for a school and two students who had specific requests.

Today I read an interesting article in *OZY* about the possibility of programming cell phones to detect cancer, much as dogs can be trained to do. The writer believes this will be possible within the next five years. Hopefully, people will be able get earlier treatment, thus increasing their chances for successful treatment.

March 23, 2021 – Tuesday – St. Toribio of Mogrovejo
Reitoca, F.M., Honduras – 9:40 p.m.
Mostly clear – 79 F

As I write this note, two horses and a mule are walking around the Holy Cross campus, grazing.

Today is Fr. Carlos' thirty-third birthday, and he stopped by this morning to give me my Mass assignments for the week. I'll be celebrating Masses in Jardines, San Román, Tablones, and Curarén. I'll be celebrating liturgies in Curarén during Holy Week.

Oregon Governor Kate Brown announced members for a newly formed Psilocybin Advisory Board. The purpose of the board will be to oversee research into the effect of psilocybin (as found in magic mushrooms). Early research finds it can be very helpful in treating conditions such as post-traumatic stress disorder and depression, and mitigating anxiety in the dying. I'm eager to find out what the researchers find.

Ten people were killed in a Boulder, Colorado supermarket by a shooter. The shooter is believed to be a 21-year-old man with a problematic mental health background.

March 24, 2021 – Wednesday – St. Oscar Romero
Reitoca, F.M., Honduras – 8:40 p.m.
Partly cloudy - 79 F

This morning I celebrated Mass in Jardines, a community of Curarén. The last time I was there, the people had painted their church red and white. Now, it's grey and white. One of the church's leaders declared that red was an inappropriate color for a church. Because today is the feast of St. Oscar Romero, my homily dealt with his story. One of our visitor *casitas* on the Holy Cross campus is dedicated to him.

Danilo said that the Jardines church community, always one of my favorites, has suffered a setback recently. Very few people have been attending services, and the community didn't have a *Delegado*. Fr. Carlos asked Danilo to go to the community to help revitalize it. Danilo did that by going house to house inviting people to attend church services. Happily, the church is thriving once again, but they still don't have a *Delegado*. I asked Danilo to consider inviting a couple of people to enter the *Delegado* formation program.

Aaron and Shelsie dropped by this evening for coffee, and Aaron helped me with various computer issues.

March 25, 2021 – Thursday – Annunciation of the Lord
Reitoca, F.M., Honduras – 7:30 p.m.
Mostly clear – 82 F

Today I celebrated Mass in the Curarén community of San Ramón. I had always thought that community was named San Román, but *Delegado* Rubén corrected me. Because often the people don't know the spelling of their communities' names, I'm still not 100% convinced which name is correct.

Anyway, though it was 97 F in Reitoca today, in San Ramón it was downright chilly, especially when Danilo and I arrived around 8:45 this morning. Waiting for us was a newly updated church overflowing with people who were ready to celebrate Mass, and the service included fourteen baptisms. José María, the *Delegado* from the Curarén community of San Isidro, was on hand to help Rubén with the music. Rubén wants me to come back to the church on the feast of Our Lady of Fatima (May 13) to bless the new church building. I told him I'd talk with Fr. Carlos about it.

Late this afternoon, I attended a Zoom meeting of *SaludHondu*. All the Board members, except for me, were gathered in the St. Mary Health Center on the campus of the Basilica Shrine of St. Mary in Wilmington, N.C. Dr. John Cromer gave a very interesting presentation on cryptocurrency, for one of our donors is a mentor in that field. I need to learn more about it. It was nice to see Laura, John, Allen, Richard, and Michael once again, even if only online.

On the international scene, a cargo ship about one-fourth of a mile long has gotten stuck in the Suez Canal and is blocking all ship traffic. The ship is called *Ever Given* and is operated by the Evergreen Shipping Company. So far, tugboats have not been able to dislodge the ship.

March 26, 2021 – Friday
Reitoca, F.M., Honduras – 3:40 p.m.
Mostly sunny – 99 F

This morning, Cardinal Rodríguez and the priests working in the Archdiocese of Tegucigalpa had a virtual mini-retreat. Fr. Carlos walked over to my house for the retreat, and Fr. Sebastián was in Tegucigalpa visiting. I was very surprised when the cardinal led the priests in a "Happy Birthday" in Spanish for another priest and me, both of whom celebrate birthdays on March 30.

I have my Saturday and Sunday homilies done, so now I'm going to relax. Blackie and I are by ourselves at home because both Juan and Emilio are off today.

The Diocese of Raleigh sent all the priests working in the diocese a notice of new priest assignments.

Oddly, someone asked me recently about what was so important about priest assignments. I thought it was self-evident that they are critical for the life of a parish as well as the life of the priest himself. Pastors can help parishes flourish, remain stagnant, or suffer harm. Assignments can have profound effects on the priest himself. On the one hand, they give priests a new chance, a time to leave behind the problems of the parish they serve and make a fresh start. But like any major life change, they have the potential for difficult psychological and spiritual effects on the priest. Each assignment a priest receives can help to "make or break" him in many ways, steering the course of the rest of his life.

Priest assignments can also give priests a glimpse into the collective mind of the "power elite," those who make such assignments. For example, a young priest sent to be a pastor of a mega-parish is a signal that the movers and shakers have great faith in him, while a priest sent to a tiny place can be a sign that the priest is not valued too highly, at least not in terms of his leadership skills or potential growth. This, in turn, can deeply affect his mental, physical, and spiritual well-being. These, of course, are generalizations; there are exceptions in which a priest serving in a remote area becomes a bishop. After all, the priest of a little place called Ars, St. John Vianney, is the patron saint of priests, especially parish priests.

Here are the priest assignments listed today, with more to come at a later date.

Effective March 20, 2021

Rev. José Carlos Miguel López, GHM, newly ordained Glenmary Home Missioner priest, is appointed parochial vicar at Holy Spirit parish in Windsor.

Rev. Samuel M. Mungai, GHM newly ordained Glenmary Home Missioner priest, is appointed parochial vicar at Holy Trinity parish in Williamston.

Effective June 29, 2021

Pastors:

Rev. Samuel J. Buchholz, pastor of St. Peter parish in Greenville, is appointed pastor of Annunciation parish in Havelock.

Rev. Michael E. Coveyou, administrator of St. Ann parish in Fayetteville, is appointed pastor of that parish.

Very Rev. Thomas R. Davis, V.F., pastor of St. Egbert parish in Morehead City, is appointed pastor and rector of the Basilica Shrine of St. Mary in Wilmington.

Rev. Eric M. Imbao, CICM, a Missionhurst priest, parochial vicar at María Reina de las Américas parish in Mount Olive and the mission of Santa Teresa del Niño Jesús in Beulaville, is appointed pastor of St. Catherine of Siena parish in Tarboro.

Rev. John A. Kane, administrator of St. Anthony of Padua in Southern Pines, is appointed pastor of that parish.

Rev. Christopher S. Koehn, administrator of St. Mary Magdalene parish in Apex, is appointed pastor of that parish.

Very Rev. Ryszard W. Kolodziej, pastor and rector of the Basilica Shrine of St. Mary in Wilmington, is appointed pastor of St. Egbert in Morehead City.

Rev. James J. Magee, III, pastor of St. Catherine of Siena parish in Tarboro, is appointed pastor of St. Peter parish in Greenville.

Rev. Robert L. Schmid, administrator of St. Charles Borromeo parish in Ahoskie and St. Anne Mission in Scotland Neck, is appointed pastor of that parish and mission.

Rev. Michal G. Schuetz, administrator of Mother of Mercy parish in Washington, N.C., is appointed pastor of that parish.

Rev. William J. Upah, pastor of Annunciation parish in Havelock, is appointed pastor of St. Therese parish in Wrightsville Beach.

Rev. Pius S. Wekesa, administrator of St. John the Baptist parish in Roanoke Rapids, is appointed pastor of Holy Cross parish in Durham.

<u>Administrators</u>:

Rev. Msgr. Gerald L. Lewis, a retired priest of the Diocese of Raleigh and assigned Diocesan Archivist, is additionally appointed administrator of St. Mildred parish in Swansboro.

Rev. Marlon A. Mendieta-Rodas, parochial vicar of St. Patrick parish in Fayetteville, is appointed administrator of St. John the Baptist parish in Roanoke Rapids.

<u>Other</u>:

Rev. Ian C. Van Heusen, chaplain at East Carolina University and parochial vicar at St. Peter parish in Greenville, remains chaplain and is appointed priest in residence at St. Peter parish in Greenville.

March 27, 2021 – Saturday
Reitoca, F.M., Honduras – 3:50 p.m.
Partly cloudy – 97 F

I celebrated a Mass this morning in Tablones, a community of Alubarén. First, however, I celebrated Reconciliation for a number of people. After the Mass, I visited a man who said he was bothered by a "*mal espíritu*" (bad spirit) that was causing noise at his house. I blessed the house and left holy water for the family to sprinkle around the rooms.

I also sent Aaron the *MissionPriest.com* blog posts for April 4-9 so he can check them and add photos that I was not able to add.

March 28, 2021 – Palm Sunday
Reitoca, F.M., Honduras – 8:05 p.m.
Clear – 84 F

As I write this note, a full moon is shining brightly. The third full moon of the year is called the Worm Moon. From what I read, it got its name from the fact that in the northern hemisphere, the ground warms up at the end of March, and worms come out of the warmed-up soil.

This morning I celebrated Mass in Curarén with no less than seventeen altar servers. All of the servers were decked out in red cassocks and white surplices. Some of the surplices were very plain, but most of them had fine lace trim. For many of the servers, this was their first experience serving on the altar, so it was a grand occasion for them and for their proud families. I took a photo of the whole group before the Mass. Perhaps the photo will turn out to be good enough to grace the cover of one of my journals.

Because the cardinal doesn't want any Holy Week processions due to the pandemic, we blessed the palm branches in the plaza in front of the church. The community then walked into the church without ceremony and, when everyone found their places, the entrance hymn was sung and the cross and the seventeen altar servers led the entrance. Noel, who supervises the altar servers and hopes to be a priest one day, was a musician for this Mass. The altar area decorations for the day were stunning, with red bunting.

I'll be celebrating Holy Thursday, Good Friday, and Holy Saturday in that church, and that makes me very happy. I love that community and their spirit.

Blackie has a scratch on his back that might have been made by barbed wire. He sometimes crosses a field surrounded by the wire, and he travels in the dark of night.

Juan now has three days off and won't return until Thursday morning. Danilo, however, plans to come to Reitoca on Wednesday evening and stay in the *mayordomo* house for the night, since we have to leave around 6 a.m. on Thursday to get to the 9 a.m. Chrism Mass in the Basilica of Suyapa.

March 29, 2021 – Monday of Holy Week
Reitoca, F.M., Honduras – 8:50 p.m.
Clear – 82 F

The ship that had been stuck in the Suez Canal has been freed. Now the logjam has been broken; normal traffic will eventually resume. Everyone in the area is thrilled. The episode reminded the world how very important the canal is to world trade.

In Myanmar, security forces killed over one hundred people this weekend. President Biden, like many other world leaders, has condemned the violence.

March 30, 2021 – Tuesday of Holy Week
Reitoca, F.M., Honduras – 8 p.m.
Clear- 86 F

Today I turn 78, and I'm feeling fine. It was nice to have warm greetings from friends in the United States, Mexico, and Honduras. I relaxed and enjoyed the day.

March 31, 2021 – Wednesday of Holy Week
Reitoca, F.M., Honduras – 6 p.m.
Clear – 88 F

Today the Diocese of Raleigh reported the death of a retired priest of the diocese, Fr. John "Jack" Richardson. I knew his name, but I don't think I ever met him. He died at St. Joseph-of-the-Pines in Southern Pines, N.C.

March has been an interesting month. But if one is paying attention, how could one experience a boring month?

This month, in addition to turning another year older, I got my United States passport renewed for another ten years. I'm eager to use it once again to visit the United States when the pandemic comes to an end, or at least after I have received the coronavirus vaccine.

Here in our parish, the healthcare scene has seen some changes. Dr. Valencia López left and will be living in Tegucigalpa. Dr. Shelsie Vásquez Banegas will take Dr. Valencia's old job. Dr. Marco Mejía, the director of the healthcare projects of our parish, has been busy not only hiring a new microbiologist, but also a new pharmacist and pharmacy tech for Farmacia San Francisco de Asís in Reitoca, and a pharmacist and pharmacy tech for Farmacia Candelaria in Curarén. I have not met any of the new pharmacy employees, but I am looking forward to meeting them within the next couple of weeks.

In the Diocese of Raleigh, three Hispanic men have been ordained as transitional deacons. If all goes well, they'll become the newest priests of the Diocese of Raleigh, a diocese where the majority of Catholic Christians are Hispanic.

Also this month, the Diocese of Raleigh posted most of the new priestly assignments.

In this month, the cargo ship *Ever Given* got stuck in the Suez Canal for days, blocking all traffic in both directions. *Ever Given* is about one-fourth mile long, about as long as the Empire State Building is tall.

Now, I look forward to an exciting and fulfilling April.

APRIL 2021

April 1, 2021 – Holy Thursday
Reitoca, F.M., Honduras – 9 p.m.
Cloudy – 79 F

Today, the priests of two of the deaneries of the Archdiocese of Tegucigalpa, the one in the central city of Tegucigalpa and our own San Francisco de Asís deanery in the southern part of the Department of Francisco Morazán, gathered in the Basilica of Suyapa to celebrate the annual Chrism Mass. It was nice to see many priests again, and I was especially happy to see Fr. Renán, who has been studying for the past two years in Mexico City. He is now finished with his studies. I think he will be teaching philosophy in the seminary.

Little by little, I'm getting to know the priests in the archdiocese. I am always amazed, however, when someone I don't know knows me. Today, for example, the priests gathered in the crypt underneath the basilica, to bless the graves of the priests who have died during the past year. As we were walking from the sacristy to the crypt, I saw a priest who looked interesting. So, I went up to him to get acquainted. His name was Alberto. When I told him my name was "Bob," he smiled and said, "Oh, you're the missionary priest in Reitoca!" I could hardly believe it.

I did not stay for the luncheon because I knew Danilo was coming to pick me up to return to Reitoca.

This evening, I celebrated the Mass of the Lord's Supper in Curarén. The people there always do a marvelous job of decorating their altar area for special occasions, and today was no exception. It was a very beautiful Mass, but because of the pandemic, we did not perform the washing of the feet this year.

April 2, 2021 – Good Friday
Reitoca, F.M., Honduras – 6:30 p.m.
Partly cloudy – 82 F

Because of the pandemic, the cardinal asked that there be no processions this year during Holy Week. We did have a *Vía Crucis* (Way of the Cross) ceremony this year in Curarén, where I celebrated the traditional Good Friday liturgy: Proclamation of the Passion according to John; Adoration of the Cross; and Communion Service. All went very well.

As Danilo and I were leaving the area, we saw that the people were having the traditional *Procesión de los Angelitos* (Procession of the Little Angels). In this procession, the deceased Jesus is carried in a glass "coffin" accompanied by children dressed up as angels and the rest of the community. The people take Jesus from the church to the hermitage of San Antonio in another part of the *pueblo*. I think it is a nice custom, and despite the prohibition, I certainly did not want to stop it; I'm not the "liturgy police."

April 3, 2021 – Holy Saturday
Reitoca, F.M., Honduras – 9 p.m.
Partly cloudy – 80 F

The Vigil Mass of Easter went very well. The altar servers and I, accompanied by much of the community, met outdoors at a bonfire as it was just getting dark. As I said the prayers for the blessing of the New Fire and Easter Candle, the wind kept whipping in different directions, so we had to be very careful not to catch fire. All went well during the Mass, which included one baptism. I love celebrating Holy Week with the Curarén community, for they have such excellent spirit and leadership. I'm happy to report that the *pueblo* is making excellent progress on their new social hall.

April 4, 2021 – Easter Sunday
Reitoca, F.M., Honduras – 3 p.m.
Mostly sunny – 91 F

I spent Easter Sunday morning celebrating Masses in La Libertad and San Miguelito. In San Miguelito, we had one baptism. The people had decorated a beautiful little baptistry on their new altar steps.

I have no Masses scheduled for the rest of the week, so I'm going to spend it reading, writing, gardening, and relaxing. In short, I'm planning on having a super week!

April 11, 2021 – 2nd Sunday of Easter
Reitoca, F.M., Honduras – 8 p.m.
Partly cloudy – 79 F

On this Divine Mercy Sunday, I celebrated a 4 p.m. Mass in Curarén. In our parish, San Francisco de Asís, at least two of the more than 80 churches are named Divina Misericordia (Divine Mercy). The churches are El Limón and Los Amates. The Second Sunday of Easter has been known as Divine Mercy Sunday since 2000, when Pope St. John Paul II proclaimed it. In the Catholic worldview, God's love and mercy have no limits. That is why we pray that all people will be saved.

April 12-17, 2021
Reitoca, F.M., Honduras

Because my journal entries for this week were misplaced, I will simply enter the basics of what happened during the week.

From Monday to Friday, April 12-16, the priests working in the Archdiocese of Tegucigalpa had a virtual retreat on Zoom. We "gathered" each day at 9 a.m., 11 a.m., and 3 p.m. to hear a presentation by our archbishop, Cardinal Óscar Andrés Rodríguez. Fathers Carlos and Sebastián came to my house to watch the retreat in my study, for my computer screen is quite large. Fr. Carlos had to celebrate a funeral anniversary Mass in the Curarén village of Usuyca on one of the days, but as it happened, the same day we had no power in Reitoca. So, all three of us missed one of the days of the retreat.

April 18, 2021 – Third Sunday of Easter
Reitoca, F.M., Honduras – 7 p.m.
Partly cloudy – 84 F

Today I celebrated Masses in Concepción and El Hatillo. In El Hatillo, the music ministry, having been tipped off by me before the Mass, sang a birthday song after Mass in honor of Danilo's birthday tomorrow.

April 19, 2021 – Monday of the third week of Eastertide
Reitoca, F.M., Honduras – 8 p.m.
Showers – 80 F

Danilo turned 42 years old today, and we went to Tegucigalpa and Valle de Ángeles. When we got to the bank, we learned that it was a national holiday, so the banks only had ATM service. That was fine for Danilo and me, for that is all we needed.

In Valle de Ángeles, I bought twenty *almendro* trees and four *jalapeño* pepper plants for the Holy Cross campus. I was pleasantly surprised to learn that the trees were only 45 *lempiras* each, or $1.87. Little by little, the campus is being beautified. Someday, it will be quite a lovely place.

April 20, 2021 – Tuesday of third week of Eastertide
Reitoca, F.M., Honduras – 7:25 p.m.
Showers – 79 F

Today I received a very strange Facebook request from someone I had never heard of. The message was written in Russian. When I looked up the person's "mutual friends," I saw many people I know who live in

Curarén or who have connections to our parish. I also discovered that the "My Files" folder was in the trash, and that many files, including all those beginning with the letters A, B, C, and part of D, were being deleted. I stopped the process and contacted Aaron. He'll come over to see what he can do to recover the lost folders and files. I have no idea if the unknown Facebook request person had anything to do with the trashed files. I immediately reflected, however, on the late Fr. Andrew M. Greeley's misadventures losing months' worth of work when his computer crashed.

Today the Diocese of Raleigh notified the priests that Fr. Frank Maloney, a retired priest of the diocese, fell at the St. Joseph of the Pines center where he lives in Southern Pines, N.C. He will have surgery tomorrow.

In the United States today, the big news of the day was that a jury found a former police officer, Derek Chauvin, guilty of three different felonies. Chauvin knelt on a handcuffed black man (George Floyd) for an extended period of time, and George died, triggering a major reawakening about police brutality in the US. I am very glad the ex-officer was found guilty.

April 21, 2021 – Wednesday – St. Anselm of Canterbury
Reitoca, F.M., Honduras – 8:15 p.m.
Cloudy – 82 F

Aaron was here this afternoon. My presumably lost files were recovered, but they are not labeled. It'll take a lot of time and patience to recover what I need. However, I'm not too upset; there are worse things in life than losing data.

Many news and opinion pieces have been written on the George Floyd murder case. Almost all of them concentrate on the black skin of George Floyd, while the more basic fact that he was a man is ignored. Violence against men is so traditional and widespread that it is invisible. The violence is legalized in such things as male-only drafts and male-only combat laws, and it is enshrined in sports such as American football and boxing. Perhaps one of my next books will be a series of essays discussing misandry in everyday life.

April 22, 2021 – Thursday in the third week of Eastertide
Reitoca, F.M., Honduras – 7:50 p.m.
Partly cloudy – 84 F

This morning I celebrated Mass in Lodo Negro. We had two baptisms in the Mass, and there was a nice crowd. Danilo showed me the land where hopes the church community can build a social hall one day. I encouraged him to begin writing down design ideas, costs of materials, and the like. Once things are on paper, action tends to move more quickly, and others can more readily be made interested in becoming invested.

Before coming to pick me up in Reitoca, Danilo brought three workers from Lodo Negro to work on the Holy Cross campus. They were joined by Juan and Juan's father. They not only cleaned up the northern and western sides of Holy Cross Hill, but also planted the twenty *almendro* trees that I bought recently. Juan also helped me plant four bamboo plants on my deck.

In the late afternoon, the power in Reitoca and Curarén went off. I am happy that I have an iPad to be able to read, and that I had already printed my homily for tomorrow and Saturday.

April 23, 2021 – Friday – St. George; St. Adalbert of Prague
Reitoca, F.M., Honduras – 8:35 p.m.
Partly cloudy – 81 F

This morning I celebrated Mass in Chaparral, and we had a very nice crowd. I think back on my very first Christmas Eve in Honduras in 2018, in which I celebrated an evening Mass at Chaparral. There were so many people at the Mass that evening that many were standing outside. It is amazing how different a church appears to a newcomer compared to how it seems when one has been around for a while. As one becomes used to a church, the building seems to shrink. Likewise, churches look vastly different between night and day. The Chaparral community is a very loving and joyful group.

When Danilo and I got back to Reitoca from Chaparral, the electricity had been restored for about ten minutes. It is so wonderful to have electricity again! I have to charge my phone and write and print some homilies. In just a half-day without electricity, I have sixty emails to read or delete.

April 24, 2021 – Saturday – St. Fidelis of Sigmaringen; St. Peter of St. Joseph de Betancur
Reitoca, F.M., Honduras – 3:45 p.m.
Sunny – 93 F

My first task this morning, around 6 a.m., was to give water to the twenty new *almendro* trees we planted yesterday. I discovered that *zampopos*, insects that love to eat certain plants, had already paid a visit to two of the trees. All the leaves were gone from one of the little trees, and the other one was half-eaten. This evening, as it gets dark, I'll put Raid around all the new trees. Danilo has an effective chemical that we can use. Perhaps he'll bring some of the treatment tomorrow.

Danilo and Juan were here by 7 a.m., and they planted three bougain-villeas on the hills on either side of my house. In time, these beautiful vines will grow and cascade down the side of the hills.

Danilo and I went this morning to Cumulina, a community of Curarén, for a 10 a.m. Mass. The community is about an hour and ten minutes from Reitoca. I preached on St. Fidelis of Sigmaringen, one of the men in my book, *Saintly Men of Nursing: 100 Amazing Stories*. The little church in Cumulina has been remodeled, and the new floor is particularly striking with beautiful tiles. The church was overflowing, and many young men stood in the doorway during the Mass. We also celebrated six baptisms, and I stayed for photos with each of the families. All though the Mass, firecrackers went off to celebrate this special day of the community.

The community of Cumulina is a very vibrant, friendly, and socially conscious place. All but a couple of the people wore masks during the Mass, removing them only for photos.

Danilo reported today that on Monday, when we go to Tegucigalpa, we will get the laminate for the overhang by my kitchen window. A young man named Alexi will install it. I think that the roof will make the kitchen much cooler, for in the morning, the eastern sun heats the kitchen uncomfortably.

April 25, 2021 – Fourth Sunday of Easter
Reitoca, F.M., Honduras – 2:45 p.m.
Mostly sunny – 99 F

Today is known as Good Shepherd Sunday, to commemorate Jesus' telling a group of Pharisees that he is the Good Shepherd. Unlike a hired hand who would not be committed to the sheep in his care, a good shepherd would even lay down his life for the sheep.

This is also the 58th anniversary of the World Day of Prayer for Vocations. And although all people have vocations, this day focuses specifically on vocations to the ordained ministries (diaconate and priesthood), religious life, secular institutes, and missions.

In my homily today, I focused on Pope Leo XIII, who guided the Church during the Industrial Revolution. Although Leo applauded the rapid progress the revolution produced, he knew that not all was to the good. He saw the devastating effects this revolution had on men and their families. For the first time in history, millions of men were forced from the comfort and security of their homes to work in other places. For the first time, children saw their fathers leave in the morning and not return until the evening, with no idea what their fathers did for a living.

Leo also saw how poorly workers were often treated. So, he wrote one of the most powerful encyclicals in the 2,000-year history of Catholic Christianity called *Rerum Novarum* (known as "On Capital and Labor"). This document has been used as a foundation for much Catholic social teaching in politics, business, health, education, science, the arts, and other fields.

Today I also read a very interesting article about Ernest Grant, the first African American – and the first man – to be President of the American

Nurses' Association. Dr. Grant, who lives in Chapel Hill, North Carolina, is in his second term. Standing at 6-feet 6-inches, he is a major presence, with a heart and personality as big as his size. He has received many accolades in his years as an R.N., including the Nurse of the Year Award from President George W. Bush. Because of his solid background in piano, he sometimes plays for services at Raleigh's St. John's Metropolitan Community Church.

I'm looking forward to a beautiful afternoon and evening of writing, watering my new trees and other plants, reading, and watching some *Grey's Anatomy* episodes. I won't be doing any watering until after 5 p.m. when it will get cooler; right now, it's a scorcher.

April 26, 2021 – Monday of the 4th week of Eastertide
Reitoca, F.M., Honduras – 6:40 p.m.
Partly cloudy – 84 F

As I write this note, the first of two "supermoons" of the year has risen, a giant yellow-orange globe over the eastern and northern mountains, lighting up the whole valley. This supermoon is called the Full Pink Moon; the second supermoon will appear on May 26 and will be called the Full Flower Moon. It is convenient that the moon is casting so much light, for all the power of Reitoca has been out.

It was 97 F in Reitoca today, but I was in Tegucigalpa with Danilo for most of the day. I had hoped to get the laminate for the overhang over the kitchen window, but no one had ordered it, and the store didn't have the color I need in stock. However, a young man named Dagoberto said the store would have the right color next week. We placed an order for it. Danilo and I brought Fr. Carlos back from Tegucigalpa with us, for his red pickup truck is being repaired in the city.

I'll be celebrating Confirmations in Curarén on Pentecost Eve in Curarén this year. Fortunately, I have a nice bilingual book on the Confirmation ritual to follow.

I was delighted to read that Apple plans to spend $80 billion over the next five years in the United States, with over $1 billion on a new office in the Raleigh-Durham, N.C. area. The new North Carolina office is expected to provide 3,000 new jobs, many in high-tech fields such as machine learning and artificial intelligence.

April 27, 2021 – Tuesday of the 4th week of Eastertide
Reitoca, F.M., Honduras – 9:10 p.m.
Partly cloudy – 81 F

My homilies for upcoming Masses are finished, so now I can work on blog posts.

Today I reflect on how many people talk about growing older. Often, one hears people say things like, "It's hard to grow older" or "Getting old is only for the tough." The emphasis is on the negative. But I have not yet found that. In fact, each decade of life is much better than the one before it. As I approach the 80s in two years, my tune might change, but I hope not.

May Sarton, in her book *At Seventy: A Journal*, shares her views of life at the age of seventy, an age she calls the "autumn of life." She captures many of my feelings in her September 25th entry, saying, "The autumn of life is also a matter of saying farewell, but the strange thing is that I do not feel it is autumn. Life is so rich and full these days. There is so much to look forward to, so much here and now, and also ahead…"
Ms. Sarton continues, "I do not feel I am saying farewell yet but only beginning again, as it used to be when school started."

April 28, 2021 – Wednesday – St. Peter Chanel; St. Louis Grignion de Montfort
Reitoca, F.M., Honduras – 3:25 p.m.
Partly cloudy – 93 F

As one enters the Holy Cross campus, the first thing one encounters is a triangle in the roadway, in which I planted an *almendro* tree last October 1. Since that day, I have watered it every morning and late afternoon, and it has grown nicely. It has grown from its original height of two feet to about six feet. This morning, I was very sad to see that some cows had nearly destroyed the tree during the night. They do not eat *almendro* trees, but such big animals can cause harm just by bumping into things. My tree illustrates the term, "bull in a china shop." We had to cut off the broken lower branches. In time, however, I think the tree will survive and become a very beautiful tree giving lots of shade.

Today the priests of the Diocese of Raleigh received invitations to the priesthood ordination of Tyler Sparrow and Steven Thomas DiMassimo. Tyler will celebrate his First Mass of Thanksgiving in St. Ann Church in Clayton, and Steven will celebrate his at St. Luke Church in Raleigh. I hope they both find the ordained priesthood as wonderful as I have.

Danilo is in Comayagua today buying new tires for my car. Because of the pandemic, I have not had to travel much this past year, and my tires have lasted for over a year. That is very unusual because in our parish, we generally must replace tires every six months because none of the roads in between parish communities are paved.

President Biden will address Congress this evening for the first time in his presidency. I look forward to hearing his message.

April 29, 2021 – Thursday – St. Catherine of Siena
Reitoca, F.M., Honduras – 8:45 p.m.
Mostly clear – 79 F

This evening I celebrated a 7 p.m. Mass in Reitoca. I told the story of St. Peter Claver, a great missionary and proto-martyr of Oceania. The homily reflected on how the missionary life of the early Catholic church, as documented in the Acts of the Apostles, has continued for more than 2,000 years of Catholic Christianity.

In his address to Congress last evening, President Biden laid out an extremely expansive and hopeful vision for the United States. President Biden's plan focuses on beefing up infrastructure, ending the COVID-19 pandemic, looking out for workers, giving more support for families and students, and ensuring civil rights. The president's plans will cost a lot of money, but he has a plan for that, taxing huge corporations that pay little to no tax as well as taxing the super-rich.

My little canine friend Henry had a very difficult time walking yesterday. He came to my deck with his friend Andy, and according to Juan, he was walking well at that time. Later, however, Henry could barely walk. I have no idea what is wrong with him. He didn't seem to sustain any injury while on the deck. I'm curious if perhaps he has arthritis that is exacerbated before a rain, for rain is predicted for us soon.

Insects called *zampopos*, which look like ants, love to destroy various types of plants. After dark Emilio will go around this evening to sprinkle anti-*zampopo* insecticide around the new little *almendro* trees that Juan and Danilo planted the other week. There is never a dull moment around here.

Lately I have been thinking of how "busy" I always am, even when I have no events or duties to attend to. I have figured out that the "busy-ness" of my life is mostly in my head, because my brain never shuts down. I'm forever thinking of new adventures and projects, all of which will cost me plenty in terms of time and psychic energy. In *Letters to a Loving God: A Prayer Journal*, the late, great Chicago priest-sociologist-novelist-professor, Fr. Andrew M. Greeley wrote this in his March 4, 2001 entry that describes the same phenomenon:

> Last night as I was going to bed, my head filled with ideas for poems, articles, books, chapters, Blackie interludes, columns — a creative imagination run amok. Where will I get the time to do all of them or even some of them? I have the sense of falling behind.

April 30, 2021 – Friday – St. Pius V
Reitoca, F.M., Honduras – 7:25 p.m.
Mostly cloudy – 81 F

As I write this note on the last day of April, rain has finally come to Reitoca, and it was a very powerful one. The land will suddenly become greener again, and Juan and I won't have to water the bushes and *plantitas* (little plants) twice a day.

I made bean and bacon soup for the first time ever today, and it turned out very well. I'm sure I would have appreciated it more in snowy weather, but that will never happen here in Reitoca - or anywhere else in Honduras, for that matter.

In northern Israel, at least forty-five people were killed in a stampede at a religious celebration of ultra-Orthodox Jews. Many more people were injured. Government officials say that over 100,000 people were gathered, at Mount Meron.

In Poland, Catholic Christians today are remembering how one-fifth of the ordained priesthood was killed during Nazi German occupation in World War II. Around 2,000 of Poland's 10,000 diocesan priests were killed by the Nazis.

April was an interesting month. Unlike last year, when the pandemic prevented us from celebrating liturgies during Holy Week and Easter, we were able to celebrate the ceremonies, although there were proper precautions such as wearing masks, not having processions, and the like.

This month also saw the planting of twenty new almendro trees on the Holy Cross campus. In my mind's eye, I can envision the beautiful shade the trees will provide in the future.

Also, this month, my website/blog, MissionPriest.com, celebrated its first anniversary on April 26. Unfortunately, due probably to a hack, I lost much of the work I did on future blog posts, so now I am devoting a portion of every day to re-writing them. But they will be even better for the re-writing.

I now look forward to the merry, merry month of May!

MAY 2021

May 1, 2021 – Saturday – St. Joseph the Worker
Reitoca, F.M., Honduras – 7:35 p.m.
Partly cloudy – 79 F

Today is the feast of St. Joseph the Worker, a fine way to begin the merry, merry month of May. In Honduras, as well as many Latin American countries, people are desperate for work. Job opportunities are limited in Honduras, and advanced education is no guarantee that one will find a job. For example, thousands of medical doctors are unemployed in this country. People with little education, such as many who work in agriculture, are paid very little. Because Pope Francis has declared this the Year of St. Joseph, one wishes governments around the world will seek new solutions to help workers, especially the poorest.

May begins the so-called "winter" here in Honduras. "Winter" simply means we have more chance of afternoon and evening rains. Although most trees here are green all year round, some lose their leaves in the "summer," which is November through April. Because we had some rain last week, the trees that were bare for the summer are now becoming green once again.

In May, farmers are busy planting corn and beans among other things. Danilo is hoping to plant a corn field on the east side of my house. We must have a fence because often cows come onto the Holy Cross campus and would eat the seedlings.

My special goal for May is to become more focused and disciplined in my writing. I have high hopes for the month.

May 2, 2021 – 5th Sunday of Easter
Reitoca, F.M., Honduras – 8:35 p.m.
Partly cloudy – 79 F

Today I had a morning Mass in Reitoca and an afternoon Mass in Curarén. Reitoca has a beautiful "May altar" dedicated to Mary, and a beautiful statue of Joseph in honor of 2021, the Year of St. Joseph.

Fr. Carlos came over in late afternoon after I returned from Curarén, to let me know about a deanery Zoom meeting on Tuesday and to give me my assignments for this week. I'll be celebrating Masses in El Arado, El Portillo, Tapope, Aniz, La Libertad, and San Miguelito.

May 3, 2021 – Monday – Exaltation of the Holy Cross (Honduras)
Reitoca, F.M., Honduras – 7:25 p.m.
Mostly cloudy – 79 F

In her book, *At Seventy: A Journal,* the late May Sarton writes in her November 19 entry: "What luxury these days to wake up and know there is an entire day ahead for work and silence." I know the feeling so very well. On most weeks, I celebrate Masses only on Thursdays through Sundays, so I am blessed to have at least three such days every week. And although I love sacramental ministry, traveling to the various mountain villages and doing everything in a language other than my native one is stressful.

Today I woke up feeling what Sarton was talking about. My first task was to water certain of my bushes and new trees. I suddenly discovered, an army of *zampopos* (or some other type of giant ants) marching up the south side of my house. It took me about a half an hour to get rid of them with water spray and then Raid. It astonishes me how well-organized and determined the insect kingdom can be.

I also learned that Claro, the company that I use for phone and internet service, will be coming tomorrow to install devices in my house and in at least one of the *casitas*. I asked Danilo to come tomorrow to be able to help the Claro visitors, but he has been a bit sick the last few days. Juan has tomorrow off, so I'll be here alone and know absolutely nothing about electricity.

In Honduras, May 3 is the feast of the Exaltation of the Cross. I'm not sure why it is celebrated on this day instead of September 14 as the rest of the Catholic Church does. I made a batch of cherry pie cups to celebrate on the "Holy Cross Campus."

Fr. Frank Maloney, the retired priest of the Diocese of Raleigh, who fell last week at St. Joseph-of-the-Pines in Southern Pines, N.C., died in neighboring Pinehurst. He was a very gentle, humble and compassionate priest, a hard worker who was well-loved by his fellow priests. I didn't know Frank well, but I do remember how warmly he greeted me when I was a seminarian in my pastoral year, and had to preach at all his Masses one weekend at St. Brendan the Navigator in Shallotte, N.C. May he rest in peace.

India has reached 20,000,000 cases of COVID. Some countries, such as Australia, are banning anyone from India from entering the country. North Korea is threatening the United States and South Korea, which is nothing new.

May 4, 2021 – Tuesday – Ss. Philip & James (in Honduras)
Reitoca, F.M., Honduras – 9 p.m.
Mostly cloudy – 75 F

Because Honduras celebrates the feast of Holy Cross on May 3, today we celebrate the feast of Ss. Philip and James. I had no Masses today.

Today was a day of sickness around here. Dr. Aaron from Clínica Santa María is a bit sick, Fr. Carlos is sick and had to be treated at the clinic, and Danilo has been in a clinic in Comayagua overnight, hoping to be released today at noon. Fortunately, I'm doing fine.

A worker from the municipality of La Venda came to the Holy Cross campus today to install Claro antennas for television. He was able to install one for my house, but he said we will need a new contract to supply TV signals to the yellow and green visitors' houses. The blue house will have an antenna from a local Reitocan company. This is very complicated to me, but I'm happy the worker knows what he's doing.

I was able to get my Thursday and Friday homilies finished, so now I just need to do Sunday's.

At 8 p.m., Fr. Sebastián joined me in my study to attend a virtual Zoom meeting with the priests of our deanery. Fr. Carlos stayed in the rectory and participated from there because of his illness.

On Saturday, the priests of the deanery will be coming to Reitoca, and I'll host the meeting in my study. So, Juan and I have three days to do cleaning around the campus and in my house. It should be a very interesting and action-packed week, especially since Thursday and Friday mornings I'll be gone to celebrate Masses in various Curarén villages.

May 5, 2021 – Wednesday of the 5th week of Easter
Reitoca, F.M., Honduras – 7:25 p.m.
Partly cloudy – 80 F

Juan and I spent much of the day getting the campus ready for the deanery meeting on Saturday. I'm pretty exhausted this evening, but it is good to work hard and I can always use the exercise.

I spent some time today investigating several people on the path to sainthood about whom I knew nothing. Most of them are candidates for my "Missionary Heroes" articles that I post almost every Friday on my website, *MissionPriest.com.* I was especially intrigued by three Italian Cimatti siblings – Bl. Maria Raffaella, a Hospitaller Sister of Mercy; Ven. Luis, a Salesian Brother; and Ven. Vincent, a Salesian priest.

May 6, 2021 – Thursday of the 5th week of Eastertide
Reitoca, F.M., Honduras – 9:20 p.m.
Cloudy – 70 F

Today I celebrated Masses in the Curarén communities of El Arado and El Portillo.

The community of El Arado, which means "The Plow," is in the process of building a new church as their old one was too small for the community. We celebrated Mass in the new church. This community does not yet have electricity, but the side window provided enough light for me to see. The floor is dirt, and there are neither window panes nor doors. The people have some tiles to lay down to finish the floor, but first they need a concrete subfloor. So, after discerning what they need, I pledged enough for the concrete and remaining boxes of tiles they'll need; this will be a grant from the Red Lantern Foundation.

This community is very vibrant and hard-working. They take great pride in their church, which they named Our Lady of Suyapa in honor of the patron saint of Honduras.

The other community where I celebrated Mass was El Portillo, which means "The Wicket." Their church is dedicated to St. John Bosco, founder of the Salesian order. Our archbishop, Cardinal Óscar Andrés Rodríguez, is a member of that order.

When I arrived at the community, I visited a new building under construction that sits next to the church. It is intended for catechism and sacramental preparation classes, as well as social activities.

The El Portillo community is extremely vibrant with excellent leadership. Before the Mass, I sat in the sacristy and visited with some leaders of the community. Five boys who were preparing for their First Communion, made themselves at home and listened attentively to our conversation. Although El Portillo has ten *Delegados*, they have no catechists. Therefore, the *Delegados* must step in to fill in the catechetical work. I asked Danilo why there are so few catechists, and he explained that it is such a big and important job that few people want to take on that responsibility.

May 7, 2021 – Friday of the 5th week of Eastertide
Reitoca, F.M., Honduras – 10:15 p.m.
Cloudy – 75

This morning, I celebrated Masses in the Curarén communities of Aniz and Tapope.

In Aniz, the people have enlarged their soccer field, and in the process, they knocked down the shade tree under which Danilo and I used to park. This community, as always, was waiting outside to greet us with guitars and singers and to escort us into their church, Our Lady of Guadalupe. In the Mass, I celebrated three baptisms and eighteen First Communions. Nobody told me in advance about the extra sacraments, but fortunately Danilo and I are always ready for whatever. After the Mass, I took a photo of the First Communion class and posed for photos with each of the baptism families. The Mass was standing room only. That community has amazing spirit and definitely needs a larger church. All the people of Aniz wore masks.

The second community was Tapope. In that Mass, I celebrated three baptisms. There, almost no one in the packed church wore masks. After the Mass, I stayed for photos with the baptism families.

This evening, all the lights of Reitoca suddenly went out. The total blackness made it seem as though the whole town had vanished. The community of San Carlos, which I can see from my deck, was also dark, for it is on the same electrical circuit.

As Danilo and I pulled out of Tapope after the Mass, I received a notice on my phone that tomorrow's meeting of the deanery's priests, which had been scheduled to meet in my house, has been changed to a Zoom meeting. What wonderful news that is for all the priests, and I have a very clean house out of the deal. When I got home, I told Juan to take the rest of the day off, for he had worked extra hard cleaning the floors.

In the darkness, a young thief entered the Holy Cross campus. Fortunately, Emilio saw him and yelled; the thief ran away into the night. Emilio knows who the young man is, and is going to confront him tomorrow morning at his home. He is one of the four who broke into one of the visitors' houses on our campus during a torrential rainstorm several months ago and stole a television and coffee pot. From what I understand, the four thieves are well-known troublemakers of Reitoca.

I called my friend Dr. Aaron to walk me through the process of turning on the campus' solar energy system. So, we had electricity after all. Because my house is on the side of one of the mountains that surround the center of Reitoca, I'm pretty sure everyone saw the lights of the property, for there are lanterns and street lights on the campus.

Today, Pat Marriott, my editor, sent me the edited 2020 journal entries for November and December. I'll review them by Monday, check over the whole manuscript one more time, and send them to Pat for formatting.

May 8, 2021 – Saturday of the 5th week of Eastertide
Reitoca, F.M., Honduras – 6:50 p.m.
Mostly cloudy – 84 F

The priests of our deanery had a short deanery meeting via Zoom. Our next in-person deanery gathering is scheduled for August 28 in Sabanagrande.

I learned today that Fr. Carlos has been diagnosed with COVID, but he is recovering well. Late this afternoon I saw him outside the rectory. He looks good but is not feeling too well. When I saw him, I was leading a herd of cows out the gate of the Holy Cross campus and into the street.

May 9, 2021 – Sixth Sunday of Easter; Mother's Day
Reitoca, F.M., Honduras – 6:15 p.m.
Partly cloudy – 88 F

Today is Mother's Day in Honduras, just as it is in the United States. It has been a very sunny day, with a high temperature of 95 F. In the coming eight days, the weather forecasters are predicting highs ranging between 95-99 F with only a slim chance of rain. May, usually the second rainiest month of the year, so far is pretty dry.

This morning Danilo and I went to La Libertad and San Miguelito so I could celebrate Masses there. In both locations, the people had Mother's Day cakes for the community members.

Danilo reports that the laminate place in Comayagua did not have the red material I wanted for the overhang outside my kitchen windows, so we'll go with "café" color if they have enough of it.

May 10, 2021 – Monday of the 6th week of Eastertide
Reitoca, F.M., Honduras – 8:55 p.m.
Partly cloudy – 84 F

Today, Fr. Carlos had to go to Tegucigalpa for hospital treatment for his COVID, which does not seem to be getting better.

For me, it was a quiet day on the Holy Cross campus, and I used much of the day working on the future blog posts that were lost a few weeks ago.

In the afternoon, I attended a wonderful Zoom meeting of Rotary District 7730. There was a nice presentation on how our district, along with many others in the United States, is helping the people of India, who are swamped with COVID-19. Specifically, our district is helping supply oxygen concentrators.

We also learned about new Rotary clubs being formed in our district. Unlike traditional clubs, these new ones have a very specific focus. For example, among the new clubs in our Rotary district are ones that appeal to those in scouting, ending child abuse, and caring for the environment. Others are made up of people with specific affiliations, such as a group of Rotary Peace Fellows and a group of former Rotaract alumni from Methodist University in Fayetteville, N.C.

May 11, 2021 – Tuesday of the 6th week of Eastertide
Reitoca, F.M., Honduras – 8:20 p.m.
Partly cloudy – 82 F

Fr. Carlos sent a message to the priests of our deanery that he is feeling much better today. I'm delighted with the news.

Danilo returned from Tegucigalpa and stopped by the Holy Cross campus. Juan went with him to the city and opened a Banco de América Central account. Beginning in June, I'll be paying Juan and Emilio by direct deposit as I already do for Danilo. Not only will direct deposit be a new experience for Juan and Emilio, so will simply having a bank account. Juan, especially, needs to learn to use a bank and credit and debit cards, for he is young and has hopes of working in the United States one day.

While he was in Tegucigalpa today, Danilo learned that Promasa, the store that sells laminate for roofing, will have red laminate for us after all, coming the first week of June. So, it looks like we won't have to compromise with café color.

While Danilo was here, Dr. Aaron was here investigating some ideas for added security. He told me that Danilo has tested positive for COVID, so Juan, Emilio, and I will get rapid response tests tomorrow at Clínica Santa María. Dr. Aaron said he thought there would be no Masses anywhere in our parish this weekend.

Dr. Aaron also said that there is an opportunity on May 25 for people my age to get their first anti-COVID vaccination in Tegucigalpa. There are two choices; one is the Russian Sputnik vaccine, and the other is an American brand but not the Johnson & Johnson one that I had hoped to get because it requires only one shot. I'm very happy to learn there is an opportunity to get vaccinated, for I'm in so many mountain communities every week, and in many of them, nobody wears a mask.

May 12, 2021 – Wednesday – Ss. Nereus & Achilleus; St. Pancras Reitoca, F.M., Honduras – 8:30 p.m.
Partly cloudy – 84 F

Fr. Sebastián, Emilio, and I were tested for COVID today, and all three of us were negative, which is great news. Tomorrow, Juan will get tested, and Danilo will have further tests in Tegucigalpa. Fr. Sebastián said that there will no Masses this week or weekend in any of our parish's communities. So, I have an unexpected mini-vacation.

This evening, we had our monthly Rotary Passport 7730 meeting, with Dr. Gretchen Rivas as speaker. She is a doctor of acupuncture and gave a presentation on that broad technique.

Our club president, Lori Harris, noted that Rotary International has specifically promised to help poor countries in their fight against

COVID-19, so that is good news. Aaron and I discussed ways in which we can help fight COVID in our area of Honduras. If we play our cards right, this will not only help the people get vaccinated, but also help our club get some excellent publicity.

May 13, 2021 – Thursday – Our Lady of Fatima
Reitoca, F.M., Honduras – 4:20 p.m.
Mostly sunny – 97 F

Juan received his rapid-response test for COVID-19 this morning at Clínica Santa María, and his test also came back negative. We are all delighted with the news. Dr. Aaron gave Juan some tips on how to stay safe.

Fr. José Luis, the Discalced Carmelite pastor of the municipality of Lepaterique, sent all the priests of our deanery notice that he has cancelled all formal church activities in all the churches of his parish because of the number of COVID-19 cases. After two weeks, he will re-evaluate the situation.

May 14, 2021 – Friday – St. Matthias, Apostle
Reitoca, F.M., Honduras – 6:50 p.m.
Partly cloudy – 86 F

Today was a day for good news. Danilo learned that he most likely had COVID-19 in the past, but now he is fine. Fr. Carlos says that he also is now fine.

Today I also found a way to recapture some of the files that I lost a couple of weeks ago in a freak computer glitch. Most of the lost files were blog posts on "Missionary Heroes" for my 2022 Fridays. I have been able recapture all but one, so I'm happy about that, for the biographies take a lot of mental effort.

Today it was 97 F, but this weekend the weather people are predicting 100 F for both Saturday and Sunday. I am so grateful for air conditioning in my study.

The Centers for Disease Control in the United States has decided that people who are fully vaccinated no longer must wear masks. However, they advised that people should continue to respect establishments that require them.

A major conflict between Israelis and Palestinians has broken out and is getting worse every day.

May 15, 2021 – Saturday of the 6th week of Eastertide
Reitoca, F.M., Honduras – 3:30 p.m.
Mostly sunny – 99 F

Juan came to the Holy Cross campus for a half-day of work, and we filled five bags of trash from what we call a "road" that runs on the other side of the north wall of the Holy Cross campus. We're trying to make the stone road a little more attractive, for in the past, people have thrown bottles, old clothes, broken toys, and whatever out there. We're making good progress, but we have plenty more to do. Because some of the trash has been sitting for what might have been years, we need a hoe and a rake to uproot it. Fortunately, most of the road is shaded by large trees, but even so, it is much too hot be working outside after about 9 a.m.

As we were working near the road that runs in front of the rectory, we saw Fr. Sebastián. He said that Fr. Carlos had just returned from Tegucigalpa and is now doing much better.

One of the more interesting news items of the day is the landing of a spacecraft from China, with a rover, on Mars last Saturday. Until then, only the United States had a rover on Mars.

I spent most of the day working on Friday missionary hero biographies for future blog posts and, eventually, book chapters.

May 16, 2021 – Ascension Sunday
Reitoca, F.M., Honduras – 7:40 p.m.
Partly cloudy – 82 F

Though the weather forecasters had predicted that we would have a high temperature today of 100 F, it reached only 99 F. More of the same is on tap for tomorrow. Around 4 p.m., all the power went out in Reitoca, so I switched to solar. I am so happy to have installed it.

Yesterday and today, two herds of cows were walking and grazing all over the Holy Cross campus. This happens whenever the priests leave the front gate to the rectory open. It does provide some fun for Blackie, Henry, and Andy, who love to help me round up the cows and escort them out the gate.

May 17, 2021 – Monday of the 7th week of Eastertide
Reitoca, F.M., Honduras – 7:30 p.m.
Mostly clear – 82 F

Though it was officially a day off for him, Juan stopped by the Holy Cross campus to help me water the bougainvilleas and *almendro* trees and go into town to Anita's store to buy a few items.

This morning, I wrote a reference letter for the man who is living an eremitical life in Wilmington, N.C., who wants to become a Consecrated Hermit in the Catholic Church.

Today I discovered another new group of saints, and others on the path to sainthood, in the Catholic Church. I am amazed and delighted at how many people the Church formally honors. At the rate I'm finding new people, I'll be able to continue writing my Friday "Mission Heroes" blog posts for my *MissionPriest.com* site for years to come!

May 18, 2021 – Tuesday – St. John I
Reitoca, F.M., Honduras – 8:20 p.m.
Cloudy – 81 F

Today, Fr. Carlos walked over to my house from the rectory to give me my week's assignments. It's the first time I've seen him since he was sick. He looks excellent, although he has lost some weight. I'll be celebrating Masses in Alubarén and two of its communities – Concepción and El Hatillo – as well as in Curarén. I had been scheduled to celebrate Confirmations in Curarén at the Pentecost Vigil Mass, but they were postponed because of COVID.

Dr. Aaron was here this evening to do some work with our computers and Internet connections. He plans to spend one night in the San Oscar Romero (green) house next week. He found that the Internet connection is excellent in the Blessed Stanley Rother (yellow) house, but the connection in the green house needs a bit of work.

May 19, 2021 – Wednesday of the 7th week of Eastertide
Reitoca, F.M., Honduras – 8:25 p.m.
Partly cloudy – 82 F

Today my stepmother, Mary Jean, died in North Canton, Ohio. She had been living in the Sanctuary Grande assisted living center. My sister Chris has been watching over her and my dad (who died a couple of years ago at age 99½). My brother Larry has also helped, although he lives in Cuba, New York. My mother, Florence Elizabeth "Pat" Foley Kus, died when I was born, and I lived with my paternal grandparents in Maple Heights, Ohio (a southeastern suburb of Cleveland) until I was six. I then went to live with my father and his new wife, Mary Jean, and my brother Larry, and eventually, our sisters Jeanette and Chris came along. So, Mary Jean was "Mom" to me. She will be missed.

I will explore the possibilities of traveling to Ohio to officiate at the funeral. However, I'm not very hopeful because of the pandemic and the fact that I haven't yet been vaccinated.

Today I finished approving the inside content of my 2020 journal. Its name will be, *MissionPriest.com: Journal of a Missionary Priest – 2020*. This will be the nineteenth yearly journal I will have published through Red Lantern Press.

Emilio, the night guard of the Holy Cross campus, went to Tegucigalpa today with Danilo to open a bank account. Now, I'll be able to pay monthly salaries to the three Holy Cross employees, Danilo, Emilio, and Juan online. That will so much simpler, for currently I transfer money to Danilo, he goes to Tegucigalpa (a three-hour drive from his home in Lodo Negro), gets the money for salaries out of his bank account in Honduran *lempiras*, brings the money to Reitoca, and then I pay Emilio and Juan. That tremendous amount of unnecessary work will now be eliminated.

May 20, 2021 – Thursday – St. Bernadine of Siena
Reitoca, F.M., Honduras – 8 p.m.
Mostly cloudy – 82 F

Although the temperature only reached 93 F today in Reitoca, the heat index went to 102 F, and it definitely felt like it.

I decided not to go to Ohio for Mom's funeral. That is the prudent thing, and Chris agrees. I'll be there in spirit, however. The funeral Mass will be at Holy Family Church in Stow, Ohio where Mom and Dad were members for many years. Fr. Paul Rosing, the beloved pastor of the parish, will be the celebrant at the Mass. I have done the funeral Masses for all the other older relatives of my family: this will be the first one I must miss. I am now the oldest member of the extended family.

This evening, I celebrated Mass in Alubarén, and I preached on one of my favorite saints, St. Toribio Romo González. St. Toribio is sometimes called the "Holy Coyote," because he has often been identified as the young priest guiding people in the Mexican deserts to the United States to begin a new life. His feast day is tomorrow.

Danilo is staying overnight in the Bl. James Miller (blue) house, because we want to be on the road at 5 a.m. to head to Tegucigalpa for my first vaccine injection. Tomorrow, people ages 77-78 will be given injections in their cars.

May 21, 2021 – St. Toribio Romo González; Ss. Christopher Magallanes and Companions
Reitoca, F.M., Honduras – 8 p.m.
Mostly cloudy – 82 F

This morning, Danilo and I left the Holy Cross campus for our trip to the campus of Catholic University of Honduras in Tegucigalpa. Hundreds of cars were already waiting for the vaccination site to open. Having been warned that the wait would take hours, I brought my iPad and read while waiting.

The whole process took about four hours. Six stations were set up in a parking lot, staffed by nurses administering the shots to people aged 77-78. The type of vaccine administered today was the Sputnik variety. Assisting in the whole process were police, soldiers, and Copeco volunteers. Copeco is a volunteer agency in Honduras that assists in many ways to make life better for people, especially in special situations such as natural disasters.

When our car was only five away from the injection site, a Copeco volunteer informed us they had run out of vaccines. However, he assured us that a new supply was "on its way" and that the president of the country was coming to the site. Twenty minutes later, the new batch of vaccines arrived. When it was my turn to get an injection, the nurse gave me the injection through the car window. The whole process was quite organized, and all the people involved were incredibly friendly. Danilo and I left before the president arrived, but we did see a horde of television people and journalists waiting for his arrival. I will get my second injection June 21.

It was a good day, but now I'm exhausted … and grateful.

May 22, 2021 – Saturday – Vigil of Pentecost
Reitoca, F.M., Honduras – 7:45 p.m.
Partly cloudy – 84 F

This morning Carolyn Hax's Washington Post advice column had an interesting equation: "Happiness = Reality - Expectations." That formula is worthy of reflection.

On the international front, Israel and Hamas, who have been battling each other for the past eleven days, have declared a ceasefire.

This evening, I celebrated a Mass in Curarén along with fifteen altar servers. The church was very beautiful, all decked out in red for Pentecost. Of all the churches of our parish, I think Curarén leads the pack in decorating for special liturgical occasions. This was my first Pentecost Mass in Honduras. In my first year, I was visiting my old parish, the Basilica Shrine of St. Mary in Wilmington, N.C., and in my second year, there were no Masses because of the pandemic. Therefore, I was not aware of a special candle ceremony that takes place at the very beginning of Pentecost Mass. Fortunately, however, the altar server Noel guided me through the process.

May 23, 2021 – Pentecost Sunday
Reitoca, F.M., Honduras – 7:50 p.m.
Cloudy – 82

This morning Danilo took me to Concepción and El Hatillo to celebrate Pentecost Masses for the people. All went well in Concepción, except one of the *Delegados*, Nahún, seems very sick. I hope he'll be well soon.

After Concepción, Danilo and I went to El Hatillo. We were very surprised when we found the churchyard empty. Clementino, one of the *Delegados* of that community, came up a hill near the church and told us that Mass had been cancelled because the people had been up all night for a Vigil. So, Danilo and I were treated to more free time.

Danilo told me that the Mayor of Curarén has asked if Red Lantern Foundation could help the community of Escalón with funds to finish their new church. The municipality of Curarén will pay half, and Red Lantern Foundation will pay the other half. The total amount needed about $2,000. I'm glad we can help.

May 24, 2021 – Monday – Mary, Mother of the Church
Reitoca, F.M., Honduras – 3:25 p.m.
Partly cloudy – 97 F

This has been such a beautiful day of blue skies, fluffy white clouds, and great breezes that make the tropical plants on my deck sway hither and yon. Although it is hot, it is very comfortable in my study thanks to the air conditioning.

I have worked all morning and most of the afternoon in solitude, investigating missionary saints for my future blog posts and journals. Blackie is always happy to nap close to wherever I am.

Unfortunately, in this part of Honduras, we have still not had rain, even though May is usually noted for its rain and the beginning of the first growing season of the year. Because most of the people here in the mountains of southern Honduras are farmers, they are very fearful of a drought. There are no government assistance programs for them, so if there are no crops to sell, they are out of income.

May 25, 2021 – Tuesday – St. Gregory VII; St. Mary Magdalen de Pazzi;
St. Bede
Reitoca, F.M., Honduras – 7:45 p.m.
Cloudy – 82 F

Dr. Aaron was at my house this afternoon and evening doing some electrical work. He is just about finished with a campus security camera system. Aaron is so bright and accomplished in so many ways. I don't know what I'd do without him.

Danilo was here today to help Aaron. Like Aaron, Danilo knows a quite a bit about electricity: he has in fact installed electricity in homes and churches in our parish.

Aaron set up a meeting tomorrow with the mayor of Reitoca. We want to introduce him to Rotary and our Rotary Passport Club 7730, see what we might be able to do to help get the people of this area of Honduras vaccinated against COVID-19, and discern how else we Rotarians might help the community.

May 26, 2021 – Wednesday – St. Philip Neri
Reitoca, F.M., Honduras – 5:30 p.m.
Partly cloudy – 90 F

The weather forecasts predicted highs today and 99 F for Reitoca, and they were correct. The next two days will be about the same, and there is still no rain in sight. This is the night of the Full Flower Moon. I imagine we won't see much here because of clouds.

Fr. Carlos was at my house this morning bright and early to give me my weekly Mass assignments I have only two Masses, both on Sunday. One is a noon Mass in Alubarén, and the other is a 4 p.m. Mass in Curarén. My homily is done and ready to go, so this will be a very easy week.

This morning and afternoon, three young men from a Reitoca company came to the Holy Cross campus to install television services for the Blessed James Miller (blue) house. Unlike the visitors' *casitas* and my house, the blue house is not connected to the solar energy system.

This afternoon, Mayor Marlon Osorto of Reitoca came to the Holy Cross campus for a meeting with Aaron and me. We met in my study because it is just too hot on my deck. This was Marlon's first time on the Holy Cross campus, and he was very impressed. In the early part of the 2000s, Marlon worked for three years in Wilmington, N.C. Aaron has been to Wilmington a few times, and of course I was a priest there for a total of fourteen years. It was remarkable that the three of us, sitting together in the mountains of Honduras, had this in common.

Currently, obtaining the COVID vaccine in Honduras is difficult and complicated by politics. However, if a government such as the municipality of Reitoca, including its *aldeas,* or small villages, should get the vaccine from the United States or from a non-profit group, the process is up to them. So, I'll meeting with Drs. Marco, Aaron, and Valencia to see how we will proceed. I told the Mayor that we will see what we can do to get the vaccine here.

Marlon told us that one of Reitoca's biggest problems is roofs. Many families have no roofs on their houses, or roofs that are so badly damaged that they are basically nonfunctional. More and more, we are expecting a drought for the first planting season. Therefore, the poor people will be even poorer, and won't be able to get or repair a roof. Marlon estimates that 400 homes are in desperate need of roofs in the Reitoca municipality. Further, the laminate that the people use for roofing is in short supply, so stores have raised their prices. However, we figured at with the average cost of 4,500 *lempiras* per house, the total cost for building materials for 400 houses would be just under $75,000. I'll tell Rotary about that. Perhaps my club, or the district, can help us with that.

Marlon said that Reitoca (including its villages) has about 12,000 people, and Curarén has 25,000. However, the people are scattered over a huge area in the mountains. I'm not sure how many people are in the other three municipalities of our parish; those municipalities include Alubarén, La Libertad, and San Miguelito.

After our meeting, Aaron and I took Marlon to see the Blessed Stanley Rother (yellow) visitors' house. He was amazed at the quality of the workmanship, and he is excited about our plans for the future. I have always planned on having him and the mayor of Curarén over to see the campus, but I'm delighted he came so soon.

May 27, 2021 – Thursday – St. Augustine of Canterbury
Reitoca, F.M., Honduras – 8:55 p.m.
Partly cloudy – 84 F

The public electricity went off around 5 p.m. yesterday and didn't return until mid-morning today. Once again, I'm extremely grateful for the solar system backup.

Yesterday, Juan installed the new generator I bought months ago, which has been sitting in the garage. With this generator, we can obtain water from the cistern for the Holy Cross campus. We need to use the generator only when the regular electricity is down and we need water.

Danilo came to Reitoca today to take Fr. Carlos into Tegucigalpa for banking. Tomorrow, Danilo plans to go to Comayagua, a three-hour journey from Reitoca, but only a two-hour journey from his home in Lodo Negro.

This afternoon and early evening, the healthcare staff of our parish had a taco birthday party for Arnulfo on my deck. In addition to Arnulfo and his wife and son, we had Drs. Aaron and Marco (physicians), Dr. Shelsie (our microbiologist), Miguel, Ricci, Emilio, and Dr. Elia (pharmacist) and her son. In addition to tacos, we had pizza from Casona Lenca, a new restaurant in Reitoca. I was amazed and delighted to learn we have a pizza place in Reitoca! Aaron spent the night in the Oscar Romero (green) house.

May 28, 2021 – Friday
Reitoca, F.M., Honduras – 10:20 p.m.
Partly cloudy – 81 F

Early this morning, Dr. Aaron joined me for breakfast at my house. He enjoyed spending the night in the green visitors' house, and he gave me a few tips on tweaks to make the house a little better.

The rest of the day comprised cleaning up after the party and writing. I love days like this, just doing routine things at my own pace in solitude.

May 29, 2021 – Saturday – St. Paul VI
Reitoca, F.M., Honduras – 9:20 p.m.
Showers – 81 F

As I write this note, rain is finally falling in Reitoca, the first actual rain we've had in this area for many weeks. Though it is probably too late to help farmers much, it is a blessing.

This morning, the Holy Cross campus was buzzing with activity. Geovany, a plumber in Reitoca, fixed the drain system in the shower of the green house and the plumbing system in the Bl. Stanley Rother (yellow) house. Meanwhile, Antonio, a young man from a startup company in Reitoca, was installing equipment in the Bl. James Miller (blue) house to allow Danilo to watch television when he's on the campus. Geovany said he'd be back to fix two of the doors in my house that need attention, as a gift.

Thankfully, the afternoon was very quiet, so I devoted it to checking over the formatted text of my 2020 journal.

May 30, 2021 – Most Holy Trinity Sunday
Reitoca, F.M., Honduras – 6:25 p.m.
Mostly cloudy – 91 F

Today I celebrated Masses in Alubarén and Curarén. In Curarén, I also celebrated the baptism of Marvin Cruz.

Juan came in today to watch over the campus while Danilo and I went to our Masses, accompanied by a young man named Norbin. He is a motorcycle mechanic in Lodo Negro, but he hopes to expand his mechanical ability to include cars and trucks. As I was showing Norbin one of the visitors' houses, he saw a toaster on the counter and asked what that was, for he had never seen a toaster. So, when we got back to my house, I made some toast for an egg salad sandwich that I gave him. He loved the idea of a toaster.

I'm looking forward to the next few days off.

May 31, 2021 – Monday – Visitation of the Blessed Virgin Mary
Reitoca, F.M., Honduras – 8:40 p.m.
Mostly cloudy – 82 F

On this last day of May, I sent the proof of my 2020 journal text formatting tweaks to Pat. We're planning on using my *MissionPriest.com* website/blog logo for the front cover; that will be very different from past covers.

May begins winter here in Honduras. In most years, May is the second rainiest month of the year, behind October, and is the beginning of the first planting season. Unfortunately, here in Reitoca we have had only a little rain this May, and that was at the end of the month. Thus, it will be devastating to farmers who were not able to plant corn, beans, and other crops. Later, because of the lack of rain, there will be a dearth of plants to feed the cattle.

The biggest news of the month of May for me was the death of my stepmother, Mary Jean (Bush) Kus, in North Canton, Ohio. She was one month shy of her ninety-fifth birthday. She lived to celebrate her seventy-first wedding anniversary with my dad, who died a couple of years ago at the age of 99½. Her funeral Mass will be tomorrow. Because of the pandemic, I'm not able to travel to celebrate the Mass.

Also, this month, Fr. Frank Maloney, a retired priest of the Diocese of Raleigh, died in Pinehurst. He had been living at St. Joseph of the Pines in Southern Pines, N.C.

In May, many of the communities of our parish are busy with construction projects. In the municipality of Curarén, the biggest of our parish's five municipalities, the community of Aniz just expanded its soccer field, El Arado and Escalón are building new churches, and El Portillo is building a new facility for education and other functions. All that is in one municipality alone.

The Red Lantern Foundation has helped fund some of the building projects of the parish, and it will continue to do as it is able.

Happily, we are partnering with the Mayor of Curarén to help Escalón, a desperately poor community whose church collapsed.

Also, this month, I gratefully received the first dose of the Sputnik COVID vaccine, and plan to get the second dose on June 21.

This month the Rotary Passport 7730 Club, of which four of us here in Honduras are part, had a meeting with the Mayor of Reitoca to discuss the possibility of helping with obtaining vaccines and assisting with money for 400 houses in the municipality that have either no roofs or have roofs in such poor condition that they don't protect the families from rain. May through October is "winter" here, which means that although the temperatures remain high, chances of rain are great.

And finally, I learned that we now have a restaurant in Reitoca that sells pizza – WooHoo!

So, May has been a very eventful month, but now I'm excited to see what wonders June will bring.

JUNE 2021

June 1, 2021 – Tuesday – St. Justin, Martyr
Reitoca, F.M., Honduras – 7 p.m.
Cloudy – 75 F

Today was Mom's funeral Mass at Holy Family Catholic Church in Stow, Ohio. Because of the pandemic, I was unable to make it. It was the first time I was unable to celebrate the funeral Mass for a family member.

The Mass was livestreamed, so I was able to not only be present in spirit, but also to experience the whole event virtually. Fr. Paul Rosing, the pastor, did a wonderful job as the celebrant, and my sister Chris did a beautiful job with the eulogy/reflection at the end of the Mass. It was good to see my brother Larry and his wife Sally, my brother-in-law Skip and his wife Bev, and a host of cousins and nieces and nephews.

Danilo stopped by my house this morning with grocery items he bought for me yesterday in Tegucigalpa. He didn't stay long, for he learned that ten of his laying hens were sick; hopefully he will be able to stop the spread of the illness before it reaches the other hens. Tomorrow, he plans to take Juan to Tegucigalpa for banking.

June 2, 2021 – Wednesday – Ss. Marcellinus & Peter
Reitoca, F.M., Honduras – 7:45 p.m.
Mostly cloudy – 82 F

This is Pride Month in the United States, and many business, professional, sports, and political groups are doing special things to show support for gay, lesbian, bisexual, and transgender persons. For example, the American Embassy at the Vatican is flying the rainbow flag outside the embassy for the month, the San Francisco Giants have a special uniform they are wearing for the month that features rainbow numbers, and President Biden sent official best wishes.

One of the cutest things I read today was about a Minnesota three-year-old girl who asked for a birthday cake featuring a dead lion on it. She was enchanted by the movie *The Lion King*, and her favorite character was

Mufasa, a lion king who was killed. The little girl figured that if all her guests saw the dead lion on her cake, they would be too sad to eat. Then, she could have the whole cake for herself. Her parents decided they would just "go with it," that is, let her do what she wanted.

In Israel, several political parties formed a new coalition government. One of their first orders of business will be to replace Prime Minister Benjamin "Bibi" Netanyahu.

June 3, 2021 – Thursday – Ss. Charles Lwanga and Companions
Reitoca, F.M., Honduras – 6:35 p.m.
Showers – 82 F

As I write this note, Reitoca is having a fine shower, long overdue.

I learned today that Fr. Carlos has closed the church of San Francisco de Asís, the parish's mother church, due to the tremendous number of COVID patients in Reitoca. Other parts of the parish, however, are still open. This afternoon, for example, I celebrated Mass in Curarén along with thirteen altar servers. Because it is the feast of the Ugandan martyrs, I told their story. I have a special love for those martyrs because I was at the site of their martyrdom, Namugongo, for their feast day in 2001. At that time, the parish where I was pastor, St. Catherine of Siena in Wake Forest, N.C., had a sister parish in Uganda.

Right before I left my house to go with Danilo to Curarén, a woman dropped by to give me a bird. I thanked her but declined the gift. I like birds outside, but not indoors.

June 4, 2021 – Friday
Reitoca, F.M., Honduras – 6 p.m.
Mostly clear – 86 F

The Diocese of Raleigh today announced new priest assignments. Effective June 29:

• **Fr. Steven Thomas DiMassimo**, newly ordained, is appointed Parochial Vicar at St. Thomas More parish in Chapel Hill;

• **Fr. John Alex González**, Pastor of St. Elizabeth of Hungary parish in Raeford, is assigned Priest in Residence at Sacred Heart parish in Pinehurst;

• **Fr. Edison De Jesús Restrepo**, Administrator of St. Isidore Mission in Fayetteville, is assigned as Administrator of St. Elizabeth of Hungary parish in Raeford;

• **Fr. Tyler Sparrow**, newly ordained, is appointed Parochial Vicar at St. Patrick parish in Fayetteville.

In addition to these assignments, the bishop announced that the Missionaries of St. Francis de Sales, the "Fransalians," have accepted responsibility to assume priestly pastoral ministry of Good Shepherd parish in Hope Mills and San Isidro mission in Stedman. The Fransalians were founded in 1838 by Fr. Peter Mermier. Their initials are M.S.F.S.

The bishop also announced that **Fr. Paul Brant**, S.J., Parochial Vicar at St. Therese parish in Wilson, has been granted a "working sabbatical" from July 21, 2021 to June 30, 2022.

June 5, 2021 – Saturday – St. Boniface
Reitoca, F.M., Honduras – 3:30 p.m.
Mostly clear – 99 F

This morning I attended an online charter party for a new special-interest club called the Rotary Club of Ending Child Abuse. According to the founders, it is the first such Rotary club in the world. It is located in the same district as my Passport club, 7730. The club has 21 charter members, six men and 15 women, and members are from three states and two countries. Interestingly, 17 of the 21 charter members have never been Rotarians in the past.

Also, today, Steven Thomas DiMassimo and Tyler Sparrow were ordained priests at Holy Name of Jesus Cathedral in Raleigh, North Carolina. Tomorrow, they will celebrate their First Mass of Thanksgiving, Steven at St. Luke's in Raleigh, and Tyler at St. Ann's in Clayton. As noted above, both have already received parochial appointments. I wish them all the best!

For me, this was a fine day to work on blogs and future homilies.

June 6, 2021 – Sunday – Most Holy Body & Blood of Christ
Reitoca, F.M., Honduras – 1 p.m.
Partly cloudy – 97 F

This morning I celebrated Masses in La Libertad and San Miguelito. On the way home from the Masses, I wanted to stop at Anita's store to get a couple of items, but it was closed, as were other little stores, in Reitoca. Someone said that the stores were closed because a young woman died yesterday in Reitoca from COVID. The incidence of COVID in Reitoca is sky high.

June 7, 2021 – Monday
Reitoca, F.M., Honduras – 6:50 p.m.
Thunderstorm – 77 F

As I write this note, a thunderstorm is raging outside, and the temperature has fallen from 97 F to 77 F. Our area is so dry, that rain is a very welcome treat.

The United States Supreme Court declined to hear a case that would ban sex discrimination in the United States. Specifically, it would ban the law that requires men to sign up for the Selective Service but not women. Although there is currently no military draft, in the past the government has used this law to draft men and not women. Because of the male-only draft and male-only combat laws, men have been overwhelmingly the victims of death, bodily injury, and psychological disorders in wars. I pray that one day, Congress will grant men an equal right to life under the law that women enjoy.

June 8, 2021 – Tuesday
Reitoca, F.M., Honduras – 6:45 p.m.
Thunderstorm – 75 F

Today, Fr. Carlos is celebrating his second anniversary of priesthood ordination in the Basilica of Suyapa. He was ordained the same day that my friend, Fr. Dave Miller, was ordained at the Holy Name of Jesus Cathedral in Raleigh, N.C.

This was one of those days when nobody seemed to have the answers I needed. For example, Delta informed me that it is not flying into Tegucigalpa during the pandemic, even though its flights are listed on the Internet plane schedules every day as departing to and arriving from Atlanta. America Online was also unable to answer some simple questions. Some days are like that, so it's good to simply roll with it.

Today I learned that most 2021 North Carolina high school graduates will have their tuition and fees covered at any one of the 58 state community colleges for up to two years, thanks to the establishment of a new state program called the Longleaf Commitment grant. I think it is time for all States to offer taxpayer-funded community college tuition as they all do for grades 1-12. Today in the United States, there is not much value in the job market for a person with only a 12th grade education, but certainly not everyone needs a four-year college degree.

This afternoon, many of our healthcare staff had a birthday party on my deck for Ricci González who turns twenty-four. Ricci works as a pharmacy tech in our Reitoca pharmacy, Farmacia San Francisco de Asís. We had a chicken lasagna dinner prepared by the new Reitocan restaurant that also makes pizza. Because rain started after dinner, we retired to my kitchen for cake. At this time, Dr. Marco presented Ricci with two certificates that she earned as a pharmacy technician.

June 9, 2021 – Wednesday – St. Ephrem
Reitoca, F.M., Honduras – 7:25 p.m.
Thunderstorm – 77 F

Danilo and I went to Tegucigalpa today. My primary objective was to apply for a Banco Atlántida credit card. That was a very interesting experience. First, the clerk told me I couldn't get a credit card because I was too old. Then, however, she said that if I had someone younger than me come with me, that would be okay. Danilo, who was sitting next to me applying for credit card at the next station, said that he was with me. However, the clerk helping him told him he just needed to bring proof of employment. So, I'll take care of that for him next week. Then, the clerk helping me told me that I had to have $8,500 in my account before applying for a credit card.

The whole experience reminded me of when I first came to Honduras three years ago and was applying for a phone package with Claro. They told me I was too old for a telephone account, but later they gave me an account anyway. I strongly suspect that a lot of people make up rules as they go along.

When Danilo and I returned from Tegucigalpa, he and Juan put screening on the lower part of two steel doors of my house, to prevent frogs from entering, Chispa from entering, and Blackie from going outside.

Danilo told me that in his town, Lodo Negro, many people recently began getting sick. Naturally everyone suspected COVID-19. However, laboratory tests showed that they had dengue fever.

Fr. Carlos came over this afternoon to let me know I'll be celebrating Masses in Travesilla on Friday and Curarén on Sunday. He also informed me that our parish's churches in the municipalities of Reitoca and Alubarén are closed, so we don't have any Masses in those communities this weekend.

Late this afternoon, my Rotary Passport Club 7730 held the last meeting of this Rotary year. We went over our goals for the 2021-2022 Rotary year, and they sound very exciting.

June 10, 2021 – Thursday
Reitoca, F.M., Honduras – 8:30 p.m.
Showers – 77 F

This morning I had a very exciting Zoom call with Lori Harris and Dawn Rochelle. Lori is the president of my Rotary Passport club, and Dawn is the outgoing governor of the Rotary district in which my club is located.

We talked about the two issues that Reitocan Mayor Marlon discussed with Dr. Aaron and me last month. The greatest need is COVID-19 vaccines. The mayor estimates that about 35,000 people in the municipalities of Alubarén, Curarén and Reitoca would be eligible for the vaccine. Therefore, we would need 70,000 doses, assuming we were not getting the Johnson & Johnson vaccine that only requires one dose. The second big need is to put roofs on approximately 400 houses in the Reitoca municipality. The cost for roofs for 400 houses would be approximately $75,000.

Lori has a great network, and many have expressed interest in assisting with the financial part of the roof project. Lori thinks it might be a good to experiment with maybe five houses to see how it goes, and then commit to the rest. We are still in the assessment phase of the project.

As for vaccines, there is a group of Rotarians and their friends in North Carolina who are exploring how to obtain the vaccines.

Dawn mentioned that in Rotary, it is always best to "under promise and over deliver." Very sage advice for anyone.

Finally, I mentioned to Lori how it would be wonderful if the filmmaker who recently spoke at a Rotary Passport meeting could come to Reitoca and film our project. It would be great for public relations and publicity for our Rotary club, our Rotary district, and Rotary in general. Plus, helping with these projects will lay the foundation for future projects we have in mind here in Honduras.

Now I will share this information with Drs. Aaron and Marco of our club, and then the three of us will meet with Mayor Marlon.

A man from the Curarén community of El Arado dropped by the *casa cural* this morning, and Fr. Carlos brought him over to my house. This man told us that the community of El Arado never got the concrete we bought for them for the floor of their new church, and they never received the money to buy the remaining boxes of tiles they need. Danilo will see what's what, for he told me that he personally delivered the bags of concrete mix and gave the money to the *Delegado* there.

Today the regular electricity went out in Reitoca around 2:30 p.m. and did not come back on for the rest of the day. Fortunately, I had finished making a batch of bean and bacon soup.

June 11, 2021 – Friday – Sacred Heart of Jesus
Reitoca, F.M., Honduras – 7 p.m.
Mostly cloudy – 82 F

June is a month of special anniversary milestones in my life. Today, for example, is the 60th anniversary of my high school graduation from Maryknoll Junior Seminary in Clarks Summit, Pennsylvania. The school was more commonly called "The Venard" after a French missionary martyr, St. Théophane Venard. But when I was in high school, he was only a "Venerable." Interestingly, of my graduating class, I'm the only one who is in priestly ministry today.

One of the first things I read this morning was a news item out of Vatican City reporting that Pope Francis said yesterday, "Clericalism is a perversion of the priesthood: it is a perversion. And rigidity is one of the manifestations. When I find a rigid seminarian or young priest, I say 'something bad is happening to this one on the inside.' Behind every rigidity, there is a serious problem, because rigidity lacks humanity." What a powerful and accurate assessment this is.

This morning, I celebrated Mass in Travesilla, a community of Curarén. Because the name of this church is Sacred Heart of Jesus, and

126

today is the feast day of the Sacred Heart, the community was celebrating. When Danilo and I arrived before Mass, the people were gathering on the road leading to the church for a procession. I was able to film the procession from the front of the church.

The community had their altar decorated beautifully, and I got some great photos. I had not been to celebrate Mass there since November 1, 2018. I certainly hope that either Fr. Carlos or Fr. Sebastián was there since then. I told the community that I can only celebrate Mass in places Fr. Carlos assigns me.

After Mass, one of the *Delegados de la Palabra* of the community told me their church needs a bell. I'm not sure where the bell would go, for there is no bell tower. However, today many churches have their bells attached to a small structure outside the church building itself, and it works fine.

Before leaving Travesilla, Danilo and I had a luncheon at the home of Delores Hernández, one of the *Delegadas* of the community, and her mother.

The Diocese of Raleigh announced a few new priest assignments.

- **Fr. Dongwook Lee**, priest of the Archdiocese of South Korea, is appointed pastor of Saint Ha-Sang Paul Jung parish in Apex effective April 30, 2021;

- **Fr. Thomas Simisky**, S.J., priest of the USA East Province of the Society of Jesus, is appointed parochial vicar at St. Raphael the Archangel parish in Raleigh effective June 12, 2021;

- **Fr. Edward Tembo**, CICM, a Missionhurst Missionary, is appointed parochial vicar at María Reina de las Américas parish in Mount Olive and its mission of Santa Teresa del Niño Jesús in Beulaville, effective June 29, 2021.

- The Bishop of Raleigh also gave thanks to Jesuit **Fr. Vincent Marchionni**, parochial vicar of St. Raphael parish in Raleigh for his ministry. Fr. Vincent is being transferred to priestly ministry in another diocese by his provincial effective July 21, 2021.

June 12, 2021 – Saturday – Immaculate Heart of Mary
Reitoca, F.M., Honduras – 6:45 p.m.
Mostly cloudy – 81 F

Last night we had heavy rains. After a very dry May, at last, we are having the weather we expect during our winter months (May-October). Now, the weather folks are predicting rain in the late afternoons and early evenings for the foreseeable future. I haven't had to water the *almendro* trees or the *napoleones* (bougainvilleas) for three days now.

Fr. Carlos walked over to my house from the rectory today and told me that he and Fr. Sebastián will be going to the major seminary in Tegucigalpa tomorrow to get their first anti-COVID vaccinations. He said that all the priests and seminarians have been invited to participate, especially good news for parish priests, for we are in contact with hundreds of people every week. And in our parish in particular, with more than 80 churches to visit, we come in contact with a huge variety of people, many of whom don't wear masks. Because I have already begun the vaccination process with Sputnik vaccine, I'll stick with that. I get my second shot a week from Monday, the 21st of the month.

Fr. Carlos told me that Reitoca and Alubarén are both closed to buses and church services because COVID is out of control.

June 13, 2021 – 11th Sunday in Ordinary Time
Reitoca, F.M., Honduras – 8:40 p.m.
Cloudy – 79 F

Regular electricity goes out pretty much every day now that our "winter" has begun. Sometimes, the outage seems to be related to storms, and other times it goes out on a sunny day for reasons beyond me. But my faithful solar system is keeping me comfortable and enabling me to write.

Today, I celebrated a 4 p.m. Mass in Curarén along with ten altar servers. Danilo and I passed by many intoxicated young men who were either lying on the side of the road or sitting on the side of the plaza. During the Mass, a young man with Down's syndrome got up from his seat after Communion and began pushing an intoxicated man down the middle aisle to get him out of the church. Many people were chuckling, but I found the experience sad.

June 14, 2021 – Monday – Flag Day USA
Reitoca, F.M., Honduras – 7:25 p.m.
Mostly cloudy – 79 F

This afternoon I attended, via Zoom, the monthly meeting of the Rotary District of which my Passport Club is a member. Because the Rotary year begins on July 1, this is Dawn Rochelle's last monthly meeting as District Governor. She has done a super job in that role.

Dawn told the attendees about how we need 70,000 vaccine doses and 400 new roofs for the people of our area. Lori, our club president, and Dawn are working hard to see how American Rotarians can help us. According to Lori, the roof project will definitely happen. The vaccine project will happen only if we can somehow obtain the vaccine. Lori also mentioned that the U.S. military will deliver the vaccines to us if a drug company or other agency donates them to us. So, now is the time to pray.

Dr. Marco has set up a meeting tomorrow with Marlon, the Mayor of Reitoca, to let him know how we have followed up on our meeting of May 26 concerning vaccines and roofs.

June 15, 2021 – Tuesday
Reitoca, F.M., Honduras – 6:15 p.m.
Thunderstorm – 84 F

As I write this note, a thunderstorm is bringing heavy rains to our area. Naturally, the regular electricity went off around 4 p.m., as has occurred every day for the past several days. Fortunately, it usually returns after a while, at least briefly.   In my blog, I am featuring each church of our parish on two days. Today, I finished scheduling the churches through November 2022.

I also wrote a long note to our Passport President Lori Harris and outgoing District Governor Dawn Rochelle telling them of a meeting I'll be hosting at my house for the Mayor of Reitoca, Drs. Aaron and Marco, and me. Unfortunately, less than sixty seconds before I was ready to send the note, the Internet went out.

I invited Richard Creech, a new member of the Rotary Passport Club, to be on the International Projects Committee which I chair. Richard is not only a dear friend and super-easy person to work with, but he has also been to Reitoca several times.

Fr. Carlos was at my house in late afternoon to let me know I have Masses at 4 p.m. on Thursday and Sunday in Curarén. He also let me know that Fr. Pedro Pablo Barona is now officially part of our parish and is working with the churches in the Curarén zone of San Marcos. The churches of that zone are quite far from Reitoca, often a two-hour drive from Reitoca. He told me Fr. Pedro Pablo has been part of the parish since February, but Fr. Carlos never informed me.   Fr. Pedro Pablo is originally from Mandastá, a community of Curarén. I don't know where he is living now.

The biggest news that Fr. Carlos shared, however, is that the social hall that the parish is building in Curarén will also feature a *casa cural* (rectory) on the second floor. This house will be for the pastor in case Curarén becomes its own parish one day. That would be marvelous, for the municipality of Curarén contains over 40 of our parish's churches.

June 16, 2021 – Wednesday
Reitoca, F.M., Honduras – 6:40 p.m.
Mostly cloudy – 79 F

Two more people died today in Reitoca from COVID. Churches in the municipalities of Alubarén and Curarén are closed because the pandemic is affecting so many people.

Today, Drs. Aaron, Marco, and I hosted a meeting with Mayor Marlon of Reitoca. Aaron, Marco, and I told the mayor that our Rotary Passport 7730 Club is working on both projects on which he requested help. Though we could not make any predictions on getting vaccines for the area, we did say that the roof project is looking very good.

As the mayor was leaving the Holy Cross campus after the meeting, he mentioned that he'll be delivering some gravel to put on the "road" next to the campus, and he'll be looking for two people to help spread it. I told him I'll put the word out before he delivers the gravel. I mentioned that I am planning on constructing a driveway connecting the drive of the *casa cural* (rectory) and the Holy Cross campus. He said he'd provide the bulldozer to do the initial work.

The U.S. House of Representatives overwhelmingly approved a new federal holiday called Juneteenth National Independence Day, traditionally called Juneteenth. This day celebrates June 19, 1865, the day Union Major General Gordon Granger rode into Galveston, Texas to let enslaved persons know that slavery had ended more than two years earlier.

On the international scene, U.S. President Joe Biden is on his first European visit as president. He is meeting with major world leaders and assuring the people that "America is back."

Also, today, the Kindle edition of my 2020 journal, *MissionPriest.com – Journal of a Missionary Priest – 2020*, is now for sale on Amazon.

June 17, 2021 – Thursday
Reitoca, F.M., Honduras – 7 p.m.
Partly cloudy – 80 F

This afternoon I celebrated Mass in Curarén, and I'll be there again on Sunday. Today the theme was forgiveness.

The new hall next to the church is coming along very nicely, and a new load of concrete blocks has been delivered.

June 18, 2021 – Friday
Reitoca, F.M., Honduras – 4 p.m.
Thunderstorm – 86 F

Torrential rain is coming down as I write this note, and the regular electricity is not working.

Today, I wrote a biography of St. George Preca, the founder of the Society of Christian Doctrine. St. George Preca was a home missionary in Malta, where he devoted much time teaching catechists and writing literature to be used in teaching. He also founded a publishing house called Veritas Press.

Aaron called today and said he heard that the drive-through vaccination event I'm supposed to go to at the Catholic University of Honduras on Monday has been cancelled. He'll try to verify this when he goes to Tegucigalpa this weekend.

June 19, 2021 – Saturday – St. Romuald; Juneteenth
Reitoca, F.M., Honduras – 7:40 p.m.
Mostly cloudy – 81 F

I gave Juan the day off, so it was a very quiet day to do some writing, organizing files, and relaxing. Andy, Chispa, and Henry hung out together all day on my deck, and Blackie spent most of the day curled up next to my chair in the study.

June 20, 2021 – 12th Sunday in Ordinary Time
Reitoca, F.M., Honduras – 7:15 p.m.
Thunderstorm – 81 F

This is Father's Day in the three big countries of North America: Canada, Mexico, and the United States. Here in Honduras, we celebrate Father's Day on the first Feast of St. Joseph, March 19. In my blog today, I used one of my favorite photos of a young father and two boys, one his son and the other his nephew. In the English version of the website, there was no problem. However, in the Spanish version, the photo for Flag Day appeared. I'm not sure what the problem was, but I have two people trying to solve the problem.

In the western United States, a heat wave is scorching the land. Phoenix, Arizona, for example, is experiencing temperatures of 112-116 F.

This afternoon I celebrated Mass in Curarén. Great progress is being made on the hall next to the church.

Aaron was not able to verify that my vaccine drive-through event tomorrow has been cancelled. He thinks that maybe it was just a rumor. Whether it's on or off, I have lots to do in Tegucigalpa, so I'll be there bright and early.

June 21, 2021 – Monday – St. Aloysius Gonzaga
Reitoca, F.M., Honduras – 7:30 p.m.
Mostly cloudy – 81 F

This morning, Danilo and I promptly left the Holy Cross campus at 5 a.m. so I could get to Tegucigalpa for my second Sputnik vaccine injection. Although we made fine time to the city limits of Tegucigalpa, the traffic in the city was crawling at a snail's pace. So, we didn't get into the line of cars for the drive-thru event until 8 a.m. There were so many cars in front of us, that we could not even see the front of the line. In no time at all, cars were backed up behind us for farther than the eye could see.

Next to the line were mountainsides with no houses or stores or buildings of any kind, so there was no food or drink or bathroom facilities. Because I knew we'd be waiting, I took along my iPad and read from time to time. As the hours ticked by, many of the elderly people who were waiting for an injection had to get out of their cars to stretch their legs, and some drivers were getting testy. The man two cars in front of us, for example, would fly out of his car to confront someone trying to cut the line. Once, as the man got out to confront someone trying to cut in, a group of other men, very strong-looking, gave him assistance. Happily, nobody cut in.

Danilo and I waited in the line until 4:30 p.m., at which time someone from the front of the line walked back to tell everyone that the place had closed for the day. So, Danilo and I spent 7½ hours practicing patience. We then stopped at a Walmart to buy a few things and discovered that Walmart no longer provides bags for free; one must now buy them. After our all-day experience in line, we were not overly cheered by Walmart.

On the way home, we stopped at a restaurant on CA-5 called El Recreativo, a buffet. The restaurant apparently does a great business during the day, when busloads of people stop in. However, in the evening, the place is pretty deserted; Danilo and I were the only customers.

My friend Aaron told me his mother was in the same line to get a shot, and she didn't get one either. Somehow, she learned we are supposed to come back in August. I have to check this out.

June 22, 2021 – Ss. Thomas More & John Fisher; St. Paulinus
Reitoca, F.M., Honduras – 8:50 p.m.
Rain – 75 F

This was a perfect day for me, totally peaceful. I was able to focus on research and writing about saints for my projects.

June 23, 2021 – Wednesday
Reitoca, F.M., Honduras – 9:35 p.m.
Partly cloudy – 79 F

Mom would have been 95 today had she not died at the end of April. She will be greatly missed.

In my research for "missionary heroes," I am running into a never-ending assortment of fascinating characters, most of whom are either saints or on the sainthood path. I am avoiding writing about missionaries who are still alive. Among the group of missionaries, I have found several men who were professional nurses or practiced nursing at one time or another. I currently have forty-two candidates for my second *Saintly Men of Nursing* book.

This afternoon, Aaron dropped by to help me with some computer programs, and Fr. Carlos dropped by to let me know I'll be celebrating Masses in Alubarén, Cunimisca, La Libertad, and San Miguelito in the coming four days.

June 24, 2021 – Thursday – Nativity of St. John the Baptist
Reitoca, F.M., Honduras – 8:10 p.m.
Cloudy – 82 F

This evening, I celebrated Mass in Alubarén for the feast of the Nativity of St. John the Baptist. Fortunately, the church has solar energy, for all the regular electricity has gone out in eight municipalities, including Alubarén and Reitoca.

Because of the occasional heavy rains of late, rocks from the back of the yellow *casita* (Bl. Stanley Rother House) have been falling down, and the same has been happening in back on north side of my house, the Four Martyrs House. Juan and I will have to clean up the mess and monitor carefully.

In Surfside, Florida, parts of a 12-story apartment building collapsed. The whole world will be following this story, I'm sure.

June 25, 2021 – Friday
Reitoca, F.M., Honduras – 10 p.m.
Rain – 79 F

Today is the third anniversary of my moving to Honduras. The time has gone very fast, and I have enjoyed learning to live in a different society and culture. Part of my joy, I think, is that I no longer have the administrative responsibilities of a pastor. I have heard many priests say the same thing when they retired, but I never really grasped the concept. Now, I totally do. I absolutely love serving as a missionary, and I love the fact that I am able to devote so much time to writing.

This evening, as I was in my study writing, I noticed that the street lights of the Holy Cross campus suddenly went on. We've been without regular electricity for three days now, so that was very welcome. Now I can cook again and have unlimited running water, assuming I have it in the cistern.

Today, I went to the Curarén community of Cunimisca to celebrate Reconciliation with twenty-two young people who are preparing for their Confirmation next month, and to celebrate Mass. The church was packed, and two of the Confirmation candidates celebrated their First Communions. For the Mass, we had visiting musicians from other of our parish's churches in that zone. After the Mass, the Confirmation candidates and I posed for group photos.

Currently, the community of Cunimisca is building a fenced area in front of their campus, and they need help buying a gate. I told them that the Red Lantern Foundation will buy the gate.

The Diocese of Raleigh reported today that Kolbe Flood has left seminary training. It is always good when men learn early on their seminary career that the ordained priesthood is not their vocation, rather than waiting until after they are ordained to the diaconate or priesthood.

June 26, 2021 – Saturday
Reitoca, F.M., Honduras – 6:50 p.m.
Cloudy – 97 F

Today, Bob Rafferty, a high school classmate of mine from Stow, Ohio, sent me a note about the death of Dave Viehland, a high school classmate of ours. Of our high school class, only Dave went on to become a Maryknoll priest. He left the priesthood in the Philippines to get married. As I noted earlier, I am the only ordained priest from that class and I'm not only still engaged in active ministry, but as a missionary to boot!

Bob also told me of the deaths of two other members of our class, Hank Cooney and Frank Ciccarillo. May they all rest in peace.

June 27, 2021 – 13th Sunday in Ordinary Time
Reitoca, F.M., Honduras – 8:35 p.m.
Intermittent showers – 77 F

On this, the 23rd anniversary of my ordination to the priesthood, I celebrated two Masses, one in La Libertad, and the other in San Miguelito.

In La Libertad, I celebrated the baptisms of two children, one-year-old José Roberto, and three-year-old Yiksi. My homily focused on how, for over 2,000 years, the Catholic Church has treasured and practiced the ministry of the sick. I told how this ministry applies not only to the body, but also to the mind and spirit. I shared a story called "The Message" by Thomas Brown. The story showed how a hairdresser who had lost his faith, came to believe after the death of his mother.

In San Miguelito, I noticed that the Mass intentions were for two people. Because I wasn't sure how to pronounce one of the names, I asked a *Delegada* of the church how to pronounce it. After telling me, she shared that both people were from her family, and both died 23 years ago within a week of this date. I told her what an amazing coincidence that was, for today is my 23rd anniversary of priesthood ordination.

In the Pacific Northwest of the United States, a heat wave is underway. For example, today it was 112 in Portland, Oregon, and tomorrow it is supposed to be 111 in Seattle, Washington. The people in that part of the country are not used to such heat, so most do not have air conditioning in their homes.

Pope Francis sent special greetings in honor of Pride month, encouraging ministers always to practice "closeness, compassion, and tenderness."

June 28, 2021 – Monday – St. Irenaeus
Reitoca, F.M., Honduras – 8:50 p.m.
Thunderstorm – 75 F

A heavy thunderstorm is raging here in Reitoca as I write this note, but Blackie and I are safe, sound, and dry.

Today is the 23rd anniversary of my First Mass of Thanksgiving that I celebrated in my ordination church, St. Michael the Archangel in Cary, North Carolina. Most of the family members who were there that day have since passed on to heaven.

A technician came to the Holy Cross campus today to do some work installing television equipment, but he said he would come back tomorrow because he needed a cable longer than the one he brought.

June 29, 2021 – Tuesday – Ss. Peter & Paul
Reitoca, F.M., Honduras – 8:20 p.m.
Light rain – 75 F

The Pacific Northwest of the United States and part of southwestern Canada are breaking records with the heat wave. Yesterday, for example, Seattle was 108 F, while Portland, Oregon hit 116 F. Lytton, British Columbia hit 117 F, the highest temperature ever recorded in Canada.

Aaron came by the Holy Cross campus this afternoon and gave me a short lesson on how to determine if a picture is a good size for my blog. He is also installing some equipment that will help beef up security for the campus and provide good internet service in the two visitors' *casitas*. Aaron is staying the night in the yellow casita, dedicated to Blessed Stanley Rother, a priest of the Archdiocese of Oklahoma City who was a martyr of Guatemala.

In Florida, the current death toll from the partial collapse of the apartment building in Surfside is now listed as 12, with 149 people missing.

When such tragedies happen, I often think how easy it would be for someone who wanted a fresh start in life to simply disappear and start over somewhere new. There are many fictional and real-life stories with this theme.

June 30, 2021 – Wednesday – First Martyrs of the See of Rome
Reitoca, F.M., Honduras – 6:10 p.m.
Mostly cloudy – 81 F

On this last day of June, the month of the Sacred Heart of Jesus, I spent the morning in Tegucigalpa paying salaries for clinic staff, shopping for plants, and buying food. On the way to the city, Danilo and I picked up a young man in Reitoca from the Curarén community of San Isidro. He said he remembered me from the two times I celebrated Mass in that community. Because priests are so visible, pretty much everyone knows who they are, but the priest often only knows a small fraction of a church's congregation, especially in churches that only have Mass a couple of times a year.

When I met with Dr. Marco at the bank to pay salaries, I learned that the Honduran government is unable to get any more Sputnik vaccine, so, nobody knows what "Plan B" will be for all of us who got the first dose but not the second. Will we be able to "mix and match," having the second injection from another company? Or will we have to start from scratch? Marco said that the person in charge of the health department in Reitoca has a vaccine for me, but she needs to find out the correct protocol. Whatever will be fine with me.

I got a message from Lori Harris, president of the Rotary Passport Club of District 7730. She asked that I set up a monthly Zoom meeting with our International Project Committee. I'm aiming for this coming Tuesday, July 6.

In Florida, the death toll from the apartment building collapse is now 18, with 145 still missing.

As I look back on the month of June, I find it was action-packed. I also realize, though, that if I didn't record things that I find especially interesting, I would gloss over most of what happened, and soon they would be out of my memory.

For me personally, the month started out with the funeral for Mom at Holy Family Catholic Church in Stow, Ohio. Now, I'm the eldest member of my extended family. My brother Larry said that after the funeral, as the extended family members were gathered, someone inevitably asked, "Well, who's next?" Larry said the consensus was that I'd outlive all of them. We'll see.

The US Supreme Court was very busy this month handing down decisions. Some I liked, and some I did not. The case that was most upsetting to me was their refusal to hear a case banning discrimination against men over registering for the Selective Service. However, the court did say that was up to Congress, so the court did not say that the discrimination, which amounts to male genocide, is forever the law of the land. One day, I pray, the lives of men will be seen in American law as of equal to those of women. And by "equal," I mean "same."

This month my 2020 journal, *MissionPriest.com: Journal of a Missionary Priest – 2020*, was published in a Kindle edition, thanks to my editor, Pat Marriott. I'm waiting for the paperback to be published now.

This June, President Biden made his first European trip as American president, and he declared Juneteenth, June 19, as the newest federal holiday.

Here in the Archdiocese of Tegucigalpa, most of the priests and seminarians got their first anti-COVID injection of AstraZeneca vaccine.

Finally, for me, June is a big "anniversary month." This June, I celebrated these anniversaries: high school graduation, 60; years living in Honduras, 3; priesthood ordination and first Mass of Thanksgiving, 23.

So, it was a good month, and now I'm ready to see what God has planned for me in July.

JULY 2021

July 1, 2021 – Thursday
Reitoca, F.M., Honduras – 8 p.m.
Partly cloudy – 83 F

This evening I celebrated Mass in Reitoca, and it was the very first time I ever celebrated in that church without at least one altar server. Dr. Aaron, who was staying in the Blessed Stanley Rother House for the night, drove me and Dr. Shelsie into town. I had planned on walking, but Aaron said he'd be happy to give us a ride to town. Shelsie had walked over to the campus with Aaron earlier to get some exercise. Dr. Marco came to the Mass in his scrubs, and Fr. Carlos dropped by from his Mass in Alubarén to give me a ride home in case I needed one. It is great to have so many people looking out for me.

July 2, 2021 – Friday
Reitoca, F.M., Honduras – 9:10 p.m.
Mostly cloudy – 79 F

Today Juan and I did some gardening projects, and we learned how to make homemade root stimulator. Of the various choices we read about on the Internet, we settled on the water and honey one. After mixing our concoction of 1 Tablespoon of honey melted and mixed in two cups of hot water, we prepared six cuttings from a bougainvillea bush. After the root stimulator was no longer hot, we dipped our cuttings into the stimulator and then planted them in the soil of a pot on the deck. I also started a garden log to record when we plant things and any notes we might have. In time, this campus will be quite stunning, I hope.

July 3, 2021 – Saturday – St. Thomas, Apostle
Reitoca, F.M., Honduras – 7 p.m.
Partly cloudy – 82 F

In preparation for the Rotary Vaccine and Roof Meeting on Tuesday, I sent seventeen photos from our parish to the members of the Rotarians involved, to give them a little taste of the area. I hope they were inspired. I'm thinking of sending a photo each week.

Today, a Vatican judge ordered ten people to stand trial for various financial crimes including embezzlement, extortion, fraud, and abuse of office. The highest-ranking person ordered to stand trial is Cardinal Giovanni Angelo Becciu. This will be incredibly interesting to watch unfold.

July 4, 2021 – 14th Sunday in Ordinary Time; Independence Day USA
Reitoca, F.M., Honduras – 9:20 p.m.
Thunderstorm – 75 F

Today is Independence Day in the United States, and many folks have a three-day weekend. This date is also important to me because it was the birthday of my father. A light rain is falling, and low clouds are hiding the mountaintops. My friend Rojann sent me a Fourth of July card from the Jacquie Lawson collection.

This morning I found Henry sleeping in one of the big flowerpots on the deck, and his friend Andy was sleeping next to the flowerpot. I guess the soft soil was appealing to him.

This afternoon, Miguel Zelaya, lab tech from Clínica Santa María, took me to celebrate Mass in Curarén. Juan came to the Holy Cross campus to watch it while I was away for Mass.

July 5, 2021 – Monday – Independence Day celebrated in USA
Reitoca, F.M., Honduras – 9:10 p.m.
Cloudy – 77 F

Americans have a holiday today because this year, Independence Day fell on a Sunday. In the news today, I read that at least 150 people were killed in the United States from Friday through Sunday, with more than 400 shooting incidents. The data were collected by CNN reporters and the Gun Violence Archive. So far this year, more than 22,500 Americans have died in violent gun incidents, including 10,000 homicides and 12,000 suicides.

This was a very unusual day here in Reitoca because the temperature only got to 84 F. We did have torrential rains in the afternoon, and then a gloomy day followed with low-hanging clouds. By Wednesday, we're supposed to have a high of 95 F once again, a normal temperature for Reitoca.

This week, the priests of the Archdiocese of Tegucigalpa are celebrating, via Zoom, an annual clergy formation week – *Jornada de Formación Permanente del Clero–* with the Cardinal leading it. Frs. Carlos and Sebastián were at my house this morning for the two-hour session. We are reading a document called *Documento para Camino hacia la Asamblea Eclesial de América Latina y El Caribe* (Preparation for the Ecclesial Assembly of Latin America and the Caribbean). The document discusses issues relevant to the Catholic Church in Latin America and the Caribbean, in preparation for a Papal conference in Mexico City in November. I'm finding it very informative, and I'm very pleased that I am able to understand most of the vocabulary.

This weekend, I'll be celebrating Reconciliation for Confirmation candidates in San Marcos, a community of Curarén on Saturday, and Masses in La Libertad and San Miguelito on Sunday.

July 6, 2021 – Tuesday – St. Maria Goretti
Reitoca, F.M., Honduras – 8:30 p.m.
Cloudy – 79 F

Clergy Formation Week continues each morning this week from 9 to 11. Today we continued reading from the document on issues of the Church in Latin America and the Caribbean. Because we have the meetings on Zoom, and because most of the priests' faces and names can be seen, I'm learning to know the presbyterate little by little by using these meetings.

Today I had a Zoom meeting with the International Projects Committee (IPC) of my Rotary Passport Club and a few others who are interested in our Vaccine and Roofs projects here in Honduras. I was happy to introduce Reitocan Mayor Marlon Osorto to the group, and the group was delighted to know that Marlon had worked in Wilmington, North Carolina at one time.

Marlon reported that the mayors of Alubarén, Curarén, and Reitoca each received a few doses of anti-COVID vaccines. Alubarén received doses to fully inoculate 200 people; Curarén enough for 250 people; and Reitoca enough for 230 people. That was a nice start, but we need enough vaccines to inoculate 35,000 people in these three municipalities.

President Lori invited Marlon to become a member of the club, and I think he is interested. I asked if a member needed to be able to speak English, and Lori explained that there is now a Zoom language translator. I asked Aaron to help Marlon navigate the application process. I'd love to have him aboard.

After the meeting was over, Marlon showed Aaron and me a little video he had made describing our project that is designed to put roofs on 400 houses in the pueblo of Reitoca and its many mountain villages. The background music is "We Are the World." The music, together with vivid photos showing the desperate poverty of many of the people, will touch many hearts. However, the film needs much tweaking. So, tomorrow I'll send notes to Aaron on how the film needs to be improved, and he'll share them with Marlon.

Today the Diocese of Raleigh sent an invitation to all the priests of the diocese to the Mass of Admission to Candidacy for two men: Drew Eliot Navarro and Robert Michael Lane, to be held on August 5 at my ordination church, St. Michael the Archangel in Cary, North Carolina.

July 7, 2021 – Wednesday
Reitoca, F.M., Honduras – 8 p.m.
Partly cloudy – 81 F

This morning, bright and early, Danilo and I left the Holy Cross campus so we could be at Banco Atlántida at 9:30 to meet Dr. Marco to pay clinic salaries. Last week, when Marco and I went to the bank, we discovered that *SaludHondu*, the group that sends us money for salaries from the United States, did not send enough for the double salaries that workers in Honduras get in June. So, we went back today, only to discover that *SaludHondu* had not yet sent the second part of the payment. So, it looks like I'll be back next week. And actually, that is fine with me, for I love going to Tegucigalpa, even though five hours in traveling wears me out.

While we were in Tegucigalpa, Danilo and I stopped at one of the tropical plant stores and brought two small trees to put in front of the blue *casita*, the cottage designed for the *mayordomo* (caretaker) of the Holy Cross campus. These trees are tropical and don't grow very tall, but they spread out in a kind of clump formation and are quite beautiful.

Aaron dropped by this evening and brought Drs. Shelsie (microbiologist of the Clínica Santa María laboratory) and Elia (pharmacist of Farmacia Candelaria in Curarén). Aaron showed me the video the mayor made, and he sent a copy to all the people on our Rotary club's Vaccine & Roof Projects list.

Because Aaron has been somewhat ill and didn't want any of us to get sick, he went to the yellow *casita* to do some computer work, while Elia, Shelsie, and I sat in the kitchen and talked for about an hour. I had the chance to practice speaking Spanish, and they had a chance to practice their English. Their English is much better than my Spanish, I think. We had a wonderful time talking about politics and religion, and now they would like to come over once a week to chat about whatever. Aaron thinks it's a great idea also.

This evening, the controversial President Jovenel Moïse of Haiti was killed in his home, and his wife and first lady of Haiti, Martine, was shot but not killed. She was taken to Miami, Florida for treatment.

July 8, 2021 – Thursday
Reitoca, F.M., Honduras – 7:25 p.m.
Partly cloudy – 82 F

Weather in the United States continues to be exciting. Tropical Storm Elsa is making its rainy way up the eastern seaboard, while the far west bakes. Yesterday, Death Valley, California hit 126 F, and Saturday it is predicted to reach 130 F. Nighttime lows may stay above 100 F in many places.

Today I took a little money from one of my retirement accounts to pay for various projects. I'm especially eager to build a paved drive connecting the drive of the rectory to that of the Holy Cross campus.

Here on campus, it is very quiet. The only visitors I had, besides Frs. Carlos and Sebastián this morning for our priest formation Zoom, were Henry and Andy and some cows. I don't know where Blackie is. He left yesterday and has not returned.

July 9, 2021 – Friday – St. Augustine Zhao Rong & Companions
Reitoca, F.M., Honduras – 7 p.m.
Partly cloudy – 82 F

Blackie still has not been home since Wednesday afternoon, so I'm starting to worry a bit.

The global COVID-19 death toll has surpassed 4 million, and the United States has had more than 600,000 deaths. Current global hot spots for the virus include Brazil and Russia, and deaths in various African nations have tripled in the past month.

In Surfside, Florida, authorities say there is virtually no chance that there are any more survivors of the apartment building collapse in May. The other part of the building has been demolished. The official death toll is 78, and 62 are still listed as missing.

In a world filled with lots of negative news, it's always great to hear about positive things people are doing. Today, for example, I read how Amazon has committed $700,000,000 to aid hourly Amazon employees with tuition for high-demand fields such as aircraft mechanics, computer-aided design, machine tool technologies, medical laboratory technologies, and nursing. Amazon will pay for 95% of tuition, fees and textbooks, up to $12,000 over four years.

June 10, 2021 – Saturday
Reitoca, F.M., Honduras – 7:10 p.m.
Partly cloudy – 84 F

Danilo and I left my house this morning at 7 a.m. to go to San Marcos, a major community of Curarén, so that I could celebrate Reconciliation with Confirmation candidates. We arrived there at 8:30, and the church was overflowing. Fr. Pedro Pablo, the priest who works in the San Marcos zone of our parish, was preaching to the young people when we arrived. I immediately began hearing confessions and continued until 10 a.m. Frs. Carlos and Sebastián came a bit later to assist with the confessions in other parts of the campus.

In the center of San Marcos stands a huge tree. One of its branches was being cut down for some reason, and that was the center of attention of everyone not involved in church activities. I hope it was only one branch that had to come down, for that tree is a most precious central part of that community.

When Danilo and I got back to the Holy Cross campus, Juan told us that Blackie had returned around 10 a.m. He is a little thinner, but that is a good thing, for he needed to lose a little weight. Otherwise, he seems fine. Later in the afternoon, after eating and napping, off he went again to who-knows-where.

Danilo planted two small tropical trees in front of the Blessed James Miller House today. The people at the *vivero* (nursery) said that these trees, which grow as clumps, can reach 12 feet in height, and like to have water twice a day. I'll see to that.

Dr. Valencia, who now lives in Tegucigalpa, set up a Zoom meeting for the International Projects Committee of our Rotary Passport club for this coming Monday. We'll be meeting with Roberto Salgado Lagos of Club Rotario Tegucigalpa Sur and his board of directors at 6 p.m. I look forward to establishing relationships with local Rotary clubs.

Today, I read that the bishop of La Crosse, Wisconsin has removed a renegade pastor. This man has not only been removed from his parish, but he is not allowed to celebrate Mass in public and forbidden to preach. He has been told to make a 30-day spiritual retreat. The priest, who is outspokenly homophobic, preaches that Catholics who support the Democratic party "face the fires of hell." His preaching in general is consistent with right-wing Trumpian ideology. Intentionally or not, this officer of the Church has made himself an unofficial spokesman for the Republican party in the USA.

June 11, 2021 – 15th Sunday in Ordinary Time
Reitoca, F.M., Honduras – 7:30 p.m.
Cloudy – 84 F

Today I celebrated Masses in La Libertad and San Miguelito. Because the Old Testament reading (Amos 7: 12-15) and the Gospel selection (Mark 6: 7-13) both focused on vocational stories, I told the story of Servant of God Thea Bowman and how she used her gifts to advance the cause for African-American people in the United States.

This afternoon, Juan helped Danilo transplant two bougainvilleas. Because the soil here is much too hard to use a mere shovel, we have to use digging bars. Danilo is an expert at using them. Now, I have to patiently train the flowering plants to climb up the side of the hill next to the stairs going up to my house.

Fr. JaVan Saxon, pastor of St. Mary Parish in Laurinburg, N.C., died today at his home. He had just come home from the hospital and seemed to be recovering satisfactorily. Fr. Saxon was one of the few African-American priests of the Diocese of Raleigh.

Finally, today, Sir Richard Branson of England made history when he flew his space ship, *VSS Unity*, along with three of his Virgin Galactic company employees, over 50 miles above Earth's surface. The ship made a smooth landing in Truth or Consequences, New Mexico. Sir Richard, a billionaire, said he wants this flight to be the beginning of a new age in which average people can become astronauts. Amazon founder Jeff Bezos of the United States, plans to make his own flight to outer space on July 20.

I can just envision the far future, when kids in school will be learning about these adventures to outer space. Of course, they'll be living on different planets, and they'll see the work of Richard Branson and others much as we would see the early pioneers of air flights with planes going into the air for a hundred feet or so. And the kids will probably be saying something to the effect, "How lame! How did the people on Earth even get around in the twenty-first century when they couldn't even visit relatives and friends in other galaxies?"

July 12, 2021 – Monday
Reitoca, F.M., Honduras – 8:05 p.m.
Mostly cloudy – 84 F

This evening, the International Projects Committee met online with Roberto Salgado Lagos of Club Rotario Tegucigalpa Sur (Rotary Club Tegucigalpa South). The purpose of this meeting was to introduce our club to the Tegucigalpa Sur club so that in the future, when we apply for global grants, we might partner with them. Roberto took some information and asked if we would make a presentation to their club about our current projects and future ones. We will probably make a presentation in three weeks.

After the meeting, Dr. Elia came by with her son to bring me some homemade croissants. They are very delicious.

So far in Surfside, Florida, 94 dead bodies have been recovered and identified.

July 13, 2021 – Tuesday – St. Henry
Reitoca, F.M., Honduras – 8 p.m.
Partly cloudy – 80 F

Today was the funeral Mass for Fr. JaVan Saxon at his parish church, St. Mary in Laurinburg, North Carolina. He was buried in the priests' section of Our Lady of Guadalupe Cemetery in Newton Grove, N.C. May he rest in peace.

Reports from Surfside, Florida say the chances of finding any more survivors of the apartment building that collapsed are basically nil. The search for bodies and survivors is coming to an end.

July 14, 2021 – Wednesday – St. Camillus de Lellis
Reitoca, F.M., Honduras – 9:10 p.m.
Partly cloudy – 81 F

About 6:30 this morning, Danilo arrived on the Holy Cross campus with three young men from Lodo Negro to work with Juan in cleaning up the campus. In this winter season, the rains make everything grow like a jungle, and in no time, the place is out of control.

Meanwhile, Danilo and I went to Tegucigalpa. I tried once again to get a credit card, but this time I was not able to do so because my Honduran identity card had expired August 21, 2019. I told them that Immigration officials keep saying they'll send me a new card, but they never do. I have now begun my fourth year living in Honduras and am still waiting for permission to be here for my second year! I don't actually care, except that I fear that if I travel to the United States, I might not be allowed back into Honduras. I may have to enlist the cardinal's help in getting a new card.

After Danilo and I got back from Tegucigalpa, I attended the first regular monthly meeting of my Rotary Passport club. Aaron and I reported on our Vaccine and Roof projects and our invitation to tell the Club Rotario Tegucigalpa Sur about our club and projects.

Aaron and I spruced up the video that the mayor of Reitoca put together, and now we have to choose a background song for it.

June 15, 2021 – Thursday – St. Bonaventure
Reitoca, F.M., Honduras – 8:45 p.m.
Partly cloudy – 82 F

Today I celebrated Mass in Curarén at 4 p.m. I told the story of Venerable Nicola D'Onofrio, an Italian who was born just six days before me. As a teen, he decided to become a Camillian Father and devote his life to the care of the sick. Tragically, however, he died at 21 from cancer. Although Nicola never became either a professional nurse or an ordained priest, he is an excellent example of how one's life journey is the path to sainthood, not our earthly accomplishments. He is also an example for all the men who never got the chance to become professional nurses because they were too poor to study nursing, or because schools of nursing refused them admission because they were men, much as many schools of medicine refused to admit women long ago.

I received an estimate for a paved drive connecting the casa cural driveway and the Holy Cross drive, and it was way too much. So, I'm leaning very heavily toward making a simple gravel drive.

June 16, 2021 – Friday – Our Lady of Mount Carmel
Reitoca, F.M., Honduras – 7:30 p.m.
Mostly cloudy – 81 F

Germany and Belgium have experienced torrential rains and massive flooding. More than 125 people have been found dead, and hundreds more are missing.

In Catholic news, Pope Francis has put restrictions on the celebration of the "modernist" Tridentine Latin Mass. This Mass, which is only a few hundred years old, was largely replaced at the Second Vatican Council with the traditional practice of the ancient Church, that is, in the language of the people. Today no nation in the world has Latin as its basic language. Even in Vatican City, where Latin is still used to write official documents, citizens do not speak Latin in their homes or on the street. "Traditionalists," who are actually "modernists" if they knew their Catholic history, are in an uproar. That's nothing new, for they have been disgruntled since the Second Vatican Council (1962-1965), as a result of the Church asking Catholics to return to their roots.

This morning, Juan and I cleaned the yellow *casita* (Blessed Stanley Rother House) in preparation for Bishop Teodoro Gómez' visit. After we had it spic and span, two workers came to install cables in the two visitors' *casitas*, getting dust everywhere. So, Juan and I cleaned everything again.

My 2020 journal, *MissionPriest.com: Journal of a Missionary Priest – 2020*, finally appeared in paperback today on Amazon.com.

Around 6:15 this evening, Fr. Carlos walked Bishop Teodoro over from the rectory to see our Holy Cross campus, where he'll be sleeping. The bishop seems very nice, and plans to be here tonight and tomorrow night.

July 17, 2021 – Saturday
Reitoca, F.M., Honduras – 8 p.m.
Partly cloudy – 84

This morning, Bishop Teodoro came to my house for coffee and cookies, and then left to go to the Curarén community of San Marcos to have breakfast and celebrate Confirmation for 130 young people. Fathers Carlos and Sebastián went for the celebration also, and I stayed home doing some writing projects.

The bishop returned to Holy Cross around 5:30 p.m. and said all went well at the Confirmation, and that he was enjoying getting to know this area of the Archdiocese.

July 18, 2021 – 16th Sunday in Ordinary Time
Reitoca, F.M., Honduras – 7:45 p.m.
Partly cloudy – 84 F

I was prepared to celebrate the 9 a.m. Mass in Reitoca this morning, but the bishop said he'd like to celebrate it in order to meet more of the people of our parish. I readily agreed. Fr. Carlos, whose Mass in the Alubarén community of Tablones, was cancelled this morning because of COVID, accompanied the bishop to Reitoca for Mass. Later in the morning, the bishop came back, thanked me for the hospitality, and said he'd be back next Friday to sleep overnight so he could celebrate Confirmation in Curarén on Saturday, July 25. I'm delighted that the Holy Cross campus is being used for visitors.

At 4 p.m., I celebrated a Mass in Curarén. Because electricians were wiring the new social hall of the church community, there was no electricity. Fortunately, I am able to project very loudly, so everyone in the church was able to hear me. I preached about how destructive bad shepherds can be. The Scripture passage I used as my inspiration was from Jeremiah 23: 1 that says, "Woe to the shepherds who mislead and scatter the flock of my pasture, says the Lord." I gave an example of the Wisconsin priest who was removed from his parish this month, and a Texas bishop who supports his caustic and highly political rhetoric. I didn't use names, just the stories of these two men and how their actions are alienating thousands of people.

My dear friend Laura Vinson called this evening, to say she is planning to visit soon with John Donoghue from Cape Fear Solar Systems and two of his friends. It will be John's first visit to Honduras, and I suppose for the other men also. So, we'll be prepared to show them an amazing and inspirational time. They hope to visit in August.

July 19, 2021 – Monday
Reitoca, F.M., Honduras – 8:05 p.m.
Mostly cloudy – 82 F

Fr. Sebastián turned 60 years old today, a great milestone in anyone's life. I hope he has many joy-filled years ahead.

News from around the world about the effects of climate change fascinate me. Today, for example, I read about three areas of the world that are experiencing highly unusual weather patterns. In Russia, Alaska, and northern Canada, permafrost is thawing at an alarming pace. Without permafrost, much forest land will go to other species, and people in many regions rely on the forests for their very existence. In Germany and Belgium, historic flooding is taking many lives and destroying whole towns. And in the United States, 80 large fires have been raging in 13 states, destroying more than a million acres. In Oregon, the Bootleg Fire has drawn over 2,100 firefighters.

When I read about the fires in the United States, I thought of some of the students I taught at the University of Montana when was doing my sociology Ph.D. work. Many were forestry majors, and in the summer months, they were on call as smokejumpers. They would pray for forest fires so that they would be called up, for they earned more money on duty than they did on call, and it was certainly more exciting to be battling fires than sitting around.

156

As I was watering the small trees on the campus this morning, Fr. Carlos came by and told me that the municipality of San Miguelito is now closed because of COVID there. I'm not sure when Alubarén will open up, but that municipality is closed this weekend.

July 20, 2021 – Tuesday – St. Apollinaris
Reitoca, F.M., Honduras – 8:10 p.m.
Partly cloudy – 84 F

Today I wrote project descriptions for my Rotary Club's Reitocan Roofs Project and the Vaccine Project. I am grateful to the president of our club, Lori Harris, for giving me a template to follow. It made putting thoughts together much easier. Aaron helped me with the map of Francisco Morazán (F.M.), the "department" in which we live. A department is like an American or Mexican state or a Canadian province.

In west Texas, Amazon founder Jeff Bezos flew in his Blue Origin spaceship called *New Shepard*. He named the spacecraft after Alan Shepard, the first American in space. This flight included the youngest and oldest person ever to fly into space, an 18-year-old man and an 82-year-old woman. The spacecraft achieved an altitude of sixty-two miles.

Dr. Aaron and Mayor Marlon were at my house this afternoon to attend the Zoom meeting we arranged with the International Projects Committee of my Rotary club. Aaron and I gave a report and informed them of our projects. Basically, Lori and others have been working on getting vaccines for eligible people in the municipalities of Alubarén, Curarén and Reitoca; as expected, that is proving to be difficult. The Reitocan Roofs project, on the other hand, has its first $2,000 to work with, and the mayor will be able to begin providing roofs for the ten poorest houses very soon. I think we will be able to get some excellent public relations and publicity from the roof project.

The mayor has a bulldozer that will be available Thursday morning to carve out a drive connecting the driveway of the rectory with the Holy Cross campus. I'm very eager for that to happen.

July 21, 2021 – Wednesday – St. Laurence of Brindisi
Reitoca, F.M., Honduras – 7:15 p.m.
Mostly clear – 84 F

Danilo and I went to Tegucigalpa this morning, while three young men from Lodo Negro worked on the campus. I met Dr. Marco at Banco Atlántida to pay salaries of Clínica Santa María staff and do some grocery shopping.

While we were in Tegucigalpa, the workers transplanted some bougainvilleas (called *napoleones* in Spanish) and two tropical trees that I had growing outside my kitchen windows.

This afternoon, Aaron and I also met with Eduardo Rivera online to discuss the Red Lantern Foundation website, which he needs to finish. Eduardo is aiming to finish next week.

July 22, 2021 – Thursday – St. Mary Magdalene
Reitoca, F.M., Honduras – 9:10 p.m.
Partly cloudy – 82 F

This morning at about 11, Mayor Marlon came with his Reitoca government crew to supervise bulldozing a roadway connecting the rectory drive to the Holy Cross campus drive. The work was done in about 25 minutes. Danilo has contacted someone in Reitoca to deliver truckloads of gravel for the road on Wednesday. With this connector, we won't have to continually submit our trucks to the terrible "Calle Calvario" that runs outside the northern part of the campus. So far today, three people have driven on the connector: Danilo, Dr. Aaron, and Dr. Marco.

This afternoon I celebrated a Mass in Alubarén for the feast of St. Mary Magdalene, "Apostle to the Apostles." In the homily, I told how Bible scholars now debunk the sixth-century notion of Mary Magdalene having been a terrible sinner, when indeed she was the first missionary of Christianity.

This evening, after the Alubarén Mass, Danilo took me to Casona Lenca, a restaurant on the outskirts of Reitoca. The owners, Jancy and Jenny, have created a beautiful home and decorated their land with many tropical plants and flowers. Jancy said that during the pandemic he was bored staying at home from his job as a teacher in the high school in Reitoca, so he and Jenny started the restaurant, named after the Lenca people indigenous to this area of Central America. I first met Jancy when my house was under construction.

The reason for our visit was a 21st birthday party for Noel Pérez, the pharmacy tech at Farmacia Candelaria in Curarén. Noel, whose birthday is actually tomorrow, has an amazing history. He is from the Curarén community of El Portillo and lives with his father. Noel's mother died some time ago, and the family is very poor. After grade school (grades 1-6), Noel was determined to go to high school even though his family had to struggle to scrape up the tuition for him. For the six years of high school (grades 7-12), Noel walked to school every day, a journey of two hours each way. Sometimes, he had to swim across a river on his journey. On those days, he had two sets of clothes, so that he could change into the dry clothes once he got to the other side of the river.

As a pharmacy tech in Curarén, Noel must walk two hours to work each way, every day. The staff and I believe that walking four hours every to and from work is ridiculous. So, the staffs of Clínica Santa María, Farmacia San Francisco, and Farmacia Candelaria got together to take up a collection to buy Noel a good motorcycle. He was shocked when we gave him a brand-new motorcycle.

Noel's dream is to one day enter the university and study nursing in Tegucigalpa. He would then like to come back here, to the rugged rural mountain area, and serve the people.

What an amazing story Noel has, and what tremendous dedication and solid work ethic he has. But Noel's story is not in any way unique. It is not at all unusual for people to walk two hours, one way, to attend Mass. What an example to American citizens Noel and others like him would make.

After the party, Dr. Elia, the pharmacist of Candelaria, stayed in the yellow *casita* overnight, and Noel stayed in the green one.

July 23, 2021 – Friday
Reitoca, F.M., Honduras – 6:40 p.m.
Partly cloudy – 79 F

As I write this note, the Full Buck Moon is aglow outside my window over the southeastern mountains. If I saw it on a postcard, I probably would think it was a painting.

Dr. Elia and Noel were here for breakfast this morning before heading to Curarén for work in Farmacia Candelaria.

This morning I helped Juan dig out some weeds and roots on the new roadway. I think I overdid it, for I became a little sick. But, after resting, I was back to my usual self. One must be very careful in this climate, for by 9 a.m. on most days, the temperature can approach 90 F.

I finished approving the text for the Spanish version of my 2012 journal, so I'll send it off to Pat in the morning.

Bishop Teodoro is staying in the yellow (Blessed Stanley Rother) *casita* tonight and tomorrow night. He had Confirmations in Ojojona today, and tomorrow he'll have Confirmations in the main Curarén church, Our Lady of Candelaria.

Mayor Marlon sent a beautiful PowerPoint introduction to the Roofs Project that my Rotary club is supporting. It contains photos of the first ten houses on which we'll put roofs, the cost for each house, and the like. It is very professionally done.

July 24, 2021 – Saturday – St. Charbel Makhlouf
Reitoca, F.M., Honduras – 8 p.m.
Partly cloudy – 82 F

This morning, Bishop Teodoro celebrated Confirmations in Curarén for 230 young people. He told me that Fr. Carlos doesn't want me to go to Curarén because COVID is running rampant there.

At breakfast, the bishop told me that he is the only official auxiliary bishop of the Archdiocese of Tegucigalpa. The other new bishop, Walter,

160

serves in the archdiocese but is not considered an auxiliary in the same sense as Teodoro.

July 25, 2021 – 17th Sunday in Ordinary Time
Reitoca, F.M., Honduras – 5:15 p.m.
Partly cloudy – 90 F

Bishop Teodoro stayed overnight in the Blessed Stanley Rother House. After breakfast, he left the Holy Cross campus. He plans to do a service this evening in Valle de Ángeles for a family.

This morning I celebrated Mass in La Libertad. Because San Miguelito has a large number of COVID cases, our church there is closed. So, it was a very short Sunday morning for Danilo and me.

I am giving Juan the next three days off. On Tuesday, Danilo will take Juan to Valle de Ángeles and Tegucigalpa. I'd like Juan to get to see the *viveros* (nurseries) near Valle de Ángeles and to see the town itself. I would also like for him to learn a little more about Tegucigalpa so he can get a better feel for where Danilo and I go to obtain things for the Holy Cross campus. Juan knows only that a couple of times a month, Danilo and I "go to Tegucigalpa," but the details are a mystery for him. I would like him to expand his horizons for the future, seeing what the world has to offer outside of the rural mountain setting in which we live.

July 26, 2021 – Monday – Ss. Joachim and Anna
Reitoca, F.M., Honduras – 8:55 p.m.
Partly cloudy – 81 F

Today is the first World Day of Grandparents and the Elderly. Pope Francis declared this day to honor the elderly as they are often forgotten or treated as though their lives are unimportant because they are "retired."

I used this day to get caught up on many odds and ends.

July 27, 2021 – Tuesday
Reitoca, F.M., Honduras – 8:50 p.m.
Cloudy – 77 F

This was a nice, quiet day at home for me for research, writing, and relaxing.

A heavy rain came around 2 p.m. and continued into the evening. Darwing and his girlfriend Mari stopped by to say hello. I think Mari is planning to build a house, and Darwing told her she should see the houses on the Holy Cross campus.

July 28, 2021 – Wednesday
Reitoca, F.M., Honduras – 9:40 p.m.
Cloudy – 75 F

Blackie was out all night, and when he returned home this morning, he was hobbling along. It appears that another dog must have bit his right back leg badly. Blackie had a little to eat and spent the rest of the day sleeping.

The Diocese of Raleigh announced that Fr. Francis P. Gillespie, S.J., a priest of the East Province of the Society of Jesus, is appointed Administrator of St. Mary Parish in Laurinburg until a new pastor can be assigned. Fr. Fran will also assist in priestly ministry for Mass on Saturday evenings at Our Lady of the Snow Mission in Elizabethtown. Fran was formerly the pastor of St. Raphael parish in Raleigh, and he is a brother of Fr. John Gillespie, former pastor of St. Mary in Wilmington. The pastorate position at St. Mary parish in Laurinburg is vacant because of the recent death of Fr. JaVan Saxon.

The Diocese of Raleigh also announced the death of Donna Miller, sister of Fr. David Miller, parochial vicar of St. Catherine of Siena Parish in Wake Forest. Poor Dave has lost three sisters in nine months. Bright Funeral Home is handling arrangements for Donna. When I was pastor of St. Catherine of Siena (2000-2006), I had a most wonderful relationship with the Bright Funeral folks. I thought I'd never find a funeral home as friendly and competent as Bright's. I was gratified to find that Andrews in Wilmington was just as great, and I have very fond memories of my time working with the staffs of both places.

Danilo is here today with 15-year-old William from Lodo Negro to work on the Holy Cross campus. The main task of the day is putting poison on weeds. They were prepared to spread gravel on the new connector drive between the rectory and the Holy Cross campus drive, but the gravel could not be delivered because the river was too high for the gravel trucks.

I used much of the day preparing a PowerPoint presentation for the International Projects Committee of my Rotary Club. It is designed to summarize the need for our Reitocan Roofs Project, and to give the people an introduction to this part of Honduras.

This afternoon, Drs. Aaron and Shelsie dropped by to fly Aaron's new drone. Aaron has some amazing aerial shots of the Holy Cross campus.

July 29, 2021 – Thursday – St. Martha
Reitoca, F.M., Honduras – 8:15 p.m.
Partly cloudy - 81 F

Juan told me all about his experience on Tuesday visiting Valle de Ángeles and its various *viveros* (nurseries). He bought a few bushes for his house and some daisies for the Holy Cross campus. We planted them today with other greenery in flowerpots in the area between the Four Martyrs House (where I live) and two of the visitors' *casitas*. The presence of blooming flowers adds a fine dash of color and warmth.

This evening, I celebrated the 6 p.m. Mass in Alubarén for the feast of St. Martha. Right before the Mass, three young men approached me to ask me why I became a priest and the joys and challenges of being a priest. I think this was a pre-Confirmation project they had. I told them the biggest challenge was to learn Spanish and minister in a language that was not my native one. The joys, however, are limitless.

July 30, 2021 – Friday – St. Peter Chrysologus
Reitoca, F.M., Honduras – 8 p.m.
Partly cloudy – 84 F

My friend Richard didn't get into the diaconate formation program he had applied for. I'm very sorry to hear that. On the other hand, I told him that in my life, many doors were closed to me. Whenever that happened, I was sad. But in time, looking back on my life, I realize that the closed doors were the very best things that could have happened. I have come to the belief that when God closes a door, it is because he has a much better one to open for us.

July 31, 2021 – Saturday – St. Ignatius of Loyola
Reitoca, F.M., Honduras – 4:30 p.m.
Mostly cloudy – 90 F

On this final day of July, I celebrated a Mass in the Reitocan community of El Higuerito, also known as Las Vegas. The occasion was the first anniversary of the death of Santos Evelio Euceda Osorto. I never met Santos, but I blessed his gravesite in January of this year. His son Mainor is a best friend of Juan who works for me in the daytime on the Holy Cross campus. Santos' wife, Carmen, is one of the *Delegadas de la Palabra* of the El Higuerito community. Because the name of the church is Carmen, several men and women in that community are named Carmen. After the Mass, there was food for everyone. Danilo and I were not able to stay, however, for we had to get back to the Holy Cross campus to receive the gravel.

As we were heading home from Mass, Juan called us and said that the gravel driver, Jorge, had delivered two loads of sand. But we ordered gravel, not sand. Not only that, he delivered the loads to the road outside the campus that I have named Calle Calvario, not to the connector road. Later, we were able to talk with Jorge to be clear as to what we wanted and where we needed it. Danilo even took a sample of gravel from a pile we have left over from the construction of the campus. So, Jorge plans to deliver good gravel on Monday.

July has been an interesting month for the world and for me.

In July, Fr. JaVan Saxon died in the Diocese of Raleigh. He was a large presence for many years, especially as an advocate for African American Catholics.

This month, extreme weather patterns dominated much of the news around the world. In the United States and Canada, record-setting temperatures were recorded, Belgium and Germany experienced death-producing floods, and in parts of the world known for extreme cold, the permafrost is melting.

Around the world, over four million people have now died of COVID.

Two billionaires have successfully flown into space, opening a whole new world of travel for the super-wealthy. However, I think that one day, their flight will be seen as a very primitive step in human beings' trans-planet and trans-galactic travel.

In the Catholic world, two big news items captured my attention. One is the removal of a very hostile priest in Wisconsin who has entwined his politics and religious beliefs so closely together, that they almost seem as one belief system. This man has verbally attacked a wide host of God's children, such as gays, lesbians, women, Democrats, health experts, government officials, immigrants, and all others who don't agree with him.

On a larger scale, the Vatican courts are hearing a case involving ten men, including a cardinal, for charges such as embezzlement, corruption, and financial misconduct. It appears that there is never a scarcity of scandals in the Catholic Church.

In my little corner of the world, July was important also. Fr. Sebastián of our parish turned 60, we got a connector road between the rectory and the Holy Cross campus, my 2020 journal came out in paperback, and the new auxiliary bishop of Tegucigalpa has made himself at home in one of the casitas on days when he has to celebrate functions in Curarén, and my Rotary Passport Club began a Roofs project with the Mayor of Reitoca.

Now, I'm eager to see what adventures and growth opportunities August has in store for me.

AUGUST 2021

August 1, 2021 – 18th Sunday in Ordinary Time
Reitoca, F.M., Honduras – 8:05 p.m.
Partly cloudy – 82 F

Today I celebrated a 9 a.m. Mass in Reitoca and a 4 p.m. Mass in Curarén.

In Curarén, I noticed a table in front of the *alcaldía* (mayor's building) and some people gathering around it. When I asked about it, someone told me that it was a health table, and people were getting vaccines. As I was getting vested in the sacristy with the altar servers, I looked out the window to see a motorcycle driving by with a message blaring that free vaccinations were now in process in the town plaza on the side of the Catholic church.

After Mass, I learned that Danilo had gone over to the table and received his first Moderna vaccine. He is scheduled to receive the second dose later this month.

Then when we got back to Reitoca after the Curarén Mass, we happened to swing by the plaza that sits in front of the mother church of our parish, San Francisco de Asís. Many tables were set up, like an outdoor restaurant. However, it wasn't a restaurant at all, but a health station to administer the COVID vaccine. So, tomorrow I'll have to learn about this new development, for I need to report it to my Rotary club, which is trying very hard to get us needed vaccines.

August 2, 2021 – Monday – St. Eusebius of Vercelli; St. Peter Julian Eymard
Reitoca, F.M., Honduras – 8 p.m.
Partly cloudy – 81 F

An amazing headline caught my attention today about the state of global warming. It noted that on last Tuesday alone, Greenland experienced its most significant melting event of the year as temperatures in the Arctic surge. In fact, last Tuesday, the amount of ice that melted in Greenland would provide enough water to cover the entire state of Florida in two inches of water.

Today, two young men from Lodo Negro, Danilo and Gerson, came to the Holy Cross campus to spread out gravel that was finally brought for the drive connecting the rectory's drive to our Holy Cross drive. Later Danilo, my driver and *mayordomo* of the Holy Cross campus, had to take a sick person from Lodo Negro to Comayagua.

I learned today that Mayor Marlon will pick me up at 8 a.m. on Friday to take me to the Reitocan community of Santa Cruz. There, I'll be able to take some photos and a video of workers putting a roof on the house of a poor family. I'll then be able to show the progress of my Rotary Club's "Reitocan Roofs Project" to our International Projects Committee.

August 3, 2021 – Tuesday
Reitoca, F.M., Honduras – 7:30 p.m.
Rain – 77 F

As I write this note, a steady rain is falling. Earlier in the evening, we had very hard rains. I definitely won't have to give the little trees on the Holy Cross campus water in the morning.

Last evening, I watched a young man named Andy Rowell on *America's Got Talent*. With a totally deadpan demeanor, he said he was going to perform a karaoke song. The song he picked was "Tequila," which has only one word for the entire song – "Tequila" – said three times during the song. The audience went wild over Andy's hilarious presentation. As I watched Andy, I couldn't help thinking, "I could have done that!" But, alas, I didn't do that. It reminds me of the "pet rock" phase we had in the United States. Like millions of other people, I said, "I could have done that!" But, alas, I didn't. So much success is doing something simple that no one else ever gives a thought to doing. It is something worthy of reflection.

More gravel for our connector driveway was delivered today, but the young men from Lodo Negro did not show up. Danilo didn't come to Reitoca today either, for he is having pain in his head. He had that symptom a month or two ago, so I hope it is not something serious.

Frs. Carlos and Sebastián went to Tegucigalpa today for the annual "sanctification day" celebrated by the priests working in the Archdiocese of Tegucigalpa on the feast of St. John Vianney, patron saint of parish priests. I did not go to that event this year. Instead, I plan to go to Tegucigalpa on another day to do many errands.

The Diocese of Raleigh reported today that Fr. Bob Diegelman, a retired priest of the Diocese of Raleigh, has died. Originally from Buffalo, New York, Bob was an educator before becoming a priest in Raleigh in 1993. I have heard of Fr. Bob, but I don't think I ever met him. May he rest in peace.

Santos Felix Cerrato Cruz, head of the *Delegados de la Palabra* at the church of Carmen in El Higuerito, dropped by my house this afternoon. The past Saturday, I asked the band to let me know how much they needed to buy shirts for the band, and Santos came by to let me know how much they needed. So, Red Lantern Foundation will give money to the band for new shirts, pants, and shoes.

August 4, 2021 – Wednesday - St. John Mary Vianney
Reitoca, F.M., Honduras – 6:25 p.m.
Cloudy – 82 F

As I write this note, ominous clouds are everywhere, flashes of lightning come and go in the southern sky and thunder rumbles. There is no rain at the moment, but we did have torrential rains around 5 p.m. I haven't had to water the little trees and bushes for two days in a row.

I was up bright and early this morning and all ready for Danilo to come to take me to Tegucigalpa for a shopping trip, but he was not able to come today. I hope tomorrow we'll be able to go. I'd like finally to buy furniture for my living room and garden tools for the campus.

Juan came in today on his day off to help spread the new load of gravel for our road connecting the driveway of the rectory with the Holy Cross campus. Again, the two young men from Lodo Negro did not show up, so I helped Juan. I discovered gravel is very heavy! Juan said this was a three-person job, and we only had two people. I told him that actually, we only have one-and-a-half; I'm the half. What I can do as a 78-year-old man weighing 120 pounds hardly counts as a whole worker. My "help" is more like that of a 3-year-old who "helps" decorate the Christmas tree. But I did my best until I was attacked by an army of vicious, biting ants. For some reason, they attack only me, never Juan. I told Juan they must like sweet things.

The Diocese of Raleigh announced that the funeral Mass for Fr. Bob Diegelman would be on August 12 at St. Matthew Catholic Church in Durham, with burial in the parish's cemetery.

August 5, 2021 – Thursday – Dedication of the Basilica of St. Mary Major
Reitoca, F.M., Honduras – 8:55 p.m.
Mostly cloudy – 79 F

This day started off weird, and by the end of the day, it was weirder.

At 7 a.m., Danilo and I left the Holy Cross campus to head for Tegucigalpa. As we entered the center of Reitoca, we saw many people in the streets talking among themselves, and in the plaza in front of San Francisco de Asís church, people were gathering. We didn't have any idea what was going on, but it was certainly unusual.

Not far from Reitoca, Danilo and I encountered many trucks full of soldiers and police. We had to wait as a large truck with about twenty soldiers turned around to head in the same direction we were going. Danilo and I were able to slip directly behind the truck of soldiers. Behind us were four or five pickup trucks of police. I joked that they were probably looking for me, as my Honduran identification card expired in August 2019. I said, "They'll never think of looking for me in a caravan of police and soldiers!"

When we got to the CA-5 highway, an hour's drive away from Reitoca, the caravan stopped to connect with other police and military. Danilo and I left the caravan to head to Tegucigalpa. I don't know what all the drama was about, but from more than three years in Reitoca, I know that there will always be drama.

In Tegucigalpa, we bought some needed tools for the Holy Cross campus and ten tropical trees for the entryway of the campus. Unfortunately, I was unable to find any furniture for my living room, but for now that's okay as I am never in the living room anyway. I'm almost always in my study where I have air conditioning.

At around 6:25 p.m., I had to walk into the center of Reitoca to celebrate a 7 p.m. Mass. Unfortunately, a ferocious storm suddenly came up, and in just a few minutes I was soaking wet, even though I had an umbrella. As I walked on the new connector drive that we built from the Holy Cross campus to the rectory, gales of wind blew me right off the drive twice. I felt like Mary Poppins, ready to fly away. Fortunately, Fr. Sebastián was at the gate of the rectory, and he gave me a ride to church as tree limbs fell on the roadway, wind howled, and rain beat down sideways.

As we entered the town, all the electricity went off. The only light was from flashes of lightning. Fortunately, the church had lights on from solar panels that the cardinal had provided. Parts of the sacristy and sanctuary were covered with water, a couple of trees were down, and broken limbs were everywhere. Fr. Sebastián came back to get me after the Mass, for which I'm eternally grateful. As we began to go back to the Holy Cross campus, the lights of the town came back on, much to the joy of the townsfolk.

Mayor Marlon had to cancel the trip we had planned for tomorrow to take photos of a roof being put on a house in the Reitocan village of Santa Cruz. He had to go to Tegucigalpa as part of the drama that unfolded in the morning, its purpose still unknown to me.

I must remember to tell him I might be a jinx for mayors. In the past, my parish in Wilmington, N.C. gave a plaque to the mayor of La Libertad, one of the five municipalities of this parish, for his help he gave us with health care. The very next day, the people of the town murdered him. Why, I don't know. Then the parish in Wilmington gave a plaque to the former mayor of Reitoca for his help with Clínica Santa María. Months later, he was sentenced to 144 years in prison for narco-trafficking.

August 6, 2021 – Friday – Transfiguration of the Lord
Reitoca, F.M., Honduras – 6:40 p.m.
Mostly cloudy – 79 F

I surveyed the Holy Cross campus first thing this morning. A few trees were fractured in half, two were completely uprooted, and debris was everywhere. The good thing is that no water came into my house or the three *casitas*, and no trees fell on them.

All the tropical trees that Danilo and I bought yesterday were fine, mostly, I suspect, because they had not yet been planted, quickly fell over in their pots as soon as the storm came.

The decorative stone on the south side entrance of my house came tumbling down, but that is not surprising because it was already coming loose. The south side of the house seems to be most vulnerable to the wild winds and rain we get quite frequently.

Today was a beautiful day of quiet. Unfortunately, I didn't get much accomplished except plenty of exercise cleaning up debris from the storm and sweeping the Holy Cross drive. I would really like to get a leaf blower.

August 7, 2021 – Saturday – Sixtus II & Companions; St. Cajetan
Reitoca, F.M., Honduras – 7 p.m.
Partly cloudy – 84 F

Jorge the gravel man finished delivering piles of gravel for the connector drive yesterday, so this morning, Juan and I finished spreading it. It was very heavy work, but we were able to finish in two hours.

Today is the feast of St. Cajetan (1480-1547), whom I wrote about in my book, *Saintly Men of Nursing: 100 Amazing Stories*. This Italian priest not only practiced nursing, but he also founded two hospitals, a hospital for incurables in his hometown of Vicenza, and another in Venice. As a founder of various Oratories, he once said their priests tried to serve God by worship, but "… in our hospital, we can say that we actually find him." I have special place in my heart for St. Cajetan, not only because he was a nurse-priest, but because he is a patron saint of two countries here in Central America – El Salvador and Guatemala.

August 8, 2021 – Nineteenth Sunday in Ordinary Time
Reitoca, F.M., Honduras – 7 p.m.
Partly cloudy – 83 F

Today I celebrated Masses in the Alubarén community of Tablones and in the pueblo of Curarén. In Tablones, there is a young woman who has just begun as an altar server along with Dennis, a young man who plans to enter the college seminary in January to begin his eight-year study for the priesthood.

Danilo and Juan planted the ten tropical trees we bought yesterday. Danilo is able to work very quickly with farm tools. He finished planting the trees in less than a half-hour.

I had a talk with Danilo and Juan today. Danilo has a family in Lodo Negro, as well as a chicken business and a petroleum business, so he doesn't have time to devote full-time to the *mayordomo* job on the Holy Cross campus. So, Juan will come to live in the blue *casita*, and will share the *mayordomo* job with Danilo. I think this arrangement will work out well. Danilo will continue his full-time job as my driver, and Juan will continue his full-time job watching over the Holy Cross campus in the daytime. Also, both Juan and Danilo will each receive half the salary of a *mayordomo*.

August 9, 2021 - Monday - St. Teresa Benedicta of the Cross (Dr. Edith Stein)
Reitoca, F.M., Honduras – 7:20 p.m.
Partly cloudy – 82 F

This was a quiet day of organizing files, researching, and writing. In other words, it was pretty much perfect.

August 10, 2021 – Tuesday – St. Lawrence
Reitoca, F.M., Honduras – 7 p.m.
Partly cloudy – 81 F

The Honduran government announced that the second dose of Sputnik V vaccine will be available on Thursday, August 19 in Tegucigalpa. I'll be watching for other details as to time and place. I told Danilo that perhaps I will stay overnight in the city so I can be closer to the front of the line if it is a drive-thru event. I definitely do not want a repeat of the previous time we were there.

In the United States today, the Senate approved a bipartisan $1.2 trillion infrastructure package, one of President Biden's prime goals. Now, the bill goes to the U.S. House of Representatives for approval.

Also, the U.S. Senate Democrats passed a $3.5 trillion bill to address climate, education, and health care policies. If passed, it will expand Medicare to include dental and vision benefits; fund climate change programs; provide medical leave benefits; and provide free pre-kindergarten and community college tuition. Much of the cost of these programs would be paid by levying additional taxes on wealthy businesses and corporations. I'm especially intrigued by the free community college, which has become practically essential for gainful employment. Today in the United States, a high school diploma, by itself, has very little value.

Also, in the news, New York Governor Andrew Cuomo said he would resign from the governorship in fourteen days. He is swamped by charges of inappropriate boundary issues with women.

Here in my little corner of the world, I approved the forematter and text for my 2012 journal's Spanish version.

August 11, 2021 – Wednesday – St. Clare of Assisi
Reitoca, F.M., Honduras – 6:35 p.m.
Rain – 81 F

This morning, I went to Tegucigalpa to visit Dr. Elmer López Lutz to have him look at a blemish on my face that will not go away. He treated it and another one with liquid nitrogen. I'll go back in a month to see how it worked.

While we were in Tegucigalpa, Danilo and I bought a couple of long hoses. With the new trees on the campus, it takes too much time to water all the plants that need watering twice a day from soda bottles full of water.

Late this afternoon, I attended the monthly meeting of my Rotary Passport club. Lynn Whitesell, partner of our club president Lori Harris, did an excellent presentation on "Habits That Hold Successful People Back."

August 12, 2021 – Thursday – St. Jane Frances de Chantal
Reitoca, F.M., Honduras – 8:30 p.m.
Partly cloudy – 84 F

This evening, I celebrated Mass in Alubarén. Before the Mass, the altar server told me that her brother knows me and even has a photo of me. He was a parishioner at the Basilica Shrine of St. Mary when I was pastor there. Now he lives in Spain. It's a small world.

For my homily, I told the story of St. Jane Frances de Chantal as this is her feast day.

August 13, 2021 – Friday – Ss. Pontian and Hippolytus
Reitoca, F.M., Honduras – 7 p.m.
Cloudy – 81 F

Today the United States presented the new 2020 census findings of the population. A census count occurs every ten years.

The United States' official population grew 22.7 million people from 2010; it is now at 331.4 million. Though the non-Hispanic white population is still the majority, the nation is rapidly on its way to be a "minority-majority" population. The most populous state in the country, California, is now majority Hispanic. Because so many Hispanics are Catholic, the Catholic Church in many parts of the country is growing. That, of course, is particularly evident in places like eastern North Carolina, where some new parishes have no Masses in English, only in Spanish.

August 14, 2021 – Saturday – St. Maximilian Kolbe
Reitoca, F.M., Honduras – 6 p.m.
Thunderstorm – 79 F

This morning, I celebrated Mass in El Portillo, a community of Curarén. Fr. Carlos told me the Mass was a 10 a.m., but it had actually been scheduled for 9 a.m. Fortunately, Danilo and I arrived at 9:20, so we were not that late. Noel, the pharmacy tech of Farmacia Candelaria in Curarén, was on hand to greet us, and he and a young *Delegado de la Palabra*, Mario, provided the music for the Mass. During the Mass I celebrated twenty baptisms.

Although today is the feast of St. Maximilian Kolbe, a martyr killed by the Nazis in World War II, I did not tell his story in the homily, for I told that story in the past to two communities in the general area of El Portillo. I figured with baptisms, some of the people from the neighboring communities would be at the El Portillo Mass. Instead, I told the story of Blessed Benildus Romançon, a Christian Brother from France. I tied Benildus' story to today's Gospel reading with Jesus' admonition not to prevent the little children from coming to him, for it is just such as they that make up the kingdom of heaven.

After delivering me back to my house, Danilo had to leave right away to get his pickup truck fixed. Yesterday, while he was driving to Comayagua on the mountain roads, his brakes failed. Fortunately, he was able to stop the truck by guiding it up the side of a hill. Having one's brakes go out while driving in the mountains is definitely not a good thing. A friend was able to get his truck to a repair station.

In Haiti, hundreds of people were killed and at least 1,800 were injured from a magnitude 7.2 earthquake. That country can't catch a break. I have always been amazed that Haiti always gets battered by something, while the Dominican Republic, which shares the same island, escapes the same fate as Haiti.

August 15, 2021 – Sunday – Assumption of the Blessed Virgin Mary
Reitoca, F.M., Honduras – 6:30 p.m.
Partly cloudy – 82 F

This morning I celebrated Masses in La Libertad and San Miguelito. In my homily I told the story of Blessed Stanley Rother, a priest of the Archdiocese of Oklahoma City who was martyred in Guatemala. One of the visitors' guesthouses on my Holy Cross campus is named after Blessed Stanley.

In the La Libertad community there were more people than usual in the Mass, because the Confirmation students were all there. After the Mass, I joined the group for a couple of photos. Years into the future, people will look back on the photos from these pandemic times and be amused that they all feature masked people. Then, they'll try to figure out who's who behind the masks.

Today I read an inspirational saying by Søren Kierkegaard: "Life can only be understood backwards; but it must be lived forwards." How very true that is. Only when we are older and able to look back on our lives, can we see how God has guided us onto unknown paths.

This afternoon, Mayor Marlon and Dr. Marco came over to my house. The mayor reported that roofs have been installed on the first six houses needing them, and the people who received the roofs are wonderfully happy.

We also talked about the Vaccine Project that the Rotary Passport 7730 club has been attempting. Unfortunately, we have had zero success in finding a vaccine donor in the United States. Our club president, Lori Harris, has devoted much time and energy, but no one has been able to help us. The good news, however, is that the Honduran government has been able to provide doses for thousands of people in the municipalities of Alubarén, Curarén, and Reitoca. Though the number of doses is not enough for all, it is still good news.

The other piece of good news is that all the priests of the Archdiocese of Tegucigalpa have received two doses of the Astra-Zeneca vaccine, and all the priests are actively encouraging their congregations to become vaccinated. In the Catholic churches of the archdiocese, pretty much every person wears a mask to church.

The bad news is that many of the Protestant clergy, for the most part Baptists, have been telling the people they don't need the vaccine and that they don't need to wear masks; they only need to trust God. Indeed, many have been spreading the same kind of right-wing American conspiracy nonsense such as that the vaccines contain micro-chips. It will be morbidly interesting to see how the *"evangélicos"* compare with the Catholic population in terms of COVID. (In Honduras, any Christian who is not a Catholic is called an *"evangélico."*)

Mayor Marlon will have a minor surgical procedure on Tuesday. When he is back to work, he would like me to go with him to see a roof being installed. I'm eager to get some great photos for our Rotary club.

August 16, 2021 – Monday – St. Stephan of Hungary
Reitoca, F.M., Honduras – 7:15 p.m.
Cloudy – 79 F

Today is the feast of St. Stephen of Hungary. I did sociological research in Budapest in 1988 when Hungary was behind the Iron Curtain, and I would sometimes go to St. Stephen's Basilica to pray. In this place is one of the hands of St. Stephen in a reliquary. The basilica is an important part of Hungarian history, for Stephen was the first King of Hungary.

Reports from Haiti today say that more than 1,400 people have been killed and more than 5,700 injured from Saturday's earthquake. And in Afghanistan, the Taliban have taken over the country. Reports say that young men have been enslaved by the Taliban to serve in the military. I assume the teenage boys will be taught to kill men. Girls and women fear further social repression, in particular that girls will be denied an education.

Today I sent reports to our Rotary Club's International Projects Committee on the Roofs and Vaccine Projects.

August 17, 2021 – Tuesday
Reitoca, F.M., Honduras – 10:10 p.m.
Rain – 77 F

Last evening, three cows came onto the Holy Cross campus to graze on the greenery. I don't mind their eating the tall grasses and weeds, but one of them has discovered that she likes to eat the coconut-based containers I use for hanging plants. Another ate the red flowers that I planted the other day in a pot by the Blessed James Miller house, and as I related last month, one of the new *almendro* trees was almost destroyed by a cow breaking some of its branches.

Fr. Sebastián is now in Tegucigalpa to take care of his mother, who has COVID. I'm not sure when Fr. Sebastián will return.

The COVID injection day for me has been changed from Thursday to Friday, so Danilo will take me to Tegucigalpa on Thursday, and I'll spend the night.

Drs. Aaron and Shelsea, both post-doctoral students, have been having difficulties with their studies because the regular electrical energy in Reitoca goes off quite frequently, especially in the later afternoon and early evening hours. So, they have been using the St. Oscar Romero and Blessed Stanley Rother houses to study here on the Holy Cross campus, for we have solar backup. This evening, unfortunately, Aaron locked the keys in the truck, so he and Shelsea had to walk back into the *pueblo* center to get a spare set.

This evening I saw something I had not seen before on the campus, a giant, hairy black spider. It was at least as big as one of my hands completely open. Aaron says that it was a tarantula. In the St. Mary House, where we have our pharmacy, tarantulas are seen from time to time.

August 18, 2021 – Wednesday
Reitoca, F.M., Honduras – 10 p.m.
Rain – 77 p.m.

The Honduran government's health department changed my vaccine day to Saturday, so Danilo and I will go to Tegucigalpa on Friday so we'll be ready to be at the injection site around 5 a.m. to join line of cars and trucks. Saturday is the day for people 77 and 78 years old.

Aaron brought over Timoteo, a young man who installed the roof of my house. He came to assess what would be needed to install an electric gate at the entrance to the rectory campus. All the pastors in the past have wished for such a gate, but this poor parish could not afford such a luxury. Timo gave me an estimate for his work, but he said one of the cinder block walls must be rebuilt before the installation. So, Fr. Carlos will see how much that will cost and get back to me. When the new electric gate is installed, pickup trucks for both the rectory and the Holy Cross campus will be able to enter and go to whatever part of the campus they want, either the rectory side or the Holy Cross side. We'll never again have to use the Calle Calvario "road."

August 19, 2021 – Thursday – St. John Eudes
Reitoca, F.M., Honduras – 9:25 p.m.
Cloudy – 75 F

The Diocese of Raleigh announced today two priest assignments: Fr. Cyriac John will be the new temporary administrator of San Isidore Mission in Fayetteville effective August 16, 2021, and Fr. Lawrence P. Searles, S.J., a priest of the USA East Province of the Society of Jesus, will be a parochial vicar at St. Raphael the Archangel parish in Raleigh. Fr. Cyriac John is from the Diocese of Mananthavady, Kerala, India.

Here on the Holy Cross campus, Juan and I finished cutting part of a tree that fell during the storm a couple of weeks ago. It is amazing what a machete can do in the right hands.

August 20, 2021 – Friday – St. Bernard
Tegucigalpa, F.M., Honduras – 6 p.m.
Cloudy – 72 F

I write this note from the Clarion Real Hotel in Tegucigalpa, where I'm staying for the night to be ready for my second injection early tomorrow morning.

This morning we went shopping for kitchen items for the Bl. James Miller *casita*, to prepare for Juan to occupy it as assistant *majordomo* of the Holy Cross campus. We were able to get many items needed. I had hoped to also find some furniture for my living room, but I didn't find anything worth buying. I did get a television for the green *casita* to replace the one that was stolen last year. I had hoped to order some plaques for the three *casitas* and my house on the Holy Cross campus, but Danilo and I couldn't find the store, and we were just too tired from shopping all morning to devote more time.

We also stopped at Promasa, the store where I ordered laminate for a new roof outside my kitchen. The store had been promising and promising my material, but now they have finally concluded they can't get it. They agreed to refund the money I spent.

Danilo will spend the night with his uncle who lives in Tegucigalpa, and plans to pick me up early in the morning so we can be at the vaccination center around 5 a.m.

Now, I'm planning on relaxing, watching some HGTV (Home & Garden Television).

August 21, 2021 – Saturday – St. Pius X
Reitoca, F.M., Honduras – 9:25 p.m.
Partly cloudy – 77 F

This morning, around 4:45 a.m., I was in front of the hotel waiting for Danilo to pick me up to go the injection site. As I waited, I chatted with a young man standing by a little booth in front of the hotel. He works twelve-hour days, six days a week. Seventy-two hours a week, every week, is definitely not for everyone. Although I worked night shifts in hospitals for 19 years, I never had a schedule that radical. It's wonderful, though, that he had a job, and he seemed to be grateful for it.

Danilo and I got to the injection site about 5:10 a.m., and we were the fifth car in line to wait for the site to open at 7 a.m. Unfortunately, after we were there about ten minutes, we learned that the site never received the Sputnik V vaccine that I need; they only had Moderna. From what I understand, the health officials do not want people to "mix and match" different types of vaccines. So, we left the line with the other cars and got back to the Holy Cross campus around 7:30 a.m.

Juan was delighted with the things we bought for his *casita* and got busy putting things in place.

We learned that Reitoca had been without regular electricity since yesterday. Fortunately, Juan knows how to transfer to the solar energy supply.

This evening, Dr. Aaron sent me a note saying that the Sputnik V has arrived and will be available on Monday. I've decided not to go, for each time I go, it takes two days away from my schedule. Rather, I'll try to receive an American vaccine even though I started with the Sputnik one. That way, I won't have to leave Reitoca to get the shot. Such is life in Honduras.

August 22, 2021 – 21st Sunday in Ordinary Time
Reitoca F.M., Honduras – 7:55 p.m.
Showers – 81 F

Today I celebrated Masses in Reitoca at 9 and in Alubarén at 12. My homily focused on St. Paul's letter to the Ephesians (5: 21-32). This passage is very repellent to many people because it demands wives being subordinate to their husbands. I explained that when Catholic Christians read the Bible, they must take into account the times and culture in which it was written. Customs in families in those days were different from today's gender roles, especially in western nations. Gender equality has come to be understood as far more consistent with God's creation of all of us as equals.

Paul, having been raised an orthodox male Jew in the middle east, simply knew no other model for the family. Today, of course, the idea of the husband being the head of the family, and the woman being subordinate, is clearly seen to disrespect both husbands and wives. It is disrespectful to husbands, because it puts the burden of a family's success or failure on him. And it is disrespectful to wives, for it makes them appear "less than" their husbands. Rather, we should take the central message of Paul, which is, that spouses should love each other.

Dr. Aaron contacted me late in the day to say the staff is planning a celebration for Dr. Elia, our pharmacist at Farmacia Candelaria in Curarén. The party could be held be at my house, but the staff isn't sure. My place is available if that's what the group decides.

I received a wonderful note from my friend, Msgr. Jerry Lewis, of the Diocese of Raleigh. At the age of 88, Jerry is working as the administrator of St. Mildred parish in Swansboro, N.C. The parish lost their pastor to death some months back. Jerry is also the archivist of the Diocese of Raleigh. I love to encounter people like Jerry who are working and thriving well into their 80s, for it gives me energy and excitement for what I can do in my own life.

August 23, 2021 – Monday – St. Rose of Lima
Reitoca, F.M., Honduras – 8:20 p.m.
Rain – 77 F

Fr. Carlos dropped by this morning to let me know my schedule for the week. I'll be celebrating Masses in the Reitocan communities of Quebracho and Saracarán, the Curarén community of Jardines, and the pueblos of Curarén, La Libertad, and San Miguelito. So, it'll be an action-packed week.

Fr. Sebastián is in quarantine in Tegucigalpa because his mother has COVID. Fr. Pedro Pablo is taking care of the churches of our San Marcos zone, and Fr. Carlos and I are covering the rest. Fortunately, every church of our parish that does not have Mass regularly, has at least Liturgy of the Word services each Thursday and Sunday. These services are conducted by one of the *Delegados de la Palabra* of the church community.

Today Fr. Carlos will be going to Tegucigalpa to pick up the next batch of *Revistas*. Each *Revista*, published four times a year, contains the Mass parts for the priest and readings for each day. The new *Revista* has everything the priest and communities need for liturgies of September, October, and November, so it carries us into Advent. Christmas is right around the corner!

This afternoon and evening, the parish's health care staffs had a birthday party at my house for Dr. Elia, pharmacist of our Farmacia Candelaria in Curarén. Because rain comes so frequently in the evening during the winter (May-October), we were able to have our dinner on the deck, but we had to dash inside for the cake when rain and wind arrived. Dr. Elia is a wonderful addition to the healthcare team. She, her 8-year-old son, and the pharmacy tech Noel, are staying in the *casitas* during the night.

August 24, 2021 – Tuesday – St. Bartholomew, Apostle
Reitoca, F.M., Honduras – 8:15 p.m.
Cloudy – 79 F

On this wonderfully quiet day, I was able to prepare three of the four homilies I'll be needing this week.

August 25, 2021 – Wednesday – St. Louis; St. Joseph of Calasanz
Reitoca, F.M., Honduras – 8 p.m.
Partly cloudy –

Today is the feast of St. Joseph of Calasanz, one of the men in my *Saintly Men of Nursing* book. During a plague, he helped his friend, St. Camillus de Lillis, nurse the sick of the city. Unlike Camillus, however, whose passion was nursing, Joseph felt more of a call to care for children, especially poor children. So, Camillus founded a religious community of men devoted to nursing and other branches of health care, and Joseph founded an order devoted to the care of children. My friend Norberto Bautista, a former parishioner of mine at the Basilica Shrine of St. Mary in Wilmington, North Carolina, is now in his final year of priesthood studies in Mexico City in the very same order, which is today formally known as the Piarist Fathers.

Today I had a delightful surprise when I went with Danilo to Tegucigalpa to pay monthly salaries for the staff of Clínica Santa María. As we were coming into the city, Dr. Marco, who comes with me to the bank for the paying of salaries, called me and told me to first go to the campus where I went for my original anti-COVID vaccine, for there were no long lines. There were only 2 cars ahead of me in the Sputnik V line! There were also stations for people needing their second dose of Moderna and Astra-Zeneca. So, now I'm all set vaccine-wise. Dr. Marco said I could get a flu shot in two weeks.

As I write this note, Dr. Shelsie is in the yellow (Bl. Stanley Rother) *casita* studying, and Dr. Aaron is in the green (St. Oscar Romero) *casita* doing the same. Both of these young people have a tremendous thirst for knowledge and perpetual growth.

August 26, 2021 – Thursday
Reitoca, F.M., Honduras – 7 p.m.
Cloudy – 81 F

Today I celebrated Masses in the Reitocan communities of Quebracho and Saracarán.

In Quebracho, in addition to the Mass, I also celebrated four baptisms and a presentation. During the Mass, three little boys about two or three years old entertained themselves by throwing balloons into the air in front of the altar. One of the balloons bounced on the altar right near a lit candle; fortunately, however, the balloon didn't pop. And as in many other Masses in the churches of the parish, children come to the altar area to walk around and check things out. The same goes for dogs. I welcome kids, dogs, and balloons. And naturally, there were plenty of firecrackers exploding outside in honor of the festivities. Fortunately, *Delegado de la Palabra* Orlando Varela kept everything under control. Orlando and I are friends on Facebook. After Mass, I blessed a nearby house, and four women of the house assisted me by sprinkling water on the walls with their hands.

In Saracarán, also known as Cafetales, the *Delegada de la Palabra* told me that this was their first Mass in 2021. So, I am guessing it was probably the first for the Quebracho community as well, for the churches are an hour-and-a-half journey from Reitoca, and I doubt Fr. Carlos or Fr. Sebastián would have made the trip without celebrating in both places. In that community, I also celebrated a Presentation and a house blessing in which I had the family dip bush branches into holy water and sprinkle the rooms.

Today I learned that Fr. Sebastián and his mother have both tested negative for COVID. I imagine that Fr. Sebastián's quarantine will soon be over, and he'll be able to return to Reitoca.

One of the most interesting things I read today was an article in the *New York Times* by Emma Goldberg. She explained that Harvard University was founded in 1630 to ensure that Protestant clergy would be literate, and they chose as their motto, "Truth for Christ and the Church." Now, almost four centuries later, Harvard's chaplains' organization voted unanimously to elect Greg Epstein, a Humanist rabbi and avowed atheist, as their new president. Greg will be responsible for overseeing the 40 university chaplains who lead various religious communities on campus, such as Buddhist, Christian, Hindu, and Jewish groups. Many in the student body say that Greg Epstein has helped them immensely on their spiritual journeys. Wonders never cease.

August 27, 2021 – Friday – St. Monica
Reitoca, F.M., Honduras – 7:30 p.m.
Partly cloudy – 80 F

One of the first things I encountered this morning in my e-mails was an article from *Religious News Service* about Mother Teresa Catholic Church in Cary, North Carolina and its leader, Fr. Dan Oschwald. The church is a mission of St. Michael the Archangel parish in Cary. St. Michael's is the church where Fr. Dan, myself and five others were ordained priests in 1998. The *Raleigh News & Observer* called us "The Magnificent Seven." This article focused on how the Mother Teresa community hoped to keep their community fairly small. (Many of the Catholic parishes in that part of the Diocese of Raleigh, such as St. Francis of Assisi and St. Michael the Archangel, have over 4,000 families each.) The article, I think, was very well done.

President Biden told the world that ISIS-K terrorists were behind twin bombings in Kabul that killed Afghans and thirteen United States military (eleven men and two women).

I celebrated baptisms in the Curarén community of Jardines this morning. I was happy to see *Delegado* Celio García after his absence for some months working in the United States. He was very happy to introduce me to his *novia* (girlfriend). The couple hopes to get married one day. Naturally, people were setting off firecrackers outside the church in honor of the priest celebrating Mass in the community.

When Danilo and I got back from Jardines, he and Juan went to the Reitoca River to gather some rocks that I'll use to create a small rock garden on the south side of my house.

In news from the Diocese of Raleigh, priests joining the Council of Priests are: Msgr. Michael G. Clay and Frs. Bill John Acosta-Escobar, Phillip R. Hurley, S.J.; Christopher S. Koehn, James J. Magee, III, Noé Ramírez de Paz, and James G. Sabak, O.F.M. The bishop thanked the men leaving the council for their service. These were: Msgrs. Gerald L. Lewis, Michael P. Shugrue, and Donald F. Staib, and Frs. Michael J. Burbeck and Peter A. Grace, C.P.

August 28, 2021 – Saturday – St. Augustine
Reitoca, F.M., Honduras – 7:55 p.m.
Mostly cloudy – 79 F

As I write this note, a gentle evening rain is falling.

Today I celebrated the wedding in Curarén of a young couple, Alex and Karen, from the Curarén community of Tapope. They are a lovely couple and were there with their three young children. The youngest of the children was dressed in a black tuxedo and kept losing his shoes, and the groom lost his tie during the photo session we had after the Mass. This was only the second wedding I have officiated at in Honduras. That is a big difference from my days at the Basilica Shrine of St. Mary, where I could do anywhere from 35 to 65 weddings a year.

Today I also got to re-connect with an R.N. friend, Nancy, who lives and works in the Los Angeles, California area. Nancy and I worked together on the night shift in a locked psychiatric unit at Harborview Medical Center in Seattle in the late 1970s and early 1980s. I treasure our friendship and love to hear how friends' lives have unfolded.

August 29, 2021 – 22nd Sunday in Ordinary Time
Reitoca, F.M., Honduras – 8 p.m.
Partly cloudy – 79 F

Today I celebrated Masses in La Libertad and San Miguelito. In San Miguelito, healthcare workers were vaccinating the population in the plaza that sits in front of the church. I stopped and chatted with two young physicians, a man and a woman. The woman told me she is part of the parish in Ojojona where Fr. Tony Salinas is the pastor. I told her I'd be seeing Fr. Tony tomorrow in Sabanagrande where I'll be going for a deanery meeting of priests.

Hurricane Ida landed in Port Fourchon, Louisiana as a Category 4 hurricane. Now, it is headed up north and is expected to go all the way into Canada.

August 30, 2021 – Monday
Reitoca, F.M., Honduras – 5:55 p.m.
Thunderstorm – 79 F

As I write this note, a heavy rain is falling while lightning and thunder rage. Miraculously, the regular electricity is still working.

The United States has officially ended its participation in a 20-year war in Afghanistan.

The United States reported that Hurricane Ida has knocked out the entire electrical grid of the city of New Orleans. It could be days or weeks before power is restored.

This morning I attended a meeting of priests of the San Francisco de Asís deanery in Sabanagrande. Our deanery includes four parishes: Lepaterique, Ojojona, Reitoca, and Sabanagrande. The largest of the parishes, in terms of the number of churches, is Reitoca, with over 80 churches in five municipalities scattered over 250 square miles. In addition to Danilo who drove me to the meeting, were our host, Fr. Gustavo of Sabanagrande, Fr. Carlos of Reitoca, Fr. Tony of Ojojona, Fr. José Luis of Lepaterique, and myself. Before the meeting, Fr. Gustavo, who was once the pastor of Reitoca, gave us a tour of the central church of the parish. I was able to get some excellent photos for my blog. The rectory has a huge porch with an amazing assortment of plants.

On our way home, Danilo and I stopped by a nursery just outside the center of Sabanagrande on CA-5. Because this nursery is right on our usual route to Tegucigalpa, I have often said to Danilo, "We should definitely stop there some day." Well, today was that day, and I bought some lemongrass, a dwarf orange tree, and a variegated yellow and green plant that looks pretty hardy, though I don't know its name.

When I got home, I learned that a young man of our parish in his early 20s was seized by five men and killed. The young man was a band member in our Espíritu Santo church in the Reitocan community of Samalares Abajo. May he rest in peace.

August 31, 2021 – Tuesday
Reitoca, F.M., Honduras – 5:15 p.m.
Showers – 79 F

As I write this note, dark clouds are coming over the northern, eastern, and western mountains, and rain is just beginning to fall. Weather forecasters are predicting rain from now until around 10 p.m. That is fine with me, for Blackie and I are dry and cozy in my study, waiting for Drs. Shelsie and Aaron to swing by to study for the evening in the green and yellow *casitas*.

On this last day of August, I can summarize it as a very exciting month in many ways.

In the Diocese of Raleigh, 80-year-old Fr. Bob Diegelman died.

In my Rotary Passport club, our Roofs project finally got off the ground. Lori Harris, our club president, reported that she has arranged meetings with other Rotary clubs in eastern North Carolina to ask for help in supporting this project. On this Thursday, I'll be joining Mayor Marlon Osorto in the Reitocan community of Santa Cruz to take photos and videos of the installation of roofs on four houses.

In the United States, President Joe Biden ended the United States' participation in the 20-year war in Afghanistan. This is war has gone on so long that many people didn't even know American military personnel were there. Before the last American plane took off from the Kabul airport, the Taliban took over the entire country.

Worldwide, August saw many interesting weather phenomena. The most interesting one was the ongoing melting of Greenland, a stark sign of global warming. In California and other western states, vast forest fires are blazing. In Haiti, an earthquake killed more than 1,400 people, and in Louisiana, Category 4 Hurricane hit with powerful force.

On the Holy Cross campus, this month we finished a gravel drive connecting the driveway of the rectory with the drive into the campus.

As for me, this month I got my second anti-COVID vaccination (Sputnik V), and on the publishing front, the Spanish version of my 2012 journal, *The Year of Clifton*, was published in paperback.

Now, I'm ready for September.

SEPTEMBER 2021

September 1, 2021 – Wednesday
Reitoca, F.M., Honduras – 7:50 p.m.
Light showers – 75 F

September is off to a good start for me. I'll be celebrating Masses on Thursday, Friday, and Sunday, and all my homilies are finished. Because I have written and saved my homilies over the years, I have a treasure-trove of homilies at my fingertips from the past. It is infinitely easier to tweak a homily from the past than to create something from scratch.

Today Pope Francis called on the Catholic faithful to celebrate the Season of Creation, which begins today and ends with the feast of St. Francis of Assisi on October 4. The Season of Creation is an ecumenical effort throughout the world to remind human beings that God has tasked us to care for creation.

Danilo took Juan to Tegucigalpa today, because Juan wanted to buy food for a birthday party he is having for his mother on September 7. It will be the first birthday party his mother has ever had, so Juan wants it to be very special. I'm sure Danilo and Juan had a great day, for they enjoy each other's company very much.

September 2, 2021 – Thursday
Reitoca, F.M., Honduras – 9:25 p.m.
Cloudy – 75 F

At 10 o'clock this morning, a young man named Miguel showed up at my house to accompany Danilo and me to the Reitocan community of Santa Cruz. The purpose of the trip was to allow me to video and photograph workers putting roofs on four houses of the poor. This is part of the project that the mayor, assisted by my Rotary club, is working on. Danilo drove the three of us to the community on some of the very worst roads I've ever seen. In fact, we got a flat tire along the way.

Mayor Marlon met us in the community. Unfortunately, the installation of the roofs will not be undertaken until tomorrow. So, we focused on just one house that needed a roof. Danilo and Miguel assisted some of the people of Santa Cruz bring sheets of laminate to the house. I was able to get two amazingly powerful photos of the house and the mother, father, and child who live there. As soon as I got back home, I sent the photos to members of the International Projects Committee of my Rotary club.

In the afternoon, Danilo took me to Curarén to celebrate Mass. Before the Mass, Dr. Marco addressed the assembly to tell them about free COVID testing on Monday in Reitoca.

September 3, 2021 – Friday – St. Gregory the Great
Reitoca, F.M., Honduras – 8:40 p.m.
Cloudy – 79 F

This morning I celebrated Mass in the Curarén community of Carbonera. In addition to Mass, I also celebrated the baptisms of three young children and one youth. After the Mass, I stayed for photographs with the families. I also got to talk with a young man named Marlon who had hoped to be accepted into the seminary. Unfortunately, however, he was not accepted, at least not at this time.

Hurricane Ida has caused many problems in the eastern United States. At least 46 people in six states were killed, and the subways of New York City had to close because of flooding. Many people believe that the flooding, fires in the western United States, and record-setting high temperatures on the planet should be seen as a powerful wake-up call that we need to pay more attention to taking care of our planet. This is exactly what Pope Francis is trying to get the world to realize, that is, that God has given us this planet, and we are to be good stewards of this gift.

September 4, 2021 – Saturday
Reitoca, F.M., Honduras – 6:45 p.m.
Light rain – 77 F

As I write this note, a gentle rain is falling. For the past two hours, however, the rains have been torrential. In fact, Emilio called to let me know he was not able to make it to work tonight, for the rivers were flooding the bridges. I told him to take the night off and enjoy his home.

Most of today I did research on saints and people on their way to canonization. I focused especially on missionaries whom I could one day include in my Friday "Missionary Hero" blog posts. It never fails to astonish me how some of these folks were able to withstand daily tortures before being martyred.

For fun, today I planted my little orange tree and lemongrass in pots on the deck. They'll stay on the deck until Juan and I decide where to plant them permanently on the south side of the house.

September 5, 2021 – 23rd Sunday in Ordinary Time
Reitoca, F.M., Honduras – 7 p.m.
Cloudy – 82 F

This day provided an unforgettable experience. I wouldn't like to relive it, but I definitely appreciate what I gained from it.

Since I've been living in Honduras as a missionary priest, whenever I celebrated the noon Mass in the church of San Lorenzo in the pueblo of Alubarén, it has always been my last Mass of the day. I always had a Mass or two before the noon Mass in one of the Alubarén communities like Concepción, El Hatillo, or Tablones. Today, however, Fr. Carlos gave me the assignment of celebrating the noon Alubarén Mass and the 4 p.m. Curarén Mass.

After the noon Mass, a young woman came up to ask for a copy of my homily, for she loves them. As always, I said, "Of course. Here, take this one," for that's what I always tell her when she asks.

In the afternoon, Danilo and I arrived in Curarén for the 4 p.m. Mass. Ten minutes before the Mass was to begin, while I was vesting and preparing for the Mass in the sacristy, I reached into my backpack and discovered, to my horror, that I didn't have my homily, for I had given it away! The panic I experienced was intense. I had no written homily with me, and I had never given a homily in Spanish without a written text. So, I had to come up with a "wing-it" plan. First, I asked the Holy Spirit to do double-time, blasting me with graces to get through the homily. Second, I decided to tell the people how I've always relied on my written homilies, and that this would be the first time ever, that I was using my Spanish to preach a homily without notes. And third, I gave the homily using the structure and story as I remembered it. When I was done, totally by the grace of God, the people applauded. Oh, I truly never want to go through that again.

After Mass, the two religious sisters who are serving in the Curarén community said they'd love to visit me on the Holy Cross campus, and I agreed to host them on Tuesday.

Juan and I are planning on where we'll be planting things, and the little bags he put on our little *almendro* trees seem to be keeping the *zampopos* away. Now, the trees that seemed to have been dying from the *zampopos* eating them, are now sprouting green leaves.

This evening, I introduced Juan to Amazon.com, opening up an entirely new world to him.

September 6, 2021 – Monday – Labor Day (U.S.A.)
Reitoca, F.M., Honduras – 7:20 p.m.
Light showers – 79 F

Danilo and I went to Tegucigalpa today. I had a meeting with a friend to discuss a project we are planning. Now, I'm ready for two very productive days off featuring writing, cooking, and gardening.

September 7, 2021 – Tuesday
Reitoca, F.M., Honduras – 10 p.m.
Cloudy – 75 F

This morning I had a wonderful visit from Sisters Dolores Edilda Andino and Lidia Nolasco. Both of them are members of the Missionary Sisters of the Sacred Heart of Jesus. Theirs is a small Honduran order with Sisters also in Guatemala and Ecuador. Sr. Dolores is from the Reitocan community of Guadalupe, and Sr. Lidia is from the Department of Copán. After talking and taking some photos, we toured the campus. I assured them that they were always welcome to use a visitors' casita for a private retreat.

Today, Juan is hosting a birthday party for his mother. Heavy rains came at 1 p.m. today, but then it cleared up. I hope the party went well.

September 8, 2021 – Wednesday - Birthday of the Blessed Virgin Mary
Reitoca, F.M., Honduras – 9 p.m.
Cloudy – 77 F

Today I learned that my friend, Dr. John Cromer, will join my Rotary Passport club. That is great news, for he knows most of us here in Honduras and has visited in the past. He was the first president of *SaludHondu*, a 501(c)(3) organization to raise funds for Clínica Santa María here in Reitoca. He and his wife Penny have devoted a great deal of time and energy to the organization. I hope he will like the club.

This afternoon I attended the monthly meeting of our club. The featured speaker heads up a "backpack project" that gathers food for poor children in coastal communities of North Carolina. If I lived near there, I think that would be a ministry I'd be involved in.

September 9, 2021 – Thursday – St. Peter Claver
Reitoca, F.M., Honduras – 8:40 p.m.
Showers – 75 F

Each morning, one of the first things I do is make rounds on the three *casitas*. I turn off the outdoor lanterns in each place, open the windows and drapes, and sweep the porches. This morning, I noticed that one of the screens in the front of the green *casita* had been bent a bit. That was strange because the *casita* has steel bars over the windows.

Then, this afternoon around 3:30, Blackie and his friends Andy and Henry, who were sleeping on the deck, began barking furiously and running down the stairs on the southside of my house to the green *casita*. Juan followed them, and he discovered a *ladrón* (thief) trying to get into the *casita* through the bathroom window (which does not have steel bars).

Juan brought the man to me. Probably in his twenties or thirties, he was disheveled and said he was hungry. I invited him to sit on the steps while I made him a couple of sandwiches and got him a bottle of water. I also asked Juan to take some photos and a video of the man while I distracted him with the sandwiches and talk. After eating one of the sandwiches, the man said he would take the other sandwich to his mother.

Juan captured the whole interaction on his cell phone, and when Emilio (the night watchman) came to work, he identified the man as one of the four thieves who stole the television and coffee pot some months back.

I called Darwing Zelaya, and he'll come in a few days to measure the bathroom windows of my house and the three *casitas* for steel bars.

It was pouring rain this evening at my time to walk into town to celebrate the 7 p.m. Mass in Reitoca. Fortunately, however, Aaron came to give me a ride to and from the Mass. When we got back to my house, Aaron explored the cameras on my computer to get a glimpse of the thief drama of the day. He recommends that I install a security camera on the south side of the green *casita*, for that side is not visible from my house's deck.

September 10, 2021 – Friday
Reitoca, F.M., Honduras – 9:30 p.m.
Rain – 75 F

This morning, Danilo came from his home in Lodo Negro to take me to a special 9 a.m. Mass in La Libertad on the occasion of the ninth-day-after-death of a woman named Consuelo. Before leaving for La Libertad, Juan and Danilo had breakfast. Juan told Danilo how I had made sandwiches for the yesterday's thief, and they both found that so hilarious that they could hardly eat. They are more used to the idea of shooting at intruders rather than feeding them. I told them, however, that I was just following what Jesus taught his followers to do when someone is hungry. Jesus didn't put any qualifiers on the case. They still found the story hilarious, but it did give them another perspective to consider.

Timoteo Flores dropped by the Holy Cross campus today to take measurements for purchasing laminate for the roof over the deck outside the kitchen. He also took measurements for material to put over my deck, for the polygal material does not block the sun's heat adequately. Now he'll work out cost estimates and get back to me.

Juan and I started decorating the triangle at the entrance of the Holy Cross campus. In the center is the little *almendro* tree that we planted last fall. The little two-foot tree is now well over our heads. In one corner of the triangle, we have purple flowers, and in another corner, we have yellow-green plants. I'm not sure what kind of plants we'll have in the third corner, but it'll have to be something that can handle flooding, as that corner sometimes collects water after heavy rains.

September 11, 2021 – Saturday
Reitoca, F.M., Honduras – 9 p.m.
Cloudy – 82 F

Today is the twentieth anniversary of the September 11, 2001, terror attacks on the United States. On the day of the attacks, I was pastor of St. Catherine of Siena parish in Wake Forest, N.C. What an incredible day that was. People were stunned, for we were not used to having attacks like that on our shores. According to the news, the attacks killed 2,977 people in three separate incidents: planes flying into the World Trade Center in New York City and the Pentagon in Washington, D.C., and another hijacked plane that crashed in Pennsylvania.

From the attack, air travel has changed immensely. Gone are the days when folks can stand around the gate areas waiting for their loved ones to arrive or depart, and a host of costly and time-consuming safety measures have been put into place.

Today I noted an article in *Axios*, an online news source that presents the world news in small bites and explains why it should matter to us. *Axios* reported that Michael Morell, former acting director of the Central Intelligence Agency, told their reporter: "We've learned in the last 20 years that ... huge armies on the ground are actually a bad idea because they incentivize people to join terrorist groups." Retired Gen. David Petraeus reported that the focus should be on providing partners in places such as Syria or Africa's Sahel regions with drones, air support and intelligence.

I don't think most people realize the enormous importance of this thought. It could drastically reduce traditional combat fatalities and injuries, with men being most of the victims.

Late this afternoon, I received a surprise visit from Fr. Renán Carrillo López and two seminarians, Darwin Medina and Juan Ángel. Fr. Renán spent his first three years of priesthood in our parish and then went to Mexico City to study philosophy. Now he has finished his studies, and the cardinal has assigned him to teach in the seminary in Tegucigalpa and to be in charge of priestly vocations. Darwin, from Reitoca, has only one more month of studies to complete in the major seminary. He'll then work in a parish to gain practical ministerial experience. Then, as time goes on, he'll be ordained to the transitional diaconate and then to the priesthood. Juan Ángel is a second-year philosophy student and artist. I have always liked Darwin, and Juan Ángel seems to be a person who will make a very pastoral priest. I wish them all well.

I gave them a tour of the Holy Cross campus and talked about my vision for the future. Afterwards, Darwin's father, Marcelino Medina, joined us for a few minutes.

September 12, 2021 – 24th Sunday in Ordinary Time
Reitoca, F.M., Honduras – 9:50 p.m.
Partly cloudy – 75 F

As I write this note in my mountainside study, the *pueblo* of Reitoca is pitch black except for my house, which is lit by solar energy. The sky is filled with stars.

Fr. Carlos arrived at my house bright and early this morning to tell me that I'll have a 7 a.m. Mass in Curarén this Wednesday in honor of Independence Day. It was two hundred years ago, September 15, 1821, that Honduras, Costa Rica, El Salvador, Guatemala, and Nicaragua declared themselves to be nations independent of Spain. Unfortunately, because of the pandemic still raging in this part of the world, celebrations will be very muted.

September 13, 2021 – Monday – St. John Chrysostom
Reitoca, F.M., Honduras – 9:05 p.m.
Partly cloudy – 79 F

As we begin a new week, North Korea has demonstrated weapons capable of hitting Japan, Tropical Storm Nicholas is heading to Texas and Louisiana, Pope Francis is visiting Hungary where the week-long 52nd International Eucharistic Congress is concluding, and then visiting Slovakia where he is meeting with the Ecumenical Council of Churches.

Today I prepared a homily for Wednesday, the feast of Our Lady of Sorrows. Then, at 5 p.m., Fr. Carlos came by my house to let me know that the cardinal does not want any of the priests to celebrate that feast on Independence Day. Rather, he has provided a different set of Scripture readings and prayers for the day. So, I prepared a new homily discussing how Catholic Christians can show good citizenship by practicing Catholic social teaching in their communities.

In late afternoon, Darwing came over to measure the windows for the bathrooms of my house and the three *casitas*. Now, he'll get estimates on the cost of the steel bars and installation.

September 14, 2021 – Tuesday – Exaltation of the Holy Cross
Reitoca, F.M., Honduras – 8:25 p.m.
Rain – 79 F

As I write this note, a heavy rain is falling here in the mountains. Although it is the feast of the Holy Cross internationally, here in Honduras that feast is celebrated earlier in the year for reasons I don't know.

Earlier today, Danilo and I were in Tegucigalpa. I had a dermatology appointment with Dr. Elmer López in his office in the new Clínica Milenio Building. It's a very modern building, and the office space is fine, but the place was much too cold due to the air conditioning.

Danilo and I also stopped by Walmart this morning so I could withdraw some money from the ATM for shopping. Walmart is beginning to put up their Christmas decorations!

September 15, 2021 – Wednesday – Honduras Bicentennial
Reitoca, F.M., Honduras – 8:40 p.m.
Showers – 75 F

Today is the bicentennial of Honduras' Independence. Though there were firecrackers in isolated places, and there was a military and police parade in the capital, it was a quiet day for the most part because of the pandemic and because people were not traveling to and from work.

As Danilo and I drove to Curarén for Mass, we picked up a number of people to give them a ride, and we passed many others walking to the *pueblo*. I was thinking that the Mass would be packed and that everyone was going to church. But it turned out that most of the people were on their way to the health center to get vaccinated against COVID. Nevertheless, there were plenty of people for the Mass.

Another sobering piece of news regarding COVID-19 is that in the past nineteen months, approximately 1 in 500 Americans have died from the illness.

A friend sent me a set of funny cartoons and sayings about people who refuse to wear masks and to get vaccinated. Often, these are the same people are also very much into guns to protect themselves and their possessions. One of the funniest pictures was of a young woman wearing a t-shirt that said, "If you don't need a mask because God will protect you, why do you need a gun?"

Meanwhile in Cape Canaveral, Florida, four "amateur astronauts" lifted off from Kennedy Space Center on a SpaceX craft, making history by becoming the first crew to go into orbit without a professional astronaut aboard. Their "space tour" is expected to take three days, orbiting Earth every 90 minutes.

Danilo brought my car back to the Holy Cross campus early this morning. He had had the brakes adjusted. The roads in this parish are absolutely horrible, and they will most likely get much worse during October, traditionally the rainiest month of the year in Honduras.

This evening, I had Mass in Alubarén at 6 p.m. Because Danilo had a conference out of town, he was not able to take me. The man who promised to give me a ride to the Mass did not show up, and naturally, there was heavy rain when it was time to go. Fortunately for me, Fr. Sebastián was in the rectory, and he took me to the church. During the Mass, a drunk man kept shouting every few minutes or so, especially during my homily. I kept going, but when the man staggered down the center aisle and approached within about three feet of me, a young man took him by the arm and led him back to his pew. After the Mass, one of the leaders of the church community told me with embarrassment that the drunk man was her brother. Following the Mass, a young man named Alex gave me a ride to the rectory, and then I walked to my house on the Holy Cross campus. Fortunately, the rain had ceased.

September 17, 2021 – Friday – St. Robert Bellarmine
Reitoca, F.M., Honduras – 8 p.m.
Partly cloudy – 77 F

One of the staff members of Clínica Santa María has tested positive for COVID, so he'll be out of work for two weeks. Fortunately, he is fully vaccinated, as are all other members of the parish's healthcare entities.

September 18, 2021 – Saturday
Reitoca, F.M., Honduras – 9 p.m.
Partly cloudy – 80 F

Today I sent a note to the Honduran members of our Rotary Club. In the note, I asked whether or not we should continue pursuing a Rotary Global Grant to gain funds to buy needed laboratory equipment, or whether we should seek another way. I'm not sure that all the requirements of the Global Grant process are worth the hassle.

After many days of rain, today there was none. This year, Reitoca has had more rain than usual. Unfortunately, however, because we didn't have rain in the first month of "winter" (May), many farmers missed out on planting for the first growing season of the year for corn, beans, and other crops.

A friend of mine from Wilmington, North Carolina, John McLaughlin, will be coming for a visit in October. He visited this parish in April 2016 when I was still pastor of the Basilica Shrine of St. Mary. I am very eager to see him once again.

September 19, 2021 – 25th Sunday in Ordinary Time
Reitoca, F.M., Honduras – 9 p.m.
Partly cloudy – 79 F

This morning I celebrated Mass in Reitoca and then at noon in Alubarén.

In the 9 a.m. Reitoca Mass, an intoxicated man was shouting gibberish, especially during the homily. Whenever he would stagger down the center aisle of the church, someone would lead him back to his seat. After Mass, he lay down in the church plaza with a couple of young men watching out for him.

Juan decided to raise a couple of piglets. He bought one black one and one white one. He has a nice pen for them, and the shade from the trees by his house should keep them comfortable.

September 20, 2021 - Monday - Ss. Andrew Kim Taegon & Companions
Reitoca, F.M., Honduras – 7:20 p.m.
Mostly cloudy – 79 F

As I write this note, a magnificent Harvest Moon is rising over the eastern mountains, illuminating the valley.

This was a very strange day. Stocks were down in the United States, our Clínica Santa María treated some very serious COVID cases including one who died, and the regular electricity kept coming on and off all day.

In the morning, I saw a couple of young men walk past the visitors' *casitas*. At first, I supposed they were more thieves. However, when I questioned them, I learned that they were volunteers from the Reitocan communities of Rebalse and San José. Fr. Carlos had asked them to cut down some of the brush around the *casitas* so that thieves would not have places to hide.

I used the day to do a bit of writing and relaxing.

September 21, 2021 – Tuesday – St. Matthew
Reitoca, F.M., Honduras – 9:40 p.m.
Mostly cloudy – 75 F

Today I learned that a former parishioner of mine in Wilmington, North Carolina, Aaron Preusser, is in intensive care, suffering from complications from COVID-19. His wife Amy worked in our youth ministry at the Basilica Shrine of St. Mary when I was pastor there. Fortunately, many people are showering him and his family with prayers.

September 22, 2021 – Wednesday
Reitoca, F.M., Honduras – 8 p.m.
Mostly cloudy – 77 F

The season of fall starts today in the northern hemisphere. Honduras is in the northern hemisphere, but we don't experience anything like spring or fall, only what we call "summer" (November-April) and "winter" (May-October). I like to pretend, though, that we have four seasons.

Today Danilo and I were in Tegucigalpa, and I bought some furniture for the living room and the *mayordomo casita*. Danilo and I also bought ten small bushes from the tropical plant nursery near the Clarion Real Hotel that we have come to like. Juan and I will plant the bushes later this week in the one part of the entrance triangle of the Holy Cross campus that does not have vegetation yet.

As Danilo and I got closer to Reitoca, it started to rain, so we had to stop to put plastic over the boxes of furniture we bought. Fortunately, Danilo was prepared for rain, for we have it many afternoons and evenings during "winter."

John and Penny Cromer sent a message today to let me know they have started a money tree to help the family of Aaron and Amy Preusser. Aaron's condition seems to be going downhill.

The Diocese of Raleigh reported that Fr. Doug Lawson is in the hospital in Pinehurst following a fall. Doug is ten years older than me and is the former pastor of Sacred Heart parish in Southport, North Carolina.

Today I discovered that the television in the St. Oscar Romero (green) *casita* has been stolen. It didn't even last a month! This is the second television set that's been stolen. I hope that when Darwing puts the *balcones* (bars) on the windows of the bathrooms, the thievery will stop.

September 23, 2021 – Thursday – St. Pius of Pietrelcina (Padre Pio)
Reitoca, F.M., Honduras – 9 p.m.
Mostly cloudy – 77 F

Today I was scheduled to celebrate a 7 p.m. Mass in San Francisco de Asís, but I had to cancel it because the town's electricity in that part of town was out, and the church's solar system backup was not working. The people of the parish are beginning a novena in honor of St. Francis of Assisi, patron saint of the parish, whose feast is October 4.

September 24, 2021 – Friday
Reitoca, F.M., Honduras – 8:55 p.m.
Mostly cloudy – 79 F

This morning Cardinal Rodríguez met on a Zoom call with the priests who work in the Archdiocese of Tegucigalpa for a morning spiritual gathering. Frs. Carlos and Sebastián joined me in my study for the virtual session.

September 25, 2021 – Saturday
Reitoca, F.M., Honduras – 9:20 p.m.
Mostly cloudy – 77 F

Juan needed to take the day off to go to Tegucigalpa on family matters, so I planted the new little bushes in the entrance triangle. Now that all three corners of the triangle have vegetation, we'll enjoy watching them grow and flower.

September 26, 2021 – 26th Sunday in Ordinary Time
Reitoca, F.M., Honduras – 7 p.m.
Mostly cloudy – 79 F

This morning I celebrated Masses in Concepción and El Hatillo. When Danilo and I got to El Hatillo, we encountered the community coming towards us in a procession. It turned out that they did not know we were having a Mass today, but after the procession, we celebrated a vibrant Mass. The procession was to celebrate the community's patron saint, Michael the Archangel, whose feast day is Wednesday. I also got to take video of the people coming from the road up to and into the church. In the afternoon, I celebrated Mass in Curarén.

In my homily for today, I told the story of a group of American soldiers who lost one of their own in a battle in France during World War II. They remembered a Catholic church they had passed, with a pretty cemetery encircled by a white picket fence. So, they took their friend there, only to learn from the priest that because their friend was not a Catholic, he couldn't be buried there. The priest did allow the men to bury him right outside the fence. Months later, the war ended, and the men returned to the little cemetery to give a final farewell to their friend. But they couldn't find the grave, for there were no graves outside the fence. When they asked the priest, he told them that he could not sleep after they buried their friend. He felt it was wrong not to welcome the man into the cemetery. So, he expanded the fence to include their friend.

Today's homily is very relevant for people in the world today, as in every age. Sociologists know that people in every age and in every society tend to divide their worlds into "we" and "them." When people do that, they invariably develop strategies to keep the "them" out of their inner circle. In the Catholic Church today, for example, there are clerics and others who are persecuting Catholics who don't buy into their religious-political belief systems. Even though Jesus came to Earth to teach us that we are all one, this tendency to divide people into "we" and "them," or "good guys" and "bad guys," will not change, even in the church of Christ. The challenge for all humans is to minimize the harm that can be caused by such a human tendency. The challenge for Christians is to remember.

I like to think we can make this a better world, bit by bit. However, when we consider that world powers have the capacity to destroy the planet Earth many times over with nuclear warheads, I can't help but wonder if we will be able to create a much better world before humans destroy it.

This evening I finished watching the Netflix series, *Midnight Mass.* It was a very dark but interesting series, a series I would probably not want to watch again. The real world is scary enough.

After Danilo brought me home to Reitoca from the Mass in Curarén, we stopped at the house of Timoteo the construction man. I gave him money to buy the laminate for my deck roof and overhang by the kitchen.

September 27, 2021 – Monday – St. Vincent de Paul
Reitoca, F.M., Honduras – 6:40 p.m.
Partly cloudy – 82 F

As the new work week begins, the world learned that the German people narrowly gave the majority of their votes to the center-left Social Democrats, defeating the party of outgoing Chancellor Angela Merkel, the center-right Christian Democrats. Now the Social Democrats must form a coalition government with other parties.

We also learned that the people of Switzerland overwhelmingly approved legalizing same-sex marriage. Switzerland now joins the majority of European countries that support marriage equality.

I subscribe to a website called *inspiringquotes.com.* A poignant quote today was from Isaac Asimov: "The saddest aspect of life right now is that science gathers knowledge faster than society gathers wisdom." How very true. Ethicists in various fields of ethics, for example, are continually scrambling to keep abreast with new discoveries about the human body and new variations in human behavior. What an interesting time it is to be alive and alert.

This afternoon, Timoteo was at my house to take some additional measurements on the deck area for installing a new roof. He plans to order the material this week. I hope we'll be able to get the work done before my friend John McLaughlin comes on October 12.

September 28, 2021 - Tuesday - St. Wenceslas; Ss. Laurence & Companions
Reitoca, F.M., Honduras – 8:30 p.m.
Mostly cloudy – 77 F

Fr. Carlos came over to my house last evening to give me a Mass schedule for the week. In addition to our regular Mass schedule, we'll also be celebrating Confirmation in Alubarén for some of the Alubarén communities, and the feast of St. Francis of Assisi, patron saint of our parish.

On Friday, auxiliary bishop Teodoro Gómez will celebrate Confirmation for some of the communities of Alubarén in San Lorenzo church, and the priests of our deanery will be concelebrating. Then on Monday, we'll have a special morning Mass for the feast of San Francisco de Asís in the mother church of our parish, San Francisco de Asís in Reitoca. I believe the pastor, Fr. Carlos, will celebrate that Mass and many of the rest of us will concelebrate. But because of the pandemic, we won't be having any social activities outside of the Mass itself.

Juan and Emilio are both off today, so Blackie and I had a very mellow day.

Wall Street had a bad day today. But what goes down will go up.

September 29, 2021 – Wednesday – Ss. Michael, Gabriel & Raphael
Reitoca, F.M., Honduras – 7:25 p.m.
Partly cloudy – 81 F

This morning Danilo and I went to the Curarén community of Chaparral to celebrate their patronal feast day with a Mass. The name of their church is San Miguel Arcángel. After the Mass, I blessed a child and two youth in honor of their birthdays; the child's name was Miguel Ángel. Chaparral is the church where I experienced my first Christmas Eve in Honduras in 2018. In my homily today, I talked about the virtue of courage, for which St. Michael the Archangel is noted. I told the story of an Irish-American Jesuit priest, Fr. Joseph Timothy O'Callahan, a Naval Chaplain in World War II, who received the Medal of Honor for his heroic service. Fr. Joe, as he was known, was a professor of mathematics, physics, and philosophy in addition to his priestly career.

After we returned from Chaparral, Danilo repaired the electric system in the church of San Francisco de Asís in Reitoca.

This evening, Danilo is putting together a dresser that I bought recently. Putting things together is totally beyond me. My brain is simply not wired for such things.

September 30, 2021 – Thursday – St. Jerome
Reitoca, F.M., Honduras – 7:40 p.m.
Showers – 81 F

Danilo and I went to Tegucigalpa today so I could pay salaries for three of the Clínica Santa María staff. Although I am able to pay most bills online now, the salaries of the clinic staff are an exception. Marco gave us some boxes to take to Aaron in the St. Mary House.

We got back to Reitoca around 2:45 and stopped to deliver the boxes to Aaron. He invited me to a birthday party for Miguel, one of the original workers of our clinic. When I asked him where and when the party would be, he told me it would be on my deck at 4 p.m., "if that is okay." Though I was pretty tired, I said that would be fine. Because we're all healthcare persons, we're used to spontaneity.

Miguel got his name in the way many Catholics from Latin America do, that is, from the saint whose feast day is on their birthday; Miguel was born on the feast of St. Michael the Archangel, September 29. The staff from Clínica Santa María and Farmacia San Francisco de Asís in Reitoca, and Farmacia Candelaria in Curarén, all showed up. We all ate Chinese food except Dr. Elia's son, for whom we ordered a pizza from Casona Lenca.

In reflecting on this month, I can say it was a good one. In Honduras, we celebrated the bicentennial of the country, for it was on September 15, 1821, that Honduras and four other Central American countries gained their independence from Spain.

In the Diocese of Raleigh, retired priest Fr. Doug Lawson fell and was taken to the hospital in Pinehurst, and one of my former parishioners, Aaron Preusser, is fighting for his life in an ICU in Wilmington, N.C. from COVID-19 complications.

This month saw the twentieth anniversary of "9-11," the day when Islamic terrorists attacked the United States.

And here in our parish of San Francisco de Asís, I gave a Sunday homily without notes, and I hosted two Missionary Sisters of the Sacred Heart of Jesus for the first time on the Holy Cross campus. In this month, Fr. Renán and two seminarians dropped by to visit the campus, and Juan and I planted flowers in the Holy Cross triangle. The only negative thing that happened on the campus is that the television in the St. Oscar Romero House (green *casita*) was stolen.

I'm expecting October to be even better.

OCTOBER 2021

October 1, 2021 – Friday – St. Therese of Lisieux
Reitoca, F.M. Honduras – 77 F
Partly cloudy – 77 F

This morning our parish celebrated its third set of Confirmations in the church of San Lorenzo in Alubarén, this time for seventy-eight persons. San Lorenzo, being more than 400 years old, has seen many Confirmations through the centuries.   So far this year, our parish has celebrated around 500 Confirmations. Bishop Teodoro Gómez, an auxiliary bishop of the Archdiocese of Tegucigalpa, celebrated the Mass. Six priests concelebrated the Mass: Fr. José Luis, pastor of Lepaterique; Fr. Gustavo, pastor of Sabanagrande; Fr. Tony, dean of the San Francisco de Asís deanery and pastor of Ojojona; and three of the four priests of the parish of Reitoca, Frs. Carlos, Sebastián, and myself.

The church was overflowing, and the community had set up chairs outdoors in front of the church. As always, the church was very hot, and the Confirmation candidates and their sponsors had to stand throughout the whole Mass, for there were no chairs for them. In his homily, the bishop said something nice about me, but I'm not sure what it was, and the people applauded.

After the Confirmation Mass, the community had food for the guests in the social hall across the road from the church, but my driver Danilo didn't want to eat anything, so we didn't attend the social.

Today is the first anniversary of the planting of the little *almendro* tree in the triangle of Holy Cross campus. I got some photos of Juan with the tree, for it was he who planted it on October 1, 2020, the first day I slept in my new house on the Holy Cross campus.

After a year of living here, I finally decorated the living room. Now it looks very cozy and inviting. The art work on the walls has a nautical theme. On the Cape Fear Coast of North Carolina, where I lived for many years, the shops always had an abundance of nautical art. Also, today, Danilo and Juan finished putting together dressers for the Blessed James Miller (blue) *casita* and for my bedroom in the Four Martyrs house.

October 2, 2021 – Saturday – Holy Guardian Angels
Reitoca, F.M., Honduras – 8 p.m.
Mostly clear – 81 F

Aaron Preusser died this morning at 6 from complications from COVID. He leaves his wife Amy, former youth director at the Basilica Shrine of St. Mary in Wilmington, N.C., their son, and three adopted children. I will celebrate two Masses for Aaron this weekend.

Today is the first anniversary of Juan planting bushes on the south side of my house. The little things were only a foot tall when they were planted, and at first, I didn't think they would survive because of attacks by *zampopos*. But with plenty of care and attention, they are now almost as tall as me.

October 3, 2021 – 27th Sunday in Ordinary Time
Reitoca, F.M., Honduras – 9:35 p.m.
Partly cloudy – 75 F

Today I celebrated two Masses in the "mother church" of our parish, San Francisco de Asís in Reitoca. Because my home is only a twenty-minute walk to the church., I like to walk there when I can. Some people think it's too dangerous to walk there at night, but I've never had any problems. I offered the Masses for the repose of the soul of Aaron Preusser and deceased members of our parish.

As I was getting close to the church for the morning Mass, I encountered a procession, with music, walking along the side of the church to make an entrance in the front door. The people were celebrating the feast of St. Francis of Assisi, patron saint of the parish and church.

The lector gave a special welcome to visitors from our parish's church in La Libertad, one of the five municipalities of our parish.

My homily focused on part of today's Gospel reading from St. Mark (10: 13-16), focusing on Jesus telling his disciples to stop trying to

218

prevent children from approaching him for a blessing. I told the story of Servant of God Edward J. Flanagan, a priest of Omaha, Nebraska, who founded Boys' Town.

October 4, 2021 – Monday – St. Francis of Assisi
Reitoca, F.M., Honduras – 7:45 p.m.
Mostly cloudy – 79 F

Today our parish celebrated the feast of St. Francis of Assisi with a special 9 a.m. Mass. We had visitors from many of our parish's churches. Fr. Carlos celebrated the Mass, Fr. Sebastián and I concelebrated, and we had eleven altar servers. As always, the church was hot, and the clouds of incense didn't help the stifling atmosphere.

Although I had ridden with Fr. Carlos to the church, I walked home. Even though the walk takes only twenty minutes, the blazing Reitocan sun and high humidity made it very uncomfortable. By the time I got home, my clothes were soaked with perspiration. Meanwhile, Juan was busily cutting down brush in the front of my house. Both of us have become wise as to how much heat we can take, and when are the best times of day to be outdoors. This morning was close to the limit.

October 5, 2021 – Tuesday – St. Faustina Kowalska
Reitoca, F.M., Honduras – 8 p.m.
Cloudy – 82 F

Most of the day, I spent writing Sunday homilies for the month of October.

Around 4 p.m., Blackie and his friends began barking outside, so I left my study to see what was happening. There I discovered an invasion of ants climbing up the south side of my house, the front of the garage, and the yellow and green *casitas*. This has happened before. Unfortunately, I had just a small amount of Raid left, so I began hosing down the invading hordes coming from every direction. What is so marvelous to me is how completely organized the ants were, and how intent they were on attacking my house and the two casitas. I spent over an hour hosing them down. As soon as I got those coming from one direction, along came more from other directions. Although most of the invaders were large black ants, or maybe *zampopos*, this invading army contained had a variety of other types, such as small flesh-biting brown ants.

Although this was Juan's day off, I asked him to come to give me a hand. By the time he got to the Holy Cross campus, however, I thought the battle was over. But upstairs, very small ants had covered the outside wall above my kitchen windows. They were so plentiful, that I could actually not see the wall in some places, only dark areas covered with ants. Fortunately, I was able to kill these with the small amount of Raid I had left.

October 6, 2021 – Wednesday – St. Bruno
Reitoca, F.M., Honduras – 6:45 p.m.
Showers, 81 F

As I write this note, steady showers are falling here in the mountains, and Blackie is snuggled up on his blanket sleeping near my desk.

This was a beautiful day for writing, leisurely cleaning, and catching up with friends.

Today is the feast of St. Bruno, a hermit who founded the Carthusian order. I love reading about hermits, for I fantasize about being a desert hermit when I can no longer be useful in the apostolic life. I dream that would occur when I'm 95 or so, and then when I'm around 98, I could be martyred. Of course, by then, I probably will have lost my mind. Fantasies are fun, for they allow us to live other lives without the consequences.

October 7, 2021 – Thursday – Our Lady of the Rosary
Reitoca, F.M., Honduras – 9 p.m.
Partly cloudy – 79 F

This afternoon I celebrated Mass in Curarén, and because it is the feast of Our Lady of the Rosary, I talked about the four sets of "mysteries" that show the life of Jesus.

The church's social hall in Curarén is coming along well. I was intrigued that the building's location will allow for a mostly-enclosed garden area for the convent of the Missionary Sisters of the Sacred Heart. Above the social hall is an area that Fr. Carlos hopes will one day become the *casa cural* (rectory) for a pastor.

Juan and Danilo were in Tegucigalpa today doing various chores, so it was very quiet on the campus.

The Diocese of Raleigh reported some new priest assignments today. Fr. Stanley Carl Zdancewicz, OFM, Conv., will live in the Blessed Sacrament friary in Burlington. He'll assist in pastoral ministry where needed. Fr. John P. Curran, L.C., will have a temporary appointment as interim priest chaplain at North Carolina State University in Raleigh. Very Rev. John Forbes, pastor of Sacred Heart parish in Pinehurst and dean of the Fayetteville Deanery, is additionally appointed administrator of St. Mary parish in Laurinburg, and Fr. Michael G. Schuetz, pastor of Mother of Mercy in Washington, N.C., will serve a dean of the New Bern deanery. I wish them all well in their new roles.

October 8, 2021 – Friday
Reitoca, F.M., Honduras – 7:15 p.m.
Partly cloudy – 81 F

Lightning flashed almost continuously over the southern mountains early in the evening, but it has since stopped.

Today I wrote two biographies for 2022 "missionary hero" blog posts. One is of St. María Guadalupe García Zavala, who came to be known as "Mother Lupita." She was a nurse serving in Guadalajara, Jalisco, Mexico during the early 20th Century persecution when it was dangerous to be a Catholic priest. In addition to her administrative role in her order, and her clinical nursing practice, Lupita was also famous for hiding priests and even the Archbishop of Guadalajara in her hospital.

The other biography is that of Venerable Rafael Cordero, who is called the "Father of Public Education in Puerto Rico." Some very famous people attended his little school on Luna Street, where he taught for 58 years. Today the school, which is actually a house, has been declared a historical site in the National Register of Historical Places of the United States.

Because it is so hot here in Reitoca, in the low 90s every day, I love to think of snow from time to time. And, because I'm Christmas freak of the first order, I like to think of Christmas. So, last evening, I treated myself to watching *Christmas Under Wraps*, and this evening, I watched *Christmas Inheritance*. I enjoyed both films very much, especially the latter.

October 9, 2021 - Saturday - St. John Leonardi; Ss. Denis & Companions
Reitoca, F.M., Honduras – 8:15 p.m.
Cloudy – 81 F

This was a nice quiet day of writing and relaxing for me.

On the international front, Nancy Pelosi, Speaker of the U.S. House of Representatives, met with Pope Francis in Rome. Like President Joe Biden and Chief Justice John Roberts of the U.S. Supreme Court, Nancy Pelosi is a Catholic Christian.

October 10, 2021 – 28th Sunday in Ordinary Time
Reitoca, F.M., Honduras – 7:10 p.m.
Mostly cloudy – 79 F

One of the first things I read this morning online was a wonderful article in the Wilmington, N.C. *Star News* by Sidney Hoover. The article discussed the building of an Eden Village in Wilmington for the homeless.

The first Eden Village was in Springfield, Missouri. The Wilmington village will sit on four acres of land and have 32 tiny homes, built for single homeless adults, each 400 square feet. Though the corporation has not yet put out a call for applications, the project has already received 300 applications.

In addition to the little homes themselves, the residents of the community will have a clubhouse, library, laundry area, and a one-acre community garden. The residents will also have access to computers and Wi-Fi. This project is funded by donations. What an incredibly uplifting article to begin my day.

This morning I celebrated Masses in La Libertad and San Miguelito.

Before I left for La Libertad, Fr. Carlos came over from the rectory with my truck, which he had borrowed yesterday to visit Curarén and Lodo Negro. In Curarén, he was checking on the progress of the social hall and potential rectory, and in Lodo Negro, he was celebrating a Mass and baptisms. He also gave me my schedule for this week. I need to prepare my homilies early as I'm having company from the United States coming on Tuesday. I'll be celebrating Masses in the Curarén communities of El Anís and El Arado, the Alubarén communities of Concepción and El Hatillo, and in Reitoca.

Today I had a powerful reminder of the need to keep in mind the age and location of people for whom I prepare homilies. This is very important for me as a preacher, for if I use examples that I assume "everyone knows," but they indeed don't know, my illustrations would be useless. For example, Americans often see themselves as the center of the universe, assuming that the rest of the world knows about events important to Americans. Likewise, older adults often incorrectly assume that younger people know things about the same things they do.

Today, for example, I was talking with Juan and mentioned the terrorist attacks that occurred in the United States on September 11, 2001. He hadn't heard of it. He did hear about the plane that crashed into a bridge near the Tegucigalpa airport a few years back. Likewise, many times I have encountered young people who haven't heard about Adolph Hitler, Nazis, concentration camps, and the like. But this should not surprise me too much in this part of Honduras, for the overwhelming majority of the population have never had the opportunity to go beyond sixth grade, for their families can't afford to pay the fees for uniforms or tuition.

October 11, 2021 – Monday – St. John XXIII
Reitoca, F.M., Honduras - 9 p.m.
Partly cloudy – 77 F

Today, Americans celebrate Columbus Day to honor Christopher Columbus who "discovered" the "new world." Many banks and other institutions have a holiday.

Some Americans prefer to celebrate today as Indigenous People's Day, as if Columbus was responsible for the entire history of persecution of "indigenous" Americans by people of European descent. President Biden became the first U.S. president to publicly honor this day. In the United States, the term "indigenous" has been used exclusively to refer to descendants of various "Indian" tribes. But science postulates, with considerable certainty, that the entire human species came from the continent of Africa. So logically, every American is an African American. Interesting.

Today as I was planning a whole day preparing for my guest tomorrow, the water spigot broke by the blue *casita* as I was getting ready to water the northern part of the campus. Suddenly, it looked like a busted fire hydrant. After panicking for a bit, I realized I could turn off a main valve in the little shed by the cistern. Sure enough, it worked. Around 4:30 p.m., Geovany came by and fixed the problem. I am so grateful for this man!

October 12, 2021 – Tuesday
Reitoca, F.M., Honduras – 7 p.m.
Heavy rain – 81 F

My friend John McLaughlin arrived safe and sound from Wilmington, N.C. He said the trip went very smoothly from Wilmington to Charlotte to Miami to Tegucigalpa's old TGU airport. From what I understand, the new Palmerola International Airport (XPL) will most likely open in mid-November, hosting all large international flights.

October 13, 2021 – Wednesday
Reitoca, F.M., Honduras – 8:15 p.m.
Heavy rains – 75 F

As I write this note, Blackie is with me in my study snuggled up on his little blanket, and John is in his Blessed Stanley Rother (yellow) *casita* for the night. John is the pastor of St. Jude's Metropolitan Community Church in Wilmington, N.C. I met John in Wilmington when I was at St. Mary's, and we were involved in various ecumenical projects.

Last night we had heavy rains that lasted into the morning. Here in Reitoca, rain in the morning is almost unheard-of. Fortunately, the rains stopped, so John and I walked into the center of Reitoca. I introduced John to many people that we encountered. As we got near the St. Mary House, Dr. Aaron was getting ready to take an 18-month-old child to the hospital in Tegucigalpa with Miguel driving.

In the evening, Aaron picked up John and me, and we all went to the Chinese restaurant in town. The restaurant is on the second floor of a building, and nicely decorated. We were the only customers in the restaurant, so we got all the attention. During our Kung Pao Chicken dinner, John was able to talk about his early life in Northern Ireland, his adventures as a walking pilgrim in Spain, and his current life in Wilmington, North Carolina.

October 14, 2021 – Thursday - St. Callistus I
Reitoca, F.M., Honduras – 9:55 p.m.
Heavy rain – 75 – 9:55 p.m.

This morning I celebrated Mass for the people of El Anís, one of my favorite communities. There, I celebrated four baptisms. The little church of Our Lady of Guadalupe was overflowing with people, but the leaders brought a chair to the front just for John.

This evening, Aaron and Shelsie, microbiologist in our Clínica Santa María laboratory, came to pick up John and me to take us to Casona Lenca here in Reitoca for a celebration with the clinic staff. However, there was no electricity in the town, and Casona Lenca had no backup power, so we decided to bring the party to my deck. Before we left, however, the Casona Lenca owner Jancy gave John and me a little tour of his house, which has many pieces of wooden furniture that Jancy has made. We were astonished to learn that Jancy was leaving tomorrow for a three-week vacation in Wilmington, N.C. What an incredible coincidence: a Reitocan being introduced to a visitor from Wilmington on the day before the Reitocan is getting ready to visit Wilmington. What are the odds? John hopes to get in touch with Jancy in Wilmington next week.

It turned out that the party was a surprise in honor of Aaron's birthday, which was on October 3. Fortunately, the electricity came back on, and everyone had a great time.

Today I learned about a variety of wheatgrass being developed in the USA, whose grain is called Kernza. It is perennial, so farmers do not have to replant every year. Scientists say the plant forms deep roots that store carbon and other nutrients in the soil, and because it is perennial, it helps prevent erosion and reduces the need for fertilizer. That sounds like it could benefit millions of people on the planet.

October 15, 2021 – Friday – St. Teresa of Avila
Reitoca, F.M., Honduras – 11 p.m.
Mostly cloudy – 73 F

The first thing on the agenda today was to get John to Clínica Santa María to get a test by Dr. Shelsie to be sure he is not positive for COVID, for that is a requirement of American Airlines. Fortunately, he's negative, so he should have no trouble on Monday catching his flight back to Wilmington, N.C.

226

This morning, Danilo took John and me to the Curarén community of El Arado ("plow" in English). The people there are nearing the final phases of their new church, so I gave them some money from the Red Lantern Foundation for concrete and tiles for the floor. It should be beautiful and plenty big when finished. Electricity has not yet reached this community, but the room was bright because of window spaces. I'm not sure if the people will have glazed windows or not, for many of our churches have only decorative bars on the windows.

In this dirt-floored church, which is named Our Lady of Suyapa, I celebrated Mass and seven baptisms. I stayed after the Mass for photos with each of the baptismal families, and John got some excellent photos of the congregants. In fact, one of the photos he got was of a teenage boy looking into the church from a window opening. The look on the youth's face is extremely difficult to describe; if I had to label it, I'd call it "wistful." The photo is absolutely stunning.

While John and I were busy being in photos or taking photos, the *Delegados* were busy giving out lollipops that John brought for the community.

After leaving El Arado, we went to see the church of Our Lady of Suyapa in the Curarén community of Pueblo Nuevo. I often call this the "Red Lantern Church" for indeed, it was built mostly by money from the Red Lantern Foundation. Within a minute of our arrival, about thirty people had gathered to say hello. John loved the church and the cool air in this pine forest mountainside community.

In the evening, John and I talked about capital campaigns, for his all-embracing church in Wilmington is contemplating raising funds for a building expansion. Having been through two very successful campaigns, I was happy to share with him.

October 16, 2021 - Saturday - St. Hedwig; St. Margaret Mary Alacoque
Reitoca, F.M., Honduras – 8 p.m.
Cloudy – 79 F

This was a very nice, laid-back day here on the Holy Cross campus. Juan had a day off, and the only thing on my agenda was to attend the virtual "reverse raffle" fundraiser for my Rotary Passport club. Two people won $2,500 each, one of whom was my friend Richard Creech.

In the evening, John and I had a delicious American meatloaf dinner.

October 17, 2021 – 29th Sunday in Ordinary Time
Reitoca, F.M., Honduras – 7:15 p.m.
Mostly cloudy – 79 F

The first thing this morning, my truck wouldn't start because of a dead battery. So, John, Danilo, and I crammed into Danilo's little truck and headed off to two communities of Alubarén: Concepción and El Hatillo, for Masses.

In both communities, John took some photos of various members of the congregations. One of my favorite photos was that of a little boy in El Hatillo, about 3 years old, holding his toy guitar, definitely part of the band.

Today in Vatican City, Pope Francis officially opened the diocesan part of the Synod on Synodality. Its official title is: "Synod 2021-2023: For a Synodal Church." As of October 5, 2021, there were 652 archdioceses and 2,248 dioceses in the world. The synod has great potential for change and growth.

October 18, 2021 – Monday – St. Luke, Evangelist
Reitoca, F.M., Honduras – 8:40 p.m.
Rain – 75 F

Danilo and I got John to the airport around 10 a.m. and we were home by around 2:30 p.m. It was wonderful having John here, and I look forward to his next visit.

The Diocese of Raleigh sent out a summary of its presbyteral (council of priests) consultation process that is focusing on five areas: (1) acquisition of new properties; (2) staffing new parishes; (3) ministering to Catholics in rural areas; (4) options to replace the Bishop's Annual Appeal; and (5) the roles the central diocesan office should play.

The announcement also noted that the 100th anniversary of the Diocese of Raleigh will be on December 12, 2024.

October 19, 2021 – Tuesday – St. Paul of the Cross; Ss. Isaac Jogues, etc.
Reitoca, F.M., Honduras – 6:25 p.m.
Thundershowers – 79 F

After hosting a friend for six days and celebrating Masses and baptisms in five mountain churches of our parish during the past few days, I planned today to be a nice, human-free day. But the best laid plans of mice and men …. In the morning, Darwing showed up with the *balcones* (steel bars for windows to prevent burglaries). After he got all set up to install the first *balcón*, he found that there was no regular electricity in Reitoca today, and we didn't want to take a chance using the solar system with his electrical equipment. So, we put the *balcones* in the garage for another day. Naturally, about an hour after he left, the regular electricity returned, but Darwing didn't. He'll be working with one of his brothers in Tegucigalpa for the next ten days.

Then a young man with a woman I assumed to be his mother stopped by. The young man was sick, and one of the staff members from

Clínica Santa María suggested he come to see if I could help him buy needed medicines. Of course, I did.

This afternoon, Geovany stopped by to do a little work for me and wondered if I could contribute to the music ministry of the new Church of God of Prophecy in town. I said I'd like to, but that I currently had too many commitments to churches of our own parish.

Also, this afternoon, I learned that the mother of Arnulfo died today after a long, serious illness. Arnulfo is one of the original staff members of Clínica Santa María.

Then Fr. Carlos showed up to give me my assignments for Thursday, Friday, and Sunday, and we visited for a bit.

Now, it's finally quiet except for the pattering of the rain on my roof and thunder rolling over the mountains. Blackie is curled up on his colorful blanket by my desk in the study. And I am getting ready to watch an episode from a new Netflix series called *Over Christmas*.

October 20, 2021 – Wednesday
Reitoca, F.M., Honduras – 6:30 p.m.
Thunderstorm – 77 F

Today was the quiet day that I had planned for yesterday, so I was able to get my homilies done for this coming weekend. I'll be celebrating Masses in Curarén on Thursday, Yigüilaca on Friday, and La Libertad and San Miguelito on Sunday.

This evening, I got an email from my Wilmington friend Laura Vinson, who plans to visit within the next few weeks. That'll be excellent.

October 21, 2021 – Thursday
Reitoca, F.M., Honduras – 5:55 p.m.
Partly cloudy – 81 F

This was a pretty quiet day here on the Holy Cross campus. I was able to get a blog-biography written of Blessed Titus Brandsma, a Dutch

230

Carmelite who was martyred in Hitler's Dachau concentration camp. The nurse who gave him a lethal injection was a fallen-away Catholic.

Juan was here today, and he planted the little orange tree and the lemongrass in a space on the south side of my house. I am pretty sure they'll do fine in that location.

In the afternoon, Timoteo Flores, a construction "jack-of-all-trades" of Reitoca, came by my house and said that the laminate is ready to be picked up, and he hopes to put the roof on the overhang by my kitchen. That will be so great, for it'll block the morning sun. Then, he'll replace the polygal roof over the deck and replace it with laminate. I'm not sure why everything is going so smoothly with the purchase of the laminate, when in the past the warehouse never had it in stock. But I'm delighted things seem to be going so smoothly now.

Danilo came from Lodo Negro today to take me to Curarén to celebrate a 4 p.m. Mass. We didn't get very far, however, because a big truck was blocking the road in both directions. So, the people had to have a Liturgy of the Word service today instead of Eucharist. But, here in this rugged part of the parish, people are used to such things.

Today, the Diocese of Raleigh announced three priest changes in the diocese. Fr. Giovanni de Jesús Romero Bermudez, a priest of the Diocese of Caldas, Antioquia, Colombia, has submitted his resignation as Pastor of St. Andrew parish in Red Springs, and the bishop of Raleigh has accepted the resignation. Fr. Francisco Javier García González, whom everyone knows as "Chesko," will be leaving his position as Parochial Vicar of the Basilica Shrine of St. Mary and become Pastor of St. Andrew parish in Red Springs. And finally, Fr. Cyriac John, a priest of the Diocese of Mananthavady, Kerala, India, currently Administrator of San Isidore Mission in Fayetteville, is appointed Pastor of St. Mary parish in Laurinburg, with responsibility for priestly ministry at Our Lady of the Snows Mission in Elizabethtown.

October 22, 2021 – Friday – St. John Paul II
Reitoca, F.M., Honduras – 9:50 p.m.
Cloudy – 75 F

This morning, Danilo and I went to the Reitocan community of Yigüilaca to celebrate Mass on the feast day of their patron saint, St. John Paul II. The roads to that community go from bad to worse, studded with rocks and holes and gullies. We got there safe and sound in an hour, but I'm sure my truck was not happy.

As we drove into the church area, loud music was coming from the church, and young men set off firecrackers for our arrival. The church was filling up, even though we were twenty minutes early, and the atmosphere was very festive. I celebrated Reconciliation before the Mass, mostly for old ladies, but I couldn't hear much with the loud music in the background. That, of course, doesn't matter, for it is God who hears the heart and spirit of the penitents; the ordained priest is merely the earthly instrument God uses.

I told the story of John Paul II and his strengths and weaknesses. One of my favorite stories of him is how, as a youth in Poland, his neighborhood's sports teams were divided into Catholics and Jews. Often, the Jewish team didn't have enough players, so young Karol, his name before becoming the 264th pope of the Catholic Church, would play on the Jewish team. His love of the Jewish people would come to distinguish his papacy and his relationship with the state of Israel.

After the Mass was over, Danilo went to eat something the women had fixed for him, and I sat and chatted with some of the men and women leaders of the community. The leader of the *Delegados* of the community asked if I could buy them laminate for a roof over their kitchen, and I said that the Red Lantern Foundation could do that for them. They were very excited.

October 23, 2021 – Saturday - St. John of Capistrano
Reitoca, F.M., Honduras – 8 p.m.
Partly cloudy – 81 F

Fr. Carlos had some workers come to the rectory and Holy Cross campus property, to chop down the weeds, which are six feet tall. In the winter months, the rains make things grow very quickly, even though we have some of the rockiest soil I ever saw.

Fr. Carlos took my truck today to celebrate a special anniversary Mass in the Curarén community of Usuyca for one of the brothers of Sr. Martha. The brother died a year ago, and it is the custom to have a Mass of remembrance at various intervals, such as nine days, a month, three months, and a year.

Today I began reading Dr. Pam Brink's book, *An Academic Nurse's Tale: Triumph, Tribulations, and Travels.* Pam is a nurse-anthropologist who founded the *Western Journal of Nursing Research.* She and I were faculty members at the University of Iowa College of Nursing. I've been eager to read the book ever since Pam told me she was going to write it.

October 24, 2021 – 30th Sunday in Ordinary Time
Reitoca, F.M., Honduras – 6:25 p.m.
Mostly cloudy – 79 F

Today is World Mission Sunday, a day set aside each year when the Church reminds all Catholic Christians of our "missionary mandate" to spread the good news of Jesus to the whole world. We are reminded to pray, in a special way, for "professional missionaries" who leave home to serve in poor areas of the world. As the former mission director of the Diocese of Raleigh for twelve years, I have a special fondness for World Mission Sunday. And, of course, I also treasure the day because I've had a missionary heart since I was 13 years old.

Today I celebrated Masses in La Libertad and San Miguelito. In both communities, there were fewer people than usual, but I have no idea why. I told the story of Venerable Edel Mary Quinn, an Irish layperson who, after learning that tuberculosis was going to kill her, decided to spend the last years of her life as a missionary in Africa.

This week, I'm expecting Timoteo Flores and his crew to do roof work on my deck, so I moved the plants out of the way to the south side of my house. Now, that side looks like a *vivero* (nursery). I can hardly wait to get a roof outside the kitchen window.

As Danilo and I were going around the Holy Cross hill on the way to Masses this morning, I noticed that the workers had cut down lots of brush as well as weeds, so now the rectory can be seen from the Holy Cross campus. I must take a closer look and decide on a plan for that area.

This evening I watched *Halloween IV* and *The Fundamentals of Caring*. The Halloween movie was spooky, especially since I'm here alone with Blackie on this dark night. I locked the doors of the house in case Michael Myers was lurking outside my house. The Caring movie was great, not only because I spent many years doing clinical nursing, but also because I always enjoy Paul Rudd's acting.

October 25, 2021 – Monday
Reitoca, F.M., Honduras – 9:05 p.m.
Partly cloudy – 77 F

I was hoping for the laminate to come today for the new roof over the deck, but Timoteo told Juan that it couldn't come until tomorrow as the driver was on another project.

This was a very quiet day, and I was able to finish my homilies for this week.

October 26, 2021 – Tuesday
Reitoca, F.M., Honduras – 8 p.m.
Partly cloudy – 79 F

Danilo and I went to Tegucigalpa today so I could pay salaries for three members of the clinic staff. Unfortunately, the car's air conditioner has developed a leak, and it quit part way. Danilo will get it fixed on Friday. Dr. Marco took me to True Value where I bought some supplies for the Holy Cross campus. The stores are filled with Christmas trees, lights, nativity scenes, and other items for sale.

Today the Diocese of Raleigh reported that Msgr. Jerry Sherba has died. He had been battling cancer for some time. Jerry was truly one of the "good guys" of the presbyterate.

October 27, 2021 – Wednesday
Reitoca, F.M., Honduras – 8 p.m.
Partly cloudy – 79 F

This morning, I had a nice conversation with Geoff Rowland of TIAA, the institution that provides financial services for academics. That's where the University of Iowa invested my retirement funds when I was a professor there from 1982-1992. Geoff lives in Charlotte, N.C., and he came to visit me once when I was the pastor of the Basilica Shrine of St. Mary. We are both satisfied with how my retirement funds are coming along.

Today the priests of the Diocese of Raleigh received word that Msgr. Jerry Sherba's funeral Mass will be tomorrow at Holy Name of Jesus Cathedral in Raleigh. He'll be interred in the columbarium of St. Raphael's Church in Raleigh at a future date.

In preparing for one of my upcoming missionary-hero blog posts, I came across these beautiful words of Blessed Irene Stefani, an Italian Comboni Missionary Sister who was a nurse-missionary in Tanzania and Kenya. She said, "The Missionary is the one who has a heart for loving, the hands for helping, the mouth for announcing. This is all!"

October 28, 2021 – Thursday – Ss. Simon and Jude
Reitoca, F.M., Honduras – 9:30 p.m.
Cloudy – 75 F

This evening, I celebrated Mass in Reitoca for the feast of Saints Simon and Jude. When I arrived, the people were celebrating adoration of the Blessed Sacrament, and the altar area was beautifully decorated in red in honor of Simon and Jude who were, according to tradition, martyred for the faith. For my homily illustration of how martyrdom has continued through the centuries, I told the story of Blessed Jerzy Popieluszko, a Polish activist priest killed by Polish Communist secret service agents in 1984.

October 29, 2021 – Friday
Reitoca, F.M., Honduras – 8 p.m.
Partly cloudy – 79 F

This morning, Danilo and I went to the Curarén community of San Isidro for Mass. The trip took one hour and forty minutes one-way, for the roads are very bad in this remote community. José María Ramírez, the leader of the community, has been a *Delegado de la Palabra* for 24 years. As always, he was a most gracious host, and the people of the community are always so grateful to have a Mass in their church. In honor of the Mass, the people lit firecrackers before, during, and afterwards.

The church of San Isidro is named after St. Isidore the Farmer who lived from around 1070 to 1130 in Spain. I have seen statues of him in other churches of our deanery, so he seems to be pretty popular here in Honduras.

José María asked if I would buy them a sound system that runs on batteries. With this system, the community could plug in an electric guitar and have a microphone for reading the Scriptures when they have Mass or Liturgies of the Word that they have every Thursday and Sunday. San Isidro does not yet have electricity, but they said they could recharge the system's battery in Golondrina, one of the other communities of our parish. I told him we can make that happen. So, the next time I got to Tegucigalpa, I'll look for that system.

José María is a very creative person, and he showed us a little altar he made. Though it was originally made for Christmas, during the year it has other religious pictures and candles gracing it. The top of the altar is made from coconut trees.

While Danilo and I were in San Isidro, Timoteo Flores and two young men were at my house putting laminate over the area outside of my kitchen windows. They were able to finish that area, and then the rains came. They'll be back tomorrow to do replace the current polygal roof over the deck with laminate.

The effect of the new roof by the kitchen is absolutely magical. For some reason, it makes the whole kitchen cozier. I am thrilled with it. Juan and I spent a little time sitting on *chaises longues* outside the kitchen, enjoying the patter of the rain on the new roof. I plan to hang three Boston ferns from the roof bars.

After delivering me back to Reitoca, poor Danilo had already had a very long day of driving, but he then took my truck to Tegucigalpa to get the air conditioner fixed. I think he plans to stay in Tegucigalpa overnight.

October 30, 2021 – Saturday
Reitoca, F.M., Honduras – 7:50 p.m.
Partly cloudy – 75 p.m.

Timoteo was here at 6:45 this morning to put the finishing touches on my deck's new roof, and they did a beautiful job. There were finished a little after noon. I'm quite pleased. I have more work projects for Timoteo to do, so I should be seeing a lot of him in the next several months.

While he and his crew were working on my house, three other groups of men were busy cutting away the overgrown brush around the Holy Cross campus. I didn't ask them to do it, so it must have been Fr. Carlos.

Today I received a Happy Halloween card from my dear friend Rojann Alpers in Scottsdale, Arizona. She had a bad fall and is recovering slowly at her home. Rojann and I taught together at the University of Iowa. After receiving her doctorate, she was a professor at Arizona State University and retired a year or so ago.

It was a beautiful day without rain, but for unknown reasons, the electricity in the town went out around 5 p.m. After switching to solar energy, I discovered that the Blessed Stanley Rother *casita*, the yellow one, was not receiving energy. Timoteo will look at it tomorrow afternoon. I'm thinking that one of the cables that goes from my house to the green and yellow *casitas* must have become disconnected when the workers were moving them around while working on the roof.

October 31, 2021 – 31st Sunday in Ordinary Time
Reitoca, F.M., Honduras – 8:25 p.m.
Mostly cloudy – 75 F

Today I had Masses at 9 a.m. in Reitoca, 12 noon in Alubarén, and 4 p.m. in Curarén.

In Reitoca, Darwin Medina provided the music. Darwin, a seminarian of the Archdiocese of Tegucigalpa, is a native of Reitoca, and has finished all his coursework. Now, he'll be doing pastoral work in the parish of Sabanagrande, which is part of our San Francisco de Asís Deanery. Fr. Gustavo González, former pastor of our parish here in Reitoca, is the pastor of Sabanagrande.

In Curarén, I celebrated five baptisms in addition to the Mass today, so it was a very festive occasion.

In looking back on the month, I realize that this month has been an interesting one, for all my months hold special milestones, memories, and surprises.

This month Aaron Preusser and Msgr. Jerry Sherba died in North Carolina, Aaron in Wilmington and Jerry in Raleigh. They will be missed.

In the parish of San Francisco de Asís we started off the month by celebrating the sacrament of Confirmation for 75 young people in Alubarén. This was our parish's third Confirmation ceremony this year, bringing our

238

total confirmed to approximately 500. Because we have over 80 churches in the parish, not every church celebrates Confirmation each year.

On the international level, Pope Francis opened the Synod 2021-2023, and dioceses and archdioceses throughout the world have begun the diocesan phase of the synod which is devoted to the listening and sharing of ideas about the Church moving into the future.

My friend Dr. Pam Brink, a nurse-anthropologist, published her book, *An Academic Nurse's Tale: Triumph, Tribulations, and Travels*, and my friend Richard Creech won the reverse raffle that my Rotary club had this month.

I finally got an overhang roof outside my kitchen, and it makes a world of difference in the whole ambience of the kitchen.

Now I'm ready for an exciting November, one of my favorite months.

NOVEMBER 2021

November 1, 2021 – Monday – All Saints' Day
Reitoca, F.M., Honduras – 8:15 p.m.
Partly cloudy – 77 F

Today is the first day of our so-called "summer" in Reitoca, and the school kids now begin their three-month vacation.

It was a quiet day for me, so I used the time to get many odds and ends done. I more or less got my desk cleaned off, and a clean desk always helps me focus more clearly on the tasks at hand.

Unlike the United States, where All Saints' Day is big in the Catholic Church, here in Honduras, All Souls' Day is the biggie. Tomorrow I'll celebrate two Masses.

November 2, 2021 – Tuesday – All Souls' Day
Reitoca, F.M., Honduras – 8 p.m.
Mostly clear – 77 F

Today is often called the "Day of the Dead," for it is the day Catholic Christians remember loved ones who have died. I celebrated Masses in La Libertad and San Miguelito this morning, and Danilo and I passed many people traveling to cemeteries with their arms filled with flowers or carrying wreaths to decorate graves.

Aaron came over this evening to see the new roofing Timoteo did and to discuss future projects for the campus.

November 3, 2021 – Wednesday – St. Martin de Porres
Reitoca, F.M., Honduras – 6:45 p.m.
Thunderstorm – 79 F

Darwing and his cousin Alexi were here this morning to install *balcones* (bars) on the bathroom windows of the three *casitas* and my house. After finishing their work, they stayed for a spaghetti dinner. Darwing would like me to help him with English pronunciation, so we plan to have private lessons beginning next week.

Eduardo Rivera sent me a couple of samples of a logo for Red Lantern Foundation. I originally thought of a red lantern with a yellow flame inside, but he came up with something much more dramatic – a black lantern with a red flame. I told him to go with that as the official logo. Now we have to approve the website design.

November 4, 2021 – Thursday – St. Charles Borromeo
Reitoca, F.M., Honduras – 9 p.m.
Mostly cloudy – 73 F

Juan took the day off to go to Tegucigalpa, so it was very quiet on the campus.

This was a very productive day of writing and organizing files. I wrote a biography of St. Émilie de Villeneuve, founder of the Blue Sisters of Castres for a blog post in 2022. I have to write only seven more biographies for missionary heroes of 2022, and then I'll begin writing the posts for 2022. Though my *MissionPriest.com* blog posts on Sundays, Mondays, Wednesdays, and Fridays, Fridays take the longest time by far to create. Once I'm done with them, I can breeze through the other posts relatively quickly.

Aaron and Miguel came to my house from the clinic today to measure the polygal sheets that were previously the deck's roof. They're trying to figure out how they'll be able to transport them to the St. Mary House to store them until they decide how they'll use them. They hope to use at least part of the four 30-foot sheets as a roof for the clinic's outdoor patient waiting area.

This evening, I celebrated Mass in the church of San Lorenzo in Alubarén, the oldest of our parish's churches (over 400 years old). For my homily, I talked about St. Martin de Porres, one of my favorite saints. He was one of the men featured in my book, *Saintly Men of Nursing: 100 Amazing Stories.*

244

November 5, 2021 – Friday
Reitoca, F.M., Honduras – 9 p.m.
Mostly cloudy – 73 F

This morning, I celebrated a special Mass in the Alubarén community of San Antonio. We also celebrated the baptism of a little girl named Elmy Valentina Gutiérrez Cruz. The San Antonio community is wonderfully vibrant, with an excellent band. I was able to get a video of the band. The church was overflowing with people, the majority being children and youth. What an uplifting experience it is to serve a community with such an amazing spirit.

While Timoteo was installing the new roof on the deck, Juan and I had moved all the plants that graced the perimeter of the deck to the south side of the house. Today, Juan moved them all back. Because plants grow so rapidly here in Honduras, we'll have to transplant many of the plants that we thought could share large flower pots. They can't share – each wants to take over the whole pot!

November 6, 2021 – Saturday
Reitoca, F.M., Honduras – 8:20 p.m.
Partly cloudy – 75 F

This morning I had a Mass in El Portillo, a community of Curarén. That community never fails to amaze me, for it is always so vibrant and filled with spirit. Before the Mass, I visited with some of the *Delegados* of the community in the room that still has a simple bed for the days when priests slept there overnight. But we no longer celebrate evening Masses there, and the community has had electricity for a decade, so there is no longer a need for a traveling priest's bedroom.

The church was, as always, packed, most of the attendees being children and young adults. The band provided excellent music. The El Portillo church community, dedicated to St. John Bosco, reminds me of San Antonio's in its vibrancy. The climate in El Portillo is quite different from Reitoca. A cool fresh breeze was blowing through the windows of the sacristy, making it almost chilly. During the Mass, the people closed the window by the altar so the breeze would not blow out the candle.

Today I learned that my friend Lorraine Westermark suffered a stroke and is in serious condition. Lorraine is a member of the Basilica Shrine of St. Mary in Wilmington, N.C. and was a faithful member of the music ministry. She was most famous for her teaching of Suzuki violin classes at St. Mary School. What she was able to do with students was amazing, and many have become life-long violinists.

Because Lorraine has cerebral palsy, she almost certainly does not have the strength to undergo the rigorous physical strength demanded for a post-stroke recovery program. She and her devoted husband Hans are in my prayers.

Norberto, friend and former member of the Basilica Shrine of St. Mary, contacted me today and is doing well in Mexico City. Currently, he is in his pastoral year in Tlaxcala. His job is coordinating all the pastoral work in a high school operated by his order (the Piarist Fathers). I look forward to the day, in the not-so-distant future, when he will be ordained a priest.

November 7, 2021 – 32nd Sunday in Ordinary Time
Reitoca, F.M., Honduras – 8 p.m.
Partly cloudy – 75 F

Today I celebrated Masses in Concepción and El Hatillo. The Mass in Concepción was uneventful, but El Hatillo was another story.

When Danilo and I got to El Hatillo following Mass in Concepción, a funeral was going on in the church. *Delegado de la Palabra* Clementino was leading the service. At first, Danilo and I wondered if the people would still want a 10 a.m. Mass, and some of the leaders assured us they did. Some men of the community took the casket out of the church around ten minutes before 10 and carried it down the road to the Alubarén cemetery, followed by many people carrying flowers. The man who died, Otilio Hernández, was in his early 60s, I believe.

When I was giving my homily, I became very weak and knew I could not continue standing up. So, I told the people that I was a little sick and that I needed to sit. I gave the rest of my homily sitting down. Later in the Mass, during the Our Father, I had to sit also. Otherwise, I was able to function normally. The problem was dehydration. I have been rather weak the last few days with zero appetite. But that happens to me every couple of years, so I'm not alarmed.

November 8, 2021 – Monday
Reitoca, F.M., Honduras – 8:55 p.m.
Partly cloudy – 75 F

Lorraine Westermark died today, and Ron Daniels, a long-time member of the Knights of Columbus in Wilmington, North Carolina, also died. Both will have funeral Masses this week in Wilmington: Lorraine at the Basilica Shrine of St. Mary, and Ron at St. Mark Catholic Church. May they rest in peace.

I am feeling very weak and have almost no appetite. It was a chore just trying to eat two pieces of toast. I'm sleeping a lot, but otherwise, I'm fine.

I spent part of the day exploring the lives of six Redemptorists who were beatified recently. They were killed in Cuenca, Spain during the Spanish Civil War. I need to explore their lives a bit more, for at least two of them might be candidates for inclusion in my second volume of *Saintly Men of Nursing*.

Danilo dropped by my house this evening after spending a day in Tegucigalpa. He brought me some groceries and introduced me to his brother Rony, who just returned from working in Missoula, Montana, where I studied for my Ph.D. in sociology. In the spring, Rony plans to be working in South Carolina. Like Danilo, he used his time in the United States to learn English. Danilo also brought me two Boston ferns to hang on the deck outside the kitchen window. He'll buy the third one next week.

November 9, 2021 – Tuesday - Dedication of the Lateran Basilica
Reitoca, F.M., Honduras – 9:35 p.m.
Clear – 73 F

The weather in Reitoca is almost never described as "perfect," mostly because it is usually hot. Even when the temperatures are only in the upper 80s, the sun seems searing, and the humidity is often oppressive. But beginning this month, the beginning of our six-month so-called "summer," the climate has changed dramatically. The nights are cooler, there is less humidity, and beautiful breezes are blowing. Emilio tells me that although the first four months of summer are cooler, the last two months, March and April, are usually the hottest months of the year.

Eduardo Cantillano dropped by my house this morning to bring me a "solicitation" from the Reitocan community of El Limón. They would like help building a new church. Eduardo told me he will be leaving in the morning to see if he can get into the United States. He wants to make money so he can buy a house for himself. I hope he makes it. Then, later in the day, the chief *Delegado de la Palabra* from the Curarén community of Anís came by with a request for more money to build a new roof for their church. The needs here are unending.

There is a priest retreat at Casa Mata in Tegucigalpa today, but I didn't go because I'm recovering from my weakness over the weekend. I'm doing much better, but I'm not at 100% yet.

This evening, Drs. Aaron and Shelsie walked from the St. Mary House in the center of Reitoca to my place on the outskirts of town. Aaron installed a new printer for me. I then treated myself to a "feel-good" movie, *Valentine's Day.*

November 10, 2021 – Wednesday – St. Leo the Great
Reitoca, F.M., Honduras – 7:05 p.m.
Mostly cloudy – 79 p.m.

Today is the first-ever Call to Earth Day in the world. The purpose of this day is to encourage individuals and organizations, such as schools, to raise awareness of environmental issues and to encourage conservation education.

Blessed Charles de Foucauld, one of my favorite priest-heroes, is scheduled to be canonized on May 15, 2022. Brother Charles of Jesus, as he called himself, had a very interesting life as a French soldier, Trappist monk, and hermit-missionary to Muslims in Algeria. One of the things I find so refreshing is that he showed that the eremitical (hermit) life is not incompatible with the apostolic (missionary) life. I like to see my current way of life as that of an apostolic hermit.

General Electric announced that it plans to break the company into three parts, with the three new companies focusing on the firm's health care, power, and aviation businesses.

Fr. Carlos dropped by today to let me know I'll be celebrating Masses in Curarén on Thursday and in La Libertad and San Miguelito on Sunday. So, it'll be an easy week liturgy-wise for me. I hope to use my free days wisely.

Yesterday I read about a priest of the Diocese of Cleveland sentenced to life in prison for sexual crimes against underage persons. I can't imagine what it would be like to face life in prison. What would one do for hope? What would encourage the person to go on living? Does God grant prisoners without hope special graces? I believe that of all the people in the world, prisoners most need prayers.

The media shared some of the official communications of the Diocese of Cleveland. The statements were very gracious and politically correct, expressing sorrow for the youths affected and their families, the parishioners where the priest had served, and how the diocese was going to do all it could to see that the priest is removed from the priesthood. But nowhere did it say anything about praying for the priest who had destroyed his life. I can't help contrasting that with how various Church-approved organizations treat women who commit abortion. Such groups go out of their way to help the women "heal" from aborting their children with lunches, kind words, expressions of sympathy, and the like. It is amazing how differently our society and our Church treat people on the basis of gender. Will the Catholic Church, and society in general, ever treat men and women with equal respect, sensitivity, and compassion? Maybe, but not in my lifetime.

November 11, 2021 – Thursday – St. Martin of Tours
Reitoca, F.M., Honduras – 8:10 p.m.
Partly cloudy – 75 F

Juan and I hung the two new Boston ferns on the new roof outside the kitchen window. They look great. Next week, I hope to buy a third fern, as we have space for a third.

This afternoon, I celebrated Mass in Curarén and gave a special blessing to Noel Fonseca in honor of his sixteenth birthday. We had nine servers for the Mass, and I told the amazing story of St. Martin of Tours on this, his feast day.

Today is Veterans Day in the United States, but here in Honduras it is not a holiday. I find it ironic that the feast of St. Martin of Tours, who became a conscientious objector, is the same day as Veterans Day.

I didn't get much scholarship done today except a biography of Servant of God Wanda Blenska, a physician who was a lay missionary in Uganda. She made a name for herself by developing a leprosy (Hansen's Disease) hospital into an internationally known research and teaching center. Dr. Blenska died in her native Poland at the age of 103.

Emilio told me that the *Delegados de la Palabra* from the Reitocan community of El Higuerito (where Juan lives) plan to come to the Holy Cross campus on Monday to help cut weeds. Nobody asked them to do this, so I guess they're doing it simply as an act of charity. What a wonderful thing it is to give a gift of time and talent.

This evening, I treated myself to another "feel-good" movie, *Operation Christmas Drop.*

November 12, 2021 – Friday – St. Josaphat
Reitoca, F.M., Honduras – 8:55 p.m.
Mostly clear – 75 F

I accomplished very little today except gardening. The campus is looking better and better thanks to Juan and to volunteers who come from time to time. Now that summer has arrived, there will be less rain, so we won't have eight-foot-tall weeds for a while.

This evening, I watched *Dumplin!* It was excellent, but I like any movie starring Jennifer Aniston.

November 13, 2021 – Saturday – St. Frances Xavier Cabrini
Reitoca, F.M., Honduras – 8 p.m.
Mostly clear – 76 F

Juan had the day off today, so it was quiet here on the Holy Cross campus. I dedicated most of the day to designing blog posts for the 2022 year.

This morning, Fr. Carlos met with *Delegados de la Palabra* from the sector of the parish that includes all the churches in four municipalities: Alubarén, La Libertad, Reitoca, and San Miguelito. The big feast day of the *Delegados*, Christ the King, is next Sunday, November 21.

After staying home all day, Blackie has decided to go out on the town for the night.

November 14, 2021 – 33rd Sunday in Ordinary Time
Reitoca, F.M., Honduras – 5:50 p.m.
Partly cloudy – 84 F

This was a beautiful day with plentiful sunshine but also white fluffy clouds and breezes.

This morning I celebrated Masses in La Libertad and San Miguelito. Because elections will be held throughout the nation on Sunday, November 28, many of the communities' mayors are busy doing construction on their roads to show how hard they are working. It was an obstacle course going to La Libertad and San Miguelito, but we made it thanks to Danilo's knowledge of the mountain roads.

Today is the Fifth World Day of the Poor. Pope Francis established this day in 2017 to be celebrated on the 33rd Sunday in Ordinary Time each year, to remind the world of the poor and their needs. Here in our parish, the needs are great, for the majority of the people are poor. There is plenty of work to be done, and I'm happy to be helping in my small but much-appreciated way by giving what I can.

This evening, I'll spend a little time working on 2022 blog posts and then relax with a movie.

November 15, 2021 – Monday – St. Albert the Great
Reitoca, F.M., Honduras – 7:55 p.m.
Partly cloudy – 75 F

Juan helped me put multi-colored Christmas lights on the railings around the deck and walkway outside the kitchen to prepare for next week. I always like to have my Christmas decorations in full blaze on the night of Thanksgiving. I turned the lights on this evening when it got dark, and it makes the whole place look like a party just waiting to happen.

I spent most of the day writing blog posts for 2022 and homilies, so this evening I'm watching *I Feel Pretty*.

November 16, 2021 - Tuesday - St. Margaret; St. Gertrude; Martyrs of Paraguay
Reitoca, F.M., Honduras – 8:20 p.m.
Partly cloudy – 79 F

Many employers in the US are desperately looking for workers to fill their job openings. Many workers have dropped out of the workforce during the pandemic. Some have discovered they want more pay and won't work for the low wages they had been receiving before the pandemic, and others got generous "payout" packages. If the United States would consider more people from the North American country of Mexico, it would have no problem filling positions. Likewise, millions of people from Central American nations such as Honduras would give anything to work in the United States. Unfortunately, there is too much anti-immigrant sentiment in the American population to make that a reality, I'm afraid.

Today I discovered three missionary saints of whom I had not heard. How these three men escaped my notice I'm not sure, for I try to keep up to date on missionary heroes for my blog. The three men, Jesuit missionaries in Paraguay, were killed for the faith. They are Roque González, Juan del Castillo, and Alfonso Rodríguez Olmedo. All were canonized in 1988.

November 17, 2021 – Wednesday – St. Elizabeth of Hungary
Reitoca, F.M., Honduras – 7 p.m.
Partly cloudy – 83 F

Danilo took me into Tegucigalpa for shopping today. Now that summer has begun, the rains have pretty much stopped. So, the roads are now dusty instead of muddy; dusty is much better.

I bought a beautiful cactus for my kitchen, some extra Christmas lights for Juan's house and for mine, and groceries. I find that our trips to Tegucigalpa, which take us about eight hours, tire me out. On the other hand, it's good to get a change of scenery.

Today I received my first Christmas letter. It was from Fr. Doug May, a Maryknoll priest who has worked extensively in Egypt. He now is doing mission appeal work in the United States while living and working at the parish of St. Eugene in Charlotte, North Carolina. He is going to Egypt for three weeks, so he wanted to get his annual letter out of the way.

November 18, 2021 – Thursday – St. Rose Philippine Duchesne
Reitoca, F.M., Honduras – 8 p.m.
Mostly clear – 82 F

Late this afternoon, I watched the rise of the Beaver Moon over the eastern mountains. One of the best things about living on the side of a mountain overlooking a valley is the great views of the moon and stars that it provides.

Blackie was out all night, and when he did come home, his right front leg was injured. Now he's hopping along on three legs, but his appetite is good. He slept all day.

I did some planting with Juan today, and we made a list of chores we'd like to get done in the following week or so.

November 19, 2021 – Friday
Reitoca, F.M., Honduras – 6:40 p.m.
Mostly cloudy – 82 F

Aaron and the crew from the clinic want to celebrate an American Thanksgiving with me, so I said that Thanksgiving Eve would be fine. I pretty much always have a Mass on Thursday afternoons and/or evenings, so Thanksgiving Day would be out of the question. Aaron knows someone in Tegucigalpa who prepares individually wrapped traditional Thanksgiving meals. So, I decided to put up my Christmas decorations this afternoon. It'll be very festive for the party next week.

November 20, 2021 – Saturday
Reitoca, F.M., Honduras – 8:25 p.m.
Partly cloudy – 79 F

Fr. Carlos dropped by this evening to let me know I'll be having Masses in La Libertad and San Miguelito tomorrow instead of Concepción and El Hatillo. That is fine with me. Because the roads are improved from their scraping, the extra half-hour travel each way won't make much difference.

Blackie is still hopping around on three legs, keeping his right leg off the floor while he's in the house. However, when he decides to leave the Holy Cross campus to visit his friends, he seems to walk perfectly well.

Today I worked all day on my blog posts. For the most part, it is going very well. I have all the posts through mid-April 2022 finished, and now I'm working on finishing the Friday mission hero biographies. Those, too, are going well, and reading about the lives of these missionaries are truly inspiring.

Often biographical data omit critical pieces of information, making the stories unclear. For example, I was reading about Venerable Maria Giuseppa Scandola, a Comboni missionary sister who served in the part of Sudan that today is South Sudan. The biographies that I have read say that she offered her own life to God so that a young missionary priest could continue his apostolic mission work in Africa. But there is no context provided. For example, offering one's life to God as a missionary makes sense. I think it is safe to say all missionaries do that. But to then say that because of her offering, a young priest was able to continue his missionary work, makes no sense. What does one have to do with another? Especially baffling, is that the articles say Sr. Maria Giuseppa died from "natural causes." It was not a case like St. Maximilian Kolbe who gave his life so that a man with a family could escape death from Nazi prison guards. I'll continue trying to find the missing piece of the story.

November 21, 2021 – Christ the King Sunday
Reitoca, F.M., Honduras – 7:55 p.m.
Partly cloudy – 79 F

Today I celebrated Masses in La Libertad and San Miguelito. In San Miguelito, workers were paving a patch of roadway entering the town, but Danilo and I were able to enter and leave without problems.

I gave special thanks to the *Delegados de la Palabra* in those communities, for the feast of Christ the King is their special holiday. In both La Libertad and San Miguelito, most of the leaders are women.

Today I read about a bizarre robbery of a Nordstrom store in Walnut Creek, California, near San Francisco. About 80 people drove up to the store in 25 cars and began ransacking the store, assaulting employees and stealing merchandise. They then fled in the waiting cars. What brazen madness!

November 22, 2022 – Monday – St. Cecilia
Reitoca, F.M., Honduras – 6:30 p.m.
Partly cloudy – 79 F

Today, Danilo and I went to Tegucigalpa so I could pay salaries for the clinic staff. After we were done with that task, we were on our way to a nursery to buy some flowers. For some reason, a group of taxis deliberately blocked the street at a round-about, causing a massive traffic jam. Fortunately, because we have a good pickup truck, we were able to drive up onto the green median and head in the opposite direction. We believe it was some kind of a political protest.

Because of the upcoming elections on Sunday, Tegucigalpa and other parts of Honduras are expecting other forms of political protesting. So, I'm cancelling the Thanksgiving Eve party at my house, and we'll have a party in mid-December instead.

This was a very cloudy day with strong winds in the afternoon, but there is no forecast of rain.

November 23, 2021 - Tuesday - St. Clement I; St. Columbanus; Bl. Miguel Pro
Reitoca, F.M., Honduras – 7:50 p.m.
Partly cloudy – 75 F

First thing this morning I was greeted by the little dog named Chispa, "Spark" in English. She is as hyper as always and filled with love.

She thrives on being hugged. I haven't seen her in many months, so I was afraid she had died.

This evening, at our monthly Rotary Passport Club meeting, I introduced our two newest members, Dr. John Cromer and Rev. John McLaughlin. John Cromer is a physician in Wilmington, N.C. and has been instrumental from the very beginning of the founding of Clínica Santa María. He and his wife Penny have also been very faithful in raising funds for our healthcare projects here in Honduras through our non-profit organization called *SaludHondu*. John McLaughlin, who visited here in Reitoca a month ago, is the pastor of St. Jude Metropolitan Community Church in Wilmington. I'm delighted that both will be members of the club.

Dr. Aaron believes that the traffic blockage Danilo and I experienced yesterday was a protest by taxi drivers because of their working conditions. Not only do they have to compete with Uber, but they also have to pay protection money to gangs. Causing blockages at major intersections is one of the only ways they can express their displeasure.

November 24, 2021 - Wednesday - St. Andrew Dung-Lac & Companions
Reitoca, F.M., Honduras – 7:55 p.m.
Mostly clear – 77 F

This Thanksgiving Eve finds me a bit sick with nausea and a complete lack of appetite. I don't know what I would have done if the party had gone as planned. Aaron gave me some anti-nausea medicine, so I should be okay.

The clinic staff will be taking off Monday and Tuesday of next week following the Sunday elections. Nobody knows what problems, if any, will occur because of the elections, but pretty much everyone is expecting protests all over the nation.

Today, in the United States, three white men were found guilty of murdering a black man who was doing nothing worse than jogging in their neighborhood. I think most people of goodwill will be rejoicing at the verdict.

**November 25, 2021 - Thursday - Thanksgiving – St. Catherine of Alexandria
Reitoca, F.M., Honduras – 7:55 p.m.
Mostly clear - 77 F**

This Thanksgiving Day finds me much better but a little weak. I even have a little appetite.

This afternoon I celebrated Mass in Curarén. The new social hall is coming along nicely, and the youth of the parish love exploring it and the upstairs which, Fr. Carlos hopes, will one day be a rectory for a priest.

Honduras doesn't celebrate a Thanksgiving Day, but I celebrate it no matter where I am. God has showered me with way more than my share of blessings in this life, and I am truly grateful. I'm also keenly aware, however, of Jesus' sobering words to his disciples: "Much will be required of the person entrusted with much, and still more will be demanded of the person entrusted with more" (Luke 12: 48).

I spent most of the day researching missionary heroes and people on the way to sainthood. I'm especially interested in finding famous women missionaries, for I have had less success finding women than men. I'm also looking for saintly men who did nursing at least part of their lives so I can put them in the second volume of *Saintly Men of Nursing* that I plan to write.

While I was doing my research today, at one point I glanced down at my phone. I have an app that lists each day of the Church year and what saint or feast it celebrates. As I glanced at the phone, the app was open to October, and the first name that I noticed was Blessed Dominic Collins on October 30. I had never heard of him, so I looked him up. I was intrigued to learn that he had been a soldier, but then he applied to become a Jesuit. The Jesuits had serious doubts about him, thinking he might be too "battle-scarred" for the religious life. However, they allowed him to enter the novitiate to become a lay brother. Soon after he was accepted into the novitiate, a plague struck, and Dominic nursed the plague victims without fear and with great compassion, comforting those who were dying in their last hours. After seeing Dominic at work, no one ever again expressed doubts as to his fitness for religious life.

I chalk up the experience of finding a saintly man of nursing as sign from God that what I'm doing is worthy. I love it when God goes out of his way to blast me with a good surprise!

November 26, 2021 – Friday – St. John Berchmans
Reitoca, F.M., Honduras – 9:45 p.m.
Cloudy – 75 F

Today is a free day for me, and both Juan and Emilio have the day off.

Today in Mexico a bus crashed, with passengers from the Mexican state of Michoacán going to the community of Chalma in the municipality of Manilaco. Nineteen were killed, and thirty-two were injured.

I received a nice note from my friend, Dominican Fr. Charles Johnson. Currently he is a chaplain at the University of Houston. Charles is from the parish of the Basilica Shrine of St. Mary in Wilmington, N.C. I was friends with his mother when I served there.

The DJIA tanked today on news of the highly contagious new COVID variant named Omicron. The variant was first identified in South Africa.

November 27, 2021 – Saturday
Reitoca, F.M., Honduras – 8:15 p.m.
Partly cloudy - 75 F

On this final day of the Church Year, I celebrated a wedding Mass for a couple named José Luis and Merlin in the church in Curarén. The ceremony went very smoothly, and I stayed for photos following the Mass.

I recently encountered a quote by Marcus Aurelius that said, "Very little is needed to make a happy life." That made a big impression on me, for I find it is true. What I most treasure is the ability to use my gifts to serve others. Fortunately for me, I'm able to do that as a priest and writer who has time, talent, and treasure to share. I have way more "things" than

I could possibly need. Though I appreciate the physical things I have, I often long to have a simple little place, maybe in a desert, with just enough to get by. Of course, it would have to have to have an excellent internet connection so I could do research. And, of course, I'd have to have my computer and printer and paper and who-knows-what-else. I guess what I need at this point in my life is simply the gift of detachment from material things. Bit by bit, I'm heading there.

November 28, 2021 – First Sunday of Advent C
Reitoca, F.M., Honduras – 8 p.m.
Mostly clear – 75 F

This morning, I celebrated Mass in Curarén. Noel had a beautiful Advent wreath in front of the altar, so we blessed that at the beginning of Mass.

This was Election Day in Honduras, and from all reports, it was peaceful. I think it was calm because of soldiers and police stationed around the country in readiness for disruptions. From early reports, it appears that Xiomara Castro of the Libre party will become Honduras' first woman president in January. We'll know more tomorrow.

November 29, 2021 – Monday
Reitoca, F.M., Honduras – 7:40 p.m.
Clear – 75 F

Xiomara Castro apparently has won the Honduran presidency by a landslide, thanks to many political parties coalescing behind her candidacy, and the fact that many in Honduras see the National party, which has ruled Honduras for twelve years, as corrupt. Ms. Castro, who will be the first female and first Libre party president in history, is the wife of Manuel Zelaya, who was deposed as president twelve years ago in a coup. President Castro defines herself as a Democratic Socialist. She is also a Catholic.

Though she will bring many progressive plans to the table, President Castro will have to contend with the remaining National members of the congress. I have not heard what the makeup of the congress will be in terms of political parties.

Fr. Carlos told me that the incumbent mayors of Reitoca and Curarén have been re-elected.

Fr. Carlos was in the Reitocan community of Quebracho this morning to do a funeral Mass. The woman who died was a person whose new house I blessed when I was in Quebracho in August of this year. May she rest in peace.

November 30, 2021 – Tuesday – St. Andrew the Apostle
Reitoca, F.M., Honduras – 2:55 p.m.
Sunny – 90 F

Juan and Emilio are both off today, so it's a very quiet day on the Holy Cross campus.

Barbados became an independent republic today, ending 396 years of British reign. Sandra Mason became the first president of the country at the stroke of midnight. I know nothing about Barbados, so I had to do some reading. I was very surprised to learn that it is the 18th most densely populated country in the world.

November has flown by for me, but as I reflect, every month does. The biggest news for us here in Honduras was the elections, which went smoothly.

Now, I'm ready for my December, the month of Christmas magic.

DECEMBER 2021

December 1, 2021 – Wednesday – St. Edmund Campion
Reitoca, F.M., Honduras – 6:20 p.m.
Partly cloudy – 82 F

Today is World AIDS Day. There is a new book on the market called *Hidden Mercy: AIDS, Catholics, and the Untold Stories of Compassion in the Face of Fear* by Michael J. O'Loughlin. I'm looking forward to reading it, for it sounds like a book that might have excellent material for future homilies or other writing projects.

Fr. Carlos dropped by this morning before he went to the Reitocan community of Guadalupe, to give me my Mass schedule for the week. I'll be celebrating Masses in Alubarén, Concepción, El Hatillo, and Quebracho. On Saturday, the priests of our San Francisco de Asís Deanery will be gathering in Ojojona for a meeting and a Christmas gift-exchange.

Today I learned that José Luis, a teacher and musician from one of our parish's Alubarén communities, has been elected mayor of Alubarén. I have always liked José Luis, so I'm delighted to learn this news. I had no idea he was into politics. I wish him well.

Today I uploaded my blog posts for Week 51 of 2021 which goes from December 19-25. So, there is just one more week to go, and we'll be in the new year.

December 2, 2021 – Thursday
Reitoca, F.M., Honduras – 8 p.m.
Partly cloudy – 80 F

Today I celebrated Mass in Alubarén. The people there are very excited that José Luis, a member of their community, has been elected mayor of the municipality of Alubarén. José Luis is a member of the San Antonio church and is a teacher and violinist. I think he also plays guitar. Like the mayors of Reitoca and Curarén, José Luis is a member of the Liberal Party.

The *Delegadas* of Alubarén with whom I talked, said that the Liberal Party will be the majority party in the new congress, so the new president, who is a member of the Libre Party and was backed by the Liberal and other non-National parties, won't have to battle the conservative National Party all the time. There is a widespread belief in the country that the leaders of the National Party, from the president on down, have been big narco-traffickers, and that has drained money that could have been used for the poor. I have no idea of the validity of the beliefs, but usually when there is so much smoke, there is likely a fire.

Danilo's cousin brought him from Lodo Negro today, for Danilo's truck is in Jardines.

Timoteo is busy working on improving the wall that will hold the new electric gate for the rectory's campus. And because the Holy Cross campus is attached to the rectory's campus, it will benefit us. For example, it will help keep robbers away, and it will keep cows out. Poor Fr. Carlos planted five beautiful banana trees on the side of the rectory, and promptly some cows ate them. The tree trunks are all that remain.

Today Juan and I made a list of projects for the near future. We have a lot of work ahead of us, but I love working with plants and beautifying the environment. Fortunately, I have a few acres to work with.

December 3, 2021 – Friday – St. Francis Xavier
Reitoca, F.M., Honduras – 6:20 p.m.
Partly cloudy – 81 F

As I write this note, firecrackers of red, white, and green are exploding in the Reitocan sky, lighting up the whole valley. I think it is a celebration for the victory of Xiomara Castro's win as the first woman president of Honduras and first member of the Libre Party to be elected president; the re-election of our mayor, Marlon Osorto of the Liberal Party; and the big defeat of the National Party which has been in power for the last twelve years.

This morning, I had a 9 a.m. Mass in Quebracho, and it took us one hour and fifteen minutes to get there. Quebracho is a community of the municipality of Reitoca high in the mountains, and the roads there are horrible. The *Delegado* of the community, Orlando, welcomed us. As always, he had everything prepared for us, and the church was full.

The altar area of the little church was decked out for Christmas, even though it's barely Advent. After blessing the Advent wreath, I blessed the Nativity scene. Jesus, Mary, and Joseph have already arrived in the stable, and the magi were also there. In addition to the cast of human characters, there were animals, including three giraffes. The whole Nativity scene was surrounded by twinkling Christmas lights.

This evening, I enjoyed watching *Single All the Way* on Netflix.

December 4, 2021 – Saturday – St. John Damascene
Reitoca, F.M., Honduras – 7:55 p.m.
Partly cloudy - 79 F

Today the priests of the San Francisco Deanery had a gathering at the rectory in Ojojona. Fr. Tony, the dean, had the place decorated to the hilt with beautiful Christmas decorations. He also completely renovated the backyard. Now, there is a central water fountain, and all around are lush tropical plants. Little lights hang in various nooks and crannies, making the place look like something out of a fairy tale book; I loved it.

In addition to Fr. Tony, the Reitoca parish was represented by Fr. Carlos, Fr. Sebastián, Danilo, and myself. Also present were Frs. José Luis of Lepaterique and Fr. Gustavo of Sabanagrande. Two seminarians who just finished all their seminary studies were also with us today: Darwin Medina, who will be in Sabanagrande for his pastoral experience, and Nelson Romero, who will be in Ojojona for his pastoral experience. A priest I had not met before was a special guest, Fr. Ovidio Rodríguez, who was celebrating his fortieth anniversary of priesthood ordination.

After a meeting and luncheon, I gathered up some pork bones for Blackie and his friends, including Juan's three dogs: Oso (Bear), Policía (Police); and Titán.

When Danilo brought me back to Reitoca, I was pleasantly surprised to find that Juan had spent some time cleaning the house.

December 5, 2021 – Second Sunday of Advent
Reitoca, F.M., Honduras – 6:40 p.m.
Clear – 82 F

Today I had Masses in the Alubarén communities of Concepción and El Hatillo. The *Delegados* from Concepción were delighted to learn that the Red Lantern Foundation has put money into the parish account for them to buy a motorcycle for necessary transportation between churches of that municipality.

Today I read an interesting article about people vanishing "into thin air." Thousands of people all over the world vanish without a trace every year. Some do it for financial reasons or merely to make a fresh start in life. I was amazed to learn that there are even organizations, called "night-moving companies," that help people disappear without a trace.

Fr. Carlos was over this evening to give me my Mass assignments for the week. On Christmas Eve, I'll be celebrating Masses in La Libertad at 4 p.m. and San Miguelito at 5:30 p.m. That will mean Danilo will be able to get me home around 6:30 p.m., and then can go to Lodo Negro to be with his family. He should be home between 7:30 and 8 p.m. We don't have Mass on Christmas Day.

December 6, 2021 – Monday – St. Nicholas
Reitoca, F.M., Honduras – 7:50 p.m.
Clear – 81 F

Danilo and I were in Tegucigalpa today. The road from Reitoca to CA-5, which takes an hour, is vastly improved, thanks to machines scraping the dirt. Despite this, there are a few communities on that road where people have installed their own speed bumps. In Honduras, there are no laws mandating signs where speed bumps are present, so sometimes we encounter them without slowing down sufficiently. Because we travel to Tegucigalpa so often, we pretty much know where the speed bumps are.

To get from Reitoca to Tegucigalpa takes two hours. However, there is construction on CA-5 going into the city. So, once we get to the city limits, it often takes a full hour to go a couple of miles into the city itself, prolonging the trip to three hours one way. I've learned to take my iPad so I can read for the hour that we travel at the speed of a snail.

Today, Danilo and I got our tasks done promptly, once we got into the city, and he had me back in Reitoca by 2:30 p.m.

December 7, 2021 – Tuesday – St. Ambrose
Reitoca, F.M., Honduras – 7:40 p.m.
Partly cloudy - 81 F

I spent most of the day working on homilies for upcoming Masses. Aaron came over in the late afternoon, and we had a nice Zoom meeting with Eduardo Rivera to set some dates for finishing my Red Lantern Foundation website. Eduardo has had this project for over a year and a half; it's time to get it online.

Chile has legalized same-sex marriage, becoming the thirtieth nation of the world to do so. In South America, Chile now joins Argentina, Brazil, Colombia, Ecuador, and Uruguay in marriage equality. In Central America, only Costa Rica has legalized same-sex marriage. In the three major nations of North America, Canada and the United States of America have completely legalized same-sex marriage, and in Mexico, 24 of the 32 states have legalized it. I believe that the pro-love movement will continue to move forward, bit by bit.

December 8, 2021 – Wednesday – Immaculate Concepcion
Reitoca, F.M., Honduras – 7:25 p.m.
Partly cloudy – 81 F

This morning, Danilo and I traveled to the Reitocan community of Saracarán to celebrate Mass on this, their patronal feast day. Their little church was decorated for Advent, Christmas, and the feast of the Immaculate Concepcion of Mary. While the Mass was going on, firecrackers were blazing away outside the church to celebrate the feast. The weather was perfect. Because of its location high in the mountains, the climate of Saracarán is very pleasant, not hot like Reitoca. Flowers bloom abundantly everywhere.

My homily focused on how we need to say "yes" to God's will in our lives, just as Mary did to the angel Gabriel. And, just like Mary, we do not have a crystal ball to foretell the vocational paths God has for us. We simply take it each day, believing that God is guiding us. My homily story focused on the life of St. Anna Schaffer of Germany, who lived in the late nineteenth and early twentieth centuries. Though she wanted to become a missionary sister, she had a terrible accident when she was eighteen years old, falling into a vat of boiling liquid in the laundry where she was working. She underwent thirty surgeries to repair her legs but was bed-ridden for the rest of her life. Nevertheless, she did a great deal of missionary work from her bed. Pope Benedict XVI canonized her in 2012.

We learned that the Reitocan community of Guadalupe will have a special 9 a.m. Mass on Saturday, December 11, in honor of Our Lady of Guadalupe, their patronal feast day.

Today I got a very warm email from Fr. T. Davis, new pastor of our sister parish, the Basilica Shrine of St. Mary in Wilmington, N.C..

(His name is Thomas, but he likes to be called Fr. T.) He filled me in on the latest endeavors of the parish, and he issued a blanket invitation to visit anytime. I told him I hoped that he would come to visit us here in Honduras one day also.

December 9, 2021 – Thursday – St. Juan Diego
Reitoca, F.M., Honduras – 7:05 p.m.
Clear – 81 F

Today I celebrated Masses in the Curarén community of Lodo Negro, and at that Mass, I also baptized twelve children and youth. It was a very festive occasion. In Curarén, it was a low-key, regular Thursday afternoon Mass. Because this is the feast of St. Juan Diego, I told his story, and how over nine million Mexicans were converted to Catholic Christianity as a result of his reporting his vision of Our Lady of Guadalupe.

Unfortunately, today the world learned of a truck crash in southern Chiapas, a state in Mexico. Reports say the truck was carrying about 100 people, mostly people from Central American nations, who were going north to seek a new life in the United States. What a tragedy, especially on this feast of St. Juan Diego.

Fr. Carlos dropped by this evening to ask if I would celebrate Mass for the people of El Divisadero on Monday in honor of their patronal feast of Our Lady of Guadalupe. Naturally, I said I would be delighted. Because the feast of Our Lady of Guadalupe falls on a Sunday, communities whose patronal feast day is December 12 are celebrating that feast on Saturday or Monday.

The Diocese of Cleveland reported that Fr. Donald Cozzens has died. He was a former rector of St. Mary Seminary in Wickliffe, Ohio outside of Cleveland, and he wrote on the state of the Roman Catholic priesthood. I never read his work, but that's on my "to do" list for the near future.

December 10, 2021 – Friday – Our Lady of Loreto
Reitoca, F.M., Honduras – 8 p.m.
Clear – 82 F

Today I received an online copy of *Maryknoll Interchange* November 2021 edition (Vol. 41, No. 2). Because I went to high school at Maryknoll Junior Seminary in Clarks Summit, Pennsylvania, more commonly called "The Venard," I get the *Maryknoll Interchange*. It is directed primarily to people who have a Maryknoll connection either as past seminarians, Brothers, or Sisters. It also provides news of Maryknoll Lay Missionaries and Maryknoll Affiliates.

This issue was particularly interesting to me. One of the poems tickled me. It is called "If, by Chance" and written by Allen Scheid.

> If, by chance, we become flowers
> After we die…and we have a choice,
> I'd like to be a Crocus, a purple one.
> They're pretty, and they have spunk.
> They shoot up in early Spring,
> Unafraid and impatient, just can't wait.
> Oh, God, if we have a choice,
> Put me down for a purple Crocus.
> But if by chance we can choose between flowers and birds,
> Then put me down for a bright red Cardinal
> That flies to the peak of the tallest tree
> And sings loudly, with all its heart.

This poem reminds me of a poem by a fellow nurse, Jim Cardwell, called "I Could Have Been a Rock Star." The poem talks of things he could have been, such as: a rock star who goes down in a plane crash or gets stalked by homicidal fans; a buckaroo who gets so banged up that his body is broken in many places; an Iowa farmer, poisoned by pesticides or chewed

272

up by his own feed grinder; or maybe a poet who died from alcoholism at 39, was stabbed by a jealous lover, or committed suicide over rejection. Instead, he became a Registered Nurse. His poem appears in *A Call to Nursing: Stories about Challenge and Commitment*, edited by Paula Sergi and Geraldine Gorman.

Also in this issue of *Maryknoll Interchange* were notices of two books written by former Maryknollers. Inocente Salazar, a former Maryknoll Brother who worked in Peru, wrote *Spirit, Symbols, & Change: A Blind Shaman's Guide to a Maryknoll Missionary in Peru*, and Al Stumph's *Wheels of My Life*.

December 11, 2021 – Saturday – St. Damasus I
Reitoca, F.M., Honduras – 6:05 p.m.
Partly cloudy – 82 F

Fr. Carlos went to the Reitocan community of Guadalupe today, but on the way, his truck broke down. So, he was very late in getting to that community and did not have time to celebrate the baptisms as planned. His truck is now sitting in Ojojona in front of the rectory. So, I'll go to Guadalupe on December 18 to celebrate Mass and baptisms for the community. The truck needs a new part which, apparently, is not available in Honduras. So, it's on order.

While Fr. Carlos was on his unfortunate adventure, Danilo was driving Fr. Sebastian to the Curarén community of El Anís to help them celebrate their patronal feast of Our Lady of Guadalupe.

While both priests were gone, I was responsible for going to the dedication of a new cooperative in the center of Reitoca called Comisal. The place is a few doors down the street from the St. Mary House. I figured I'd pop by, bless the place, and be back home in a flash. Wrong! The way the leaders had the tables set up, there was barely room to move. Naturally, they put me at the head table, so if I wanted to leave, everyone in four tables would have to get up, and it would interrupt the flow of the program. So, I stayed. In addition to what seemed like endless speeches by dignitaries from places such as Sabanagrande and Ojojona, there was a Protestant minister who gave an inordinately long prayer. My blessing was short and to the point when it finally came. The program took one and a half hours, and that was before the luncheon, for which I didn't stay. Instead, while people were going to get food, I was with the president of the cooperative sprinkling the walls and rooms of the very spacious place. I was glad to be there as an official Catholic presence.

In the United States, devastating tornadoes struck Kentucky and other states. An estimated 100 people have been killed.

One of the most positive things I read today was from the New York Times. Because of the pandemic, millions of people in the United States abandoned their traditional Christmastime schedules. Instead of all the stress of visiting multiple houses of relatives on Christmas Eve and Christmas Day, many families stayed home and created new customs. They were amazed at how much more peaceful these new customs were, and now they want to continue the new, less stressful, ways of celebrating Christmas. I discovered that years ago, as a person who gets energy from solitude and loses energy in groups.

December 12, 2021 – Third Sunday of Advent
Reitoca, F.M., Honduras – 6:20 p.m.
Clear – 81 F

This was a pretty quiet day. I celebrated Mass in La Libertad and San Miguelito, and both communities were delighted to hear that I'll be celebrating Christmas Eve Masses with them.

December 13, 2021 – St. Lucy
Reitoca, F.M., Honduras – 7:35 p.m.
Clear – 79 F

This morning I celebrated Mass in El Divisadero in honor of the community's patronal feast day of Our Lady of Guadalupe. Since I was last at that church, the community put beautiful tiles on the floor. This is a very warm and welcoming community, but then, it seems to me that all church communities of Alubarén are especially hospitable. On this feast of St. Lucy, I told the story of Blessed María Agustina Rivas López, whom everyone called "Aguchita." She was a Good Shepherd Sister who was killed on September 27, 1990, by members of the Shining Path, a Communist guerilla group in Peru. Pope Francis approved her beatification in May of this year.

I also learned that Sharon Marren, my friend who is the finance director of the Basilica Shrine of St. Mary in Wilmington, N.C., had open heart surgery last Saturday. From what I hear, the surgery went well.

I also heard from Dr. John Cromer in Wilmington about *SaludHondu*, a 501(c)(3) charity that raises money to help pay salaries for staff of Clínica Santa María. Thanks to the hard work of John and his wife Penny, the group was able to raise a good amount of money this year. I always love getting good news!

December 15, 2021 – Wednesday
Reitoca, F.M., Honduras – 7:45 p.m.
Partly cloudy – 79 F

Danilo and I were in Tegucigalpa today so I could pay salaries. Although I am able to pay many bills online, the clinic salaries are part of the Archdiocese of Tegucigalpa's account that cannot be accessed except by archdiocesan staff. Though there were many people downtown today, the traffic seemed less hectic than usual for some reason. We were home by 2:30 p.m.

Last evening, staff from Clínica Santa María and Farmacia San Francisco de Asís in Reitoca, and Farmacia Candelaria in Curarén, were all at my house for a party. We had games, gifts, and a turkey dinner. We also celebrated Dr. Marco's upcoming birthday (December 22) and Yesenia's university graduation. Her degree is in nutrition, and now she wants to go back for a university degree in nursing. The group of fifteen people ended the evening with firecrackers, some of which were quite impressive and colorful.

Today I came across a beautiful quote: "The happiest people don't have the best of everything, they just make the best of everything." That is so very true. When I look back, I recall many who were content with what they had, so they always lived in a good space. Others, who may have had many more worldly goods, were never satisfied. What a great quote this is.

December 16, 2021 – Thursday
Reitoca, F.M., Honduras – 8 p.m.
Mostly clear – 79 F

This is the first day of the Posadas celebration in Latin American countries. The celebration goes from December 16-24, and it commemorates Joseph and Mary's search for a *posada* (inn). Danilo explained that usually there is not just one celebration for the entire community. Rather, families and friends celebrate in small groups with prayers and food for the nine days before Christmas. At 6 p.m. this evening, I celebrated Mass in Alubarén to a full church.

December 17, 2021 – Friday
Reitoca, F.M., Honduras – 9:05 p.m.
Partly cloudy – 77 F

As I write this, the Reitocan valley is filled with music in honor of the wedding of Anita and Dago, a couple who run the little general store where I shop for soda, bread, and vegetables. Fr. Carlos officiated at the couple's wedding this evening, and a band came all the way from San Pedro Sula on the north coast of Honduras to provide the music. Dago and Anita are two of my favorite people in the town.

Pope Francis turns 85 years old today. I hope he is pope for many years to come.

December 18, 2021 – Saturday
Reitoca, F.M., Honduras – 6:15 p.m.
Partly cloudy – 82 F

The full Cold Moon is coming up as I write this, flooding the mountains with light. One of the best things about my deck is the view of the night sky, and of storms on their way to my house in the daytime.

Today I celebrated Mass in the Reitocan community of Guadalupe, and we also celebrated the baptism of a baby named Sonia. The plaza in front of the church has been renovated since I was last there, and a new Baptist church has been built.

After the Mass, Danilo and I went to the house of the *Delegado*, Julio. He is expecting the whole community to drop by his house later today to celebrate the baptism of Sonia. He had many blue and white balloons on his porch and inside his house to mark the celebrations. Blue and white are the colors of the Honduran flag.

December 19, 2021 – Fourth Sunday of Advent
Reitoca, F.M., Honduras – 6:55 p.m.
Partly cloudy – 82 F

Getting ready to celebrate a 9 a.m. Mass in Reitoca, I told Juan to be sure to keep Blackie in the house, or he would follow me to church and be with me throughout the whole Mass; Blackie did that one time. Well, Blackie indeed stayed in the house, but little Chispa, wildly energetic, followed me to church and insisted on staying with me like a shadow all through the Mass. Amazingly, she was as good as gold, just as Blackie was the one time he visited during Mass. When I walked, Chispa walked. When I sat, she sat, when I went to the ambo for the Gospel and homily, she came with me and sat at my feet the whole time. I was astonished at how good she was.

The nativity scene in the church of San Francisco de Asís in Reitoca is stunning. Not only does it have the traditional cast of characters, but also an area with dancers, little houses, and I don't know what else. I'll have to study it some more to see what other interesting things it has.

In the afternoon, I celebrated Mass in Curarén. Sr. Lidia Nolasco told me she will be leaving on December 26 for a new assignment in Guatemala near the Mexican border. I wish her well.

December 20, 2021 – Monday
Reitoca, F.M., Honduras – 7:05 p.m.
Partly cloudy – 81 F

Today Danilo and I left the Holy Cross campus in Reitoca to head to Casa Mata for the annual Christmastime event for priests who work in the Archdiocese of Tegucigalpa, with our archbishop Cardinal Óscar Andrés Rodríguez.

The Casa Mata complex has experienced new additions since I was last there, and they are absolutely stunning. The complex sits on the San

278

José Campus of Universidad Católica de Honduras. In the event room, one entire wall is of glass, giving dazzling views of the cityscape and the mountainsides. We had Morning Prayer, a talk by the cardinal, introduction of seminarians and young men beginning their post-seminary pastoral year, and Mass. The Cardinal also gave each of us a shopping bag with a bottle of wine, a box of imported cookies, a book about the Catholic Church in Honduras, and a booklet on the 275th anniversary of the story of Our Lady of Suyapa. Plus, after lunch, we got the best gift of all – personal checks.

I'm continuing to meet more people in the archdiocese. Today, for example, I met a priest in the food line. Francisco, who is 66, is from Panama. He works in a part of Tegucigalpa called El Hatillo and has been here for only four months. Like me, he has no plans to live in another place during his priesthood.

I wished the cardinal a happy birthday in advance, as he'll turn 79 on December 29. I told him I was only three months younger than him. He told me he is looking forward to turning 80, for then he'll be free like me and be able to what he wants without the responsibilities he has now. I completely understand what he meant, for it is so wonderful being a priest without all the non-priestly administrative duties a pastor is saddled with. Plus, I love having all the time in the world to garden, write, cook, and think up new adventures.

And speaking of gardening, Danilo was able to find three Miami palms that I was looking for, so he bought them for the Holy Cross campus. Juan said he'd come over on Wednesday and plant them. They will make a beautiful addition to the scenery.

After the events of the day, Danilo came to Casa Mata to pick me up. We gave a ride to two seminarians who were staying at the *casa cural* (rectory) in Ojojona, and also to Darwin, who is from Reitoca but will do his pastoral year in Sabanagrande with Fr. Gustavo. Darwin told me that he plans to bring the two seminarians to see the Holy Cross campus next week. I look forward to welcoming them.

When Danilo and I got back to Reitoca, we saw Timoteo and three of his young helpers putting finishing touches on the electric front gate to the parish's *casa cural* campus, half of which is the Holy Cross campus.

So, it was an excellent but exhausting day for me. In the early morning, I dreaded going to the priest gathering, for I am an introvert, and such events drain every ounce of energy I have. However, halfway through the event, I realized that I was being re-charged and filled with joy. The Spirit was at work.

December 21, 2021 – Tuesday
Reitoca, F.M., Honduras – 9:15 p.m.
Partly cloudy – 75 F

Most of the day I spent writing and trying to get various projects finished before the year's end. Since I love to create through writing, most of my "work" doesn't seem like a chore, but a combination of hobby, therapy, and vocation. And at the end of each project, I have something concrete to show for my effort, such as a homily, story, book, or whatever.

Today I was reading about cybercrime and how many believe that the next "war" will be conducted online. I can just imagine how terrible it would be if cybercriminals, or foreign enemies, could destroy our electricity or communication centers. Imagine what it would be like if all the lights of every airport suddenly went out, and all the air traffic control towers of the airports suddenly lost means of communication. Or if suddenly every traffic light in New York City stopped functioning during the day. Or if all bank records were lost. The list of what could go wrong is enormous!

Our new airport, Palmerola International Airport (XPL) in Comayagua, which is being called Tegucigalpa-Palmerola, currently has only one United States airline in service, Spirit Airlines. Aeroméxico is also flying there. Spirit Airlines is providing non-stop flights from Comayagua to Houston and

Miami. I hope Delta is planning on setting up flights from XPL, for I love that airline.

And speaking of air travel, my friend Laura Vinson is planning on a visit in early January. It will be so good to see her! In her last visit, Laura had the honor of being the first guest to sleep in one of the casitas of the Holy Cross campus.

December 22, 2021 – Wednesday
Reitoca, F.M., Honduras – 9 p.m.
Partly cloudy - 73 F

Amazon.com published my review today of Laura Conklin's book, *More Shocking Stories of Nursing: What Were They Thinking?* This book discusses the many ways in which nurses can get into trouble while practicing clinical nursing. Some of the problems are due to addiction, such as theft of narcotics by addicted nurses. Others are criminal, such as stealing money from patients. But most are the result of non-deliberate mistakes, such as medication errors.

When I first began practicing clinical nursing on a gynecology floor, patients would typically stay in the hospital for many days. Today, patients having the same procedures are discharged after a day or two, and in many cases, what used to require a week-long hospital stay is now done in an outpatient clinic. Thus, hospitalized patients today tend to be much more acute cases than before. Plus, nurses today must control a large array of technical equipment, any of which can malfunction at any time. One only needs to visit an intensive care unit to see all the tubes and machines at each patient's bedside.

Laura Conklin is a very clear writer, and she makes no assumptions that the reader will know technical vocabulary of nursing, medicine, law or pharmacology. She defines terms clearly and avoids using jargon and legalese, even though she is board-certified in legal nurse consulting.

Timoteo has almost finished the front gate to the rectory campus. Now, he is waiting for the electric motor and the clickers for our vehicles that will open the doors automatically. However, I discovered a big omission today: there is no entrance now for the dogs to come and go. They have been used to using a hole under the old gate to enter the rectory part of the campus and then walking over to the Holy Cross campus. I'll have to figure something out.

December 23, 2021 – Thursday
Reitoca, F.M., Honduras – 9:45 p.m.
Clear – 73 F

Usually I don't remember my dreams, but last night I had one that was exceptionally vivid. I was driving on a hill in the snow, but for some reason, I had to drive backwards down the hill. I kept going faster and faster, and I knew I couldn't keep the pace without getting into an accident. Somehow, I didn't get into an accident, but I did find myself on a psychiatric ward.

I had to admit it did seem crazy for me to be driving backwards, even though it was a necessity in my mind. So, when I shared the dream with the staff, I told them, "Yes, I can see how you'd think that is crazy," so "Let's just say probably it's a symptom of my being so busy." In the dream, I figured that by being a "cooperative" and friendly patient, I could take some medicine and get out of there without much trouble. I have no idea why I had the dream, but it is worth keeping in the back of my mind.

This evening, I celebrated Mass in Reitoca, and Darwin Medina, who is on vacation now before he begins his post-seminary pastoral experience in Sabanagrande, provided the music, along with his mother.

On the way to the Mass, I stopped off at the store of Anita and Dago. There, I dropped off a note telling them how much I love coming to their store, and that they should be proud of creating such a warm and welcoming place for the people of Reitoca.

December 24, 2021 – Friday
Reitoca, F.M., Honduras – 7:55 p.m.
Clear – 77 F

Christmas Eve, my favorite day of the year, has finally arrived. Many houses of worship around the world have cancelled in-person Christmas services, but here in our parish of San Francisco de Asís, all churches are open for either Christmas Eve Mass or Liturgy of the Word.

Christmas Eve in the rural mountain areas of Honduras is very interesting, being both the final day of the nine-day *Posadas* celebration, and also the celebration of Christmas. In La Libertad, there was a little beer stand in the plaza across the street from the church, and people were getting ready to celebrate *posadas* at 6 p.m. Meanwhile, Christmas Eve Mass was at 4 p.m. So, people were going from one celebration to another, making the afternoon and evening one big celebration.

In San Miguelito, our Mass was at 5:30 p.m. There was a new nativity scene there, featuring not only Jesus, Mary, and Joseph, but also animals such as dinosaurs, a tiger, a lion, and a panda. A beautiful dark green wreath with red twinkling lights arched over the nativity scene. I loved it.

In the United States, I read how the new, highly infectious Omicron variant of COVID has led to cancellations of thousands of flights, leaving many holiday travelers stranded.

After the Mass in San Miguelito, as Danilo and I made our way back to Reitoca on the mountain roads, we passed by many families walking to celebrate *Posadas* in their communities.

December 25, 2021 – Saturday – Christmas
Reitoca, F.M., Honduras – 9:35 p.m.
Clear – 75 F

What a beautiful, peaceful Christmas Day this has been for me. Most of the day I spent going through my 2021 journal and doing a bit of editing before sending it to my editor Pat: I'm up to June.

Blackie has been very quiet all day and seems sad because he is unable to leave the campus because of the new gate. At least that is what I infer. But he is eating fine, and he is enjoying being on the deck and enjoying the beautiful breezes. Little Chispa dropped by for dinner around 8:30 p.m. I have no idea how she got into the campus, but I'm not surprised that she did. When Chispa wants something, nothing will stop her from getting it. I'll have to find out and show it to Blackie.

December 26, 2021 – Holy Family Sunday
Reitoca, F.M., Honduras – 7:50 p.m.
Mostly clear – 79 F

On this feast of the Holy Family, Anglican Archbishop Desmond Tutu died at the age of 90 in South Africa. He was a major light of the twentieth century, a champion who fought against the apartheid government system of South Africa. Archbishop Tutu, a winner of the Nobel Peace Prize, was interesting in so many ways. What I find so fascinating about him is how much he accomplished as an individual. Of course, others helped him, and many followed him. But it was his leadership that led others to assist him and follow him.

In La Libertad today, I celebrated three baptisms in the Mass. Danilo told me that on Christmas Eve, after he left me at the Holy Cross campus in Reitoca and was heading to his home in Lodo Negro, a drunk driver hit my car. Fortunately, nobody was hurt. The car is dented a little in the left front, and the driver, a young police officer who works in Tegucigalpa, said he would take care of the repairs on Tuesday in Comayagua.

Today I learned about a group called the Northwell Health Nurse Choir. They were on the Today Show in the United States singing "We Need a Little Christmas." This group won the golden buzzer on *America's Got Talent,* and they've sung in Carnegie Hall in New York City and at the White House. They are doing nursing proud, just as the nursing profession is making the world proud of them in this pandemic!

December 27, 2021 – Monday – St. John, Apostle & Evangelist
Reitoca, F.M., Honduras – 8:30 p.m.
Partly cloudy – 79 F

Fr. Carlos brought over seminarian Edwin to see the Holy Cross campus today. Edwin has stayed in the *casa cural* in the past, but this was the first time he has seen the new campus. Edwin is beginning his final year of seminary study, making him one year behind Darwin Medina of Reitoca. Edwin seems like a fine young man.

Dictionary.com has named "allyship" as its word of the year. It is defined as "the status or role of a person who advocates and actively works for the inclusion of a marginalized or politicized group in all areas of society, not as a member of that group but in solidarity with its struggle and point of view and under its leadership." Merriam-Webster, on the other hand, proclaimed "vaccine" as its word of the year for 2021.

December 28, 2021 – Tuesday – Holy Innocents
Reitoca, F.M., Honduras – 8:10 p.m.
Clear – 79 F

This was one of those days I didn't accomplish much writing. Fortunately, such days are fewer and far between as I get older. I'm not worrying about it, for tomorrow will be better I'm sure.

This evening, I watched *The Firm* on Netflix. I rate it excellent.

December 29, 2021 – Wednesday – St. Thomas Becket
Reitoca, F.M., Honduras – 6:30 p.m.
Partly cloudy – 82 F

The big news of the day is that Ghislaine Maxwell, a British socialite who celebrated her 60th birthday a few days ago, was convicted of obtaining under-age girls for sex for her partner, Jeffrey Epstein. Mr. Epstein allegedly committed suicide in his prison cell in 2019.

Although I understand why she was found guilty, for the evidence against her was quite overwhelming, I am always sad when someone ruins their life.

In another sex abuse case, the Diocese of Cleveland announced today that the pope has removed a priest, sentenced to life in prison for sex abuse of minors, from the clerical state.

I'm finished with my homilies for Thursday, Friday, and Sunday, so tomorrow I'll be able to tie up loose ends of various projects that don't require much brainwork.

Today the Diocese of Raleigh reported that the mother of my friend Fr. Mark J. Betti, Mrs. Anne Rita Betti, died in her sleep in Parma, Ohio yesterday, December 28. Mark will have her funeral Mass on his birthday, January 18.

December 30, 2021 – Thursday
Reitoca, F.M., Honduras – 8 p.m.
Mostly clear – 80 F

Today it was 95 F in Reitoca, but because of a beautiful breeze, it didn't seem so hot. Blackie enjoyed the day napping on the deck.

This evening, I walked to Reitoca to celebrate a 7 p.m. Mass in San Francisco de Asís. In the evenings, the temperature of Reitoca is cool and refreshing.

When I got back to the Holy Cross campus from Mass, Emilio pointed out that there are hordes of *zampopos* near the triangle where my big *almendro* tree stands. So, we took some Raid and visited the area. Sure enough, we discovered thousands of *zampopos* and did out best to destroy their pathways. Next week, I'm going to investigate solutions for getting rid of *zampopos* and other insects that infect trees.

December 31, 2021 – Friday - St. Sylvester I
Reitoca, F.M., Honduras – 7:45 p.m.
Mostly clear – 81 F

On this last day of the year, an amazing American actor, Betty White, died just two weeks before her 100th birthday. Betty was an American icon, a larger-than-life personality who began her career in 1949 and never really retired from it. In addition to her roles in the TV series, The Mary Tyler Moore Show and Hot in Cleveland, she was most famous for playing the lovable and innocent featherhead, Rose Nylund, in The Golden Girls. May she rest in peace.

On this last day of the year, I find myself battling huge ants, including zampopos. The zampopos are trying to destroy the big almendro tree that Juan and I have been nurturing for more than a year now. I sometimes joke that the alternative name for the Holy Cross campus should be *Hormiga Junction*, *Hormiga* being Spanish for "ant." But if that's the biggest problem in my life, I'm a very blessed person.

Also, on this last day of the year, I celebrated Mass for the people of Alubarén in their main church, San Lorenzo. Mass on New Year's Eve is very popular with the Catholic people here, even more popular than going to church for Christmas. I preached on the gift of time.

Like all years, 2021 was an interesting one.

On the world scene, the pandemic continues. As the year comes to an end, a variant of the COVID virus called Omicron is spreading rapidly throughout the planet. This is worsening problems not only in hospitals and homes, but also in many businesses.

In the United States, the best news was the election of Joe Biden as President of the United States. President Biden is a Democrat and the second Catholic president in United States history, the first being President John F. Kennedy. Also elected was Kamala Harris as Vice President, the first woman, the first Asian, and the first person of color to be elected to that office. Democrats narrowly took control of the U.S. Senate this year also.

Of comparable note was the storming of the United States Capitol by pro-Trump vandals who called themselves "patriots."

In the Catholic Church universal, Pope Francis opened a synod to run from 2021 through 2023. This synod is designed for people from all levels of Church in the entire world to share their ideas about where the Church should be headed in the future, how it should be governed, and what changes it should make. The synod has the potential for many important changes in the life of the Church of the future.

In the Diocese of Raleigh, to which I am still subject, 2021 saw the death of six diocesan priests and one Passionist priest who was working in the diocese at the time of his death. The diocesan priests who died were Fr. Trent Watts, Fr. John "Jack" Richardson, Fr. Frank Maloney, Fr. JaVan Saxon, Fr. Bob Diegelman, and Msgr. Jerry Sherba. The Passionist was Fr. J. Hector Rangel Galván.

In my former parish, the Basilica Shrine of St. Mary, Fr. Ryszard Kołodziej was transferred to St. Mildred parish in Morehead City, N.C., and Fr. Tom "Fr. T" Davis has come to take his place. Among the many deaths of the parish were Aaron Preusser and Lorraine Westermark. Aaron was the husband of Amy, former youth director of the parish, and Lorraine was a teacher at St. Mary School, best known for the Suzuki violin program she established in the school.

Here in the parish of San Francisco de Asís – Reitoca, Fr. Sebastián Cruz turned 60, and Fr. Pedro Pablo Barona became a parochial vicar of the parish and is taking care of the churches in the San Marcos zone of Curarén.

In Honduras, people elected Xiomara Castro of the Libre Party as president by a landslide. Xiomara, a Catholic, is the first member of the Libre Party and first woman president of Honduras. She defines herself as a Democratic Socialist. The Mayors of Reitoca and Curarén were re-elected, and José Luis of our parish was elected as the new Mayor of Alubarén. All three mayors are members of the Liberal Party. Finally, our new airport, Palmerola International Airport (XPL) has opened. It will eventually handle all non-Central American international flights.

On the Holy Cross campus, we built a connector road going from the *casa cural* (rectory) part of the campus to the Holy Cross campus, planted many new trees, and put up a new overhang outside the kitchen. Little by little, the campus is becoming beautified.

Finally, in my life the biggest news was the death of my stepmother, Mary Jean Kus in May. With her death, I am now the eldest member of my extended family. In April, Aaron and I celebrated the first anniversary of our *MissionPriest.com* website/blog. In June, I celebrated the 60th anniversary of my high school graduation from Maryknoll Junior Seminary, "The Venard," in Clarks Summit, Pennsylvania.

On this day, I looked back to January 1 to check my New Year's resolution. I made only one, and that was to write and publish a book of Missionary Heroes that I featured in my blog's first year. Although I have prepared most of the material, I have not yet put it together as a book. I'll do that in 2022.

Now, I'm very eager to see what exciting adventures await me in 2022.